Enterprise Risk Management

Enterprise Risk Management

A Manager's Journey

K.H. Spencer Pickett

John Wiley & Sons, Inc.

Library of Congress Cataloging-in-Publication Data:
Pickett, K. H. Spencer.
  Enterprise risk management : a manager's journey / K.H. Spencer Pickett.
      p. cm.
  Includes index.
  ISBN-13: 978-0-471-74529-7 (cloth)
  ISBN-10: 0-471-74529-4 (cloth)
 1. Risk management. I. Title.
  HD61.P53 2006
  658.15'5—dc22
                        2006002907

Printed in the United States of America

10   9   8   7   6   5   4   3   2   1

*This book is dedicated to the lovely lady
in the yellow dress, my wife, Jennifer*

*A very special thanks to Tim Burgard
for his continuing faith in the
adventures of Bill and Jack*

CONTENTS

Contents

PROLOGUE

Bill started to dream. He was back in the Caribbean floating on his back in the warm sea. The sound of reggae music seemed to vibrate through the water and he felt strangely contented. Suddenly there was the sound of someone thrashing around close by and Bill saw a large man in distress bobbing up and down in the water. He reached out for the victim and pulled toward the shore, only to find that the person laying flat on her back was a very attractive woman. He applied mouth-to-mouth and the woman slowly opened her green eyes and said; "Kiss me again." Bill sputtered; "I wasn't kissing you, I was saving you . . ."

At this point Bill woke with a jerk and stretched out his hand, searching for his wife. He remembered that she was away as his hand met nothing but a soft pillow. In fact she was in the Caribbean taking care of her mother, who was due to undergo an operation. Bill blinked and turned over on his side. "I should have gone with her," he thought, as he slowly drifted back to sleep, searching in vain for the warm sea that had featured in his dream.

CHAPTER 1

A NEW JOURNEY

Bill emerged from his restless sleep and assumed robot mode as he showered and dressed before grabbing a muffin from the fridge, which was washed down with strong black coffee. This was so embarrassing. His sweetheart had only been away a few days and he had not had a good night's sleep ever since. Bill followed the usual daily routine of taking the train from Long Island, squeezing into the subway, and the dash to his glass-fronted office building in Manhattan. He marched through the open-plan offices and a raft of "Good mornings" from colleagues preceded his arrival at his office with his desk overlooking 8th Avenue. BILL REYNOLDS, HEAD OF CORPORATE PLANNING read the office plaque. Bill let out a short laugh. This felt good—promotion and new challenges and getting to oversee the dozens of new projects that were a feature of the large multinational company for which he had worked for many years now.

"Told you I'd make it, folks," he muttered to a picture of his parents sitting proudly on his desk. Bill's mother was dead but his elderly dad lived close by. "The kid's done good." Wow. How long had he been talking to himself? He'd better stop or people would think he was crazy and promote him to the board. Not being able to help himself, he said out loud, "E-mails first," and scanned through the morning's messages, which felt odd because his assistant who normally checked his e-mail was out sick. Bill quickly spotted the red-flagged message from his CEO, Georgina Forsythe:

Bill

Thanks for the project status summary report. Looks like most things are on track.

I need to throw something at you. Can you catch?

I have set up a working lunch today to discuss.

Call my PA to confirm and see you at 12:30.

Georgina

"Oh, no," thought Bill. Georgina has a habit of using restaurant meals to make big announcements. His apprehension got worse when he was told by the assistant that only himself and the CEO would be going to lunch. Is this good or bad? Since his wife, Ruth, was away, Bill had lived on junk food, so the thought of a good meal was fine. But being hit with a big deal was normally bad. Perhaps he could ask her if they could eat first and talk after. Actually, Georgina was quite attractive even though, in her mid-forties, she was some 10 years Bill's senior.

Bill was seated at the restaurant when Georgina flounced in, nice looking but petite, her previously blond hair now died jet-black, and sat down and crossed her booted legs. Bill stood up and sat straight down as he greeted her before ordering a chicken dish and thought about making a joke about the vegetarian meal that Georgina had decided on.

After a little small talk Georgina commanded, "Okay Bill. Let's get to it!"

Bill looked up expectantly in the middle of a vigorous effort to chew what was proving to be a tough piece of chicken.

"I am getting really interested in REM," Georgina went on, waving her hands around to emphasize the point, and suddenly stopped talking and stared at Bill with raised eyebrows. Bill realized that she was expecting some kind of comment and his mind went humming off searching for a good response. *REM*, Bill wondered. *What the hell is that? Rapid Eye Movement? That happens when you dream at night.*

Bill looked thoughtful and said in a sleepy tone, "Do you dream a lot at night?"

"What? Georgina said in a sharp tone.

"Do you, uh . . . your eyes. Do they flicker at night? I mean . . ."

Georgina seemed used to dealing with idiots and shrugged her shoulders, and said, "Look, Bill. Forget the small talk, you're hopeless at it. I've been hearing about Enterprise Risk Management, or what's called ERM, and how many big companies are getting to grips with risk management across their entire business. Not just specialist parts that have traditionally used risk assessment over the years. We have good, reliable controls thanks to the work you did last year on our internal control framework but we've been expanding pretty rapidly and I need to make sure we understand our risks and have them bolted down. That's what ERM can do. Or so I've been told."

"Yes," agreed Bill, slowly realizing that he had misunderstood his CEO and needed to make up some ground. "Bolted-down sounds good . . ." he added.

Georgina frowned. She thought a lot of Bill's competence but at times he really had to be led by the nose.

"Okay," she interrupted Bill and continued, "I need to tell you my plans. You will need to bone up on ERM and make a presentation to the next board meeting in three weeks' time. Okay?"

"Sounds good to me." Bill replied, trying to look really efficient despite a piece of greenbean hanging from his teeth.

Georgina shuddered again, frowned, and looked at her watch. "Right, Bill. So you hop a plane to London. Attend the conference and workshop and spend a few days getting your material together. Then hit us with your ideas about a first-class action plan to make ERM work here."

Bill had stopped listening after the word "London" had been said. He tweaked his left earlobe to make sure he was hearing right and said, puzzled, "Okay. Now I get the bit about making a presentation to the board but I thought I heard you say something about London? Please correct me if I'm wrong."

Georgina called for the check and looked as if she was about to make a quick getaway. She mumbled, "Oh, yes. You must have heard about the international ERM conference that's going to be in London next week. Two days of top presentations and a series of short workshops. It'll be great. Take one of your staffers with you to bounce around ideas. So get going and don't come back until you can get me a draft of the presentation before the board meeting. You know, like you did when you went on vacation last year."

Georgina stood up and said, "Gotta go. My assistant will send you your itinerary."

Bill finally got his brain into gear and stuttered with as much presence as he could gather, "Can I employ Jack?"

"Who?" Georgina looked puzzled as she paid the check with her credit card.

"You know, your old friend, Jack Durham. The guy who helped me prepare the internal control stuff last year."

"Look, Bill. Draw up a short business case. I'll look at it later today and if it makes sense, then yes, I guess it's possible to use Jack again. Remember, any extra costs come from your budget."

And with that she spun on her heel, flashed a waved in Bill's direction, and was gone.

Bill looked at the remains of the dinner and half-bottle of wine. Okay, this can work, he thought. The wife's away. Jack's a lazy cuss, sitting around the Caribbean drinking booze all day long. Didn't he say something about risk management in that e-mail he sent to Bill the other day? It'll work. We'll go to London, get the info, knock out a paper, and bag it up for the board. Sounds doable. Bill finished up the meal and walked slowly back to work, thinking through all the things he needed to do to clear his desk and get right into the new project.

Bill's wife, Ruth, sat back in her wicker chair on the veranda, watching the orange sunset as her friend's husband, Jack, sat opposite. Jack sipped his drink and asked, "How's Bill getting on? Is he working all hours as usual?"

"Pretty much" replied Ruth. "He wanted to come with me but, you know, work priorities and all of that." Ruth stretched out her long legs and her brown skin seemed to shimmer in the glow of the sunset. She was tall and slender, wearing a loose-fitting flowery dress that seemed just right for the tropical sun. Jack looked at Ruth and remembered how Bill had visited the island last year—a lonely man who did not even realize his height and good looks made him most attractive to the opposite sex. And then he ends up romancing and marrying this nice-looking Jamaican lady.

Jack, much shorter than Bill, squatted on his chair more like a bulldog with his square jaw and thick neck emphasizing his muscular frame, and years of self-defense training that had developed his physical strength and presence.

"Yes," he said, "It would be good to see my old buddy Bill again. Do you know, we spent a week driving around the island when he came for his first visit last year? It's due to him and some of his bright ideas that I managed to write my book on internal control. I sent him an e-mail last month about getting a contract for a new book. It's going to cover risk management and I wondered if he had any bright ideas. He didn't even bother to reply."

"That's Bill," replied Ruth with a frown, "too busy working to take time out."

Jack's wife swept through the veranda and threw herself down into the nearest chair. She was larger than Ruth but with a good figure and friendly open face. She assumed a thoughtful posture, which suited her status as a Florida State University professor on loan to the University of the West Indies. She stated in a matter of fact way, "Yes, Jack, my dear. Isn't it about time you started your next book? You have a contract and a deadline you know. Being fat and lazy doesn't help."

"Certainly, my dear," mimicked Jack, "I'll do it tonight and we can send it right off. That's if I can think of three hundred pages of reasonably sensible stuff. And I'm not fat, I'm just well-built."

Sharon glared and started to purse her lips and thought about taking on her bulldog, but she suddenly laughed and threw a cushion toward him.

"You're too much. You do know that my assignment is over in a few months and then it's back to Florida and you can get back to doing those consulting jobs that keep us in clover. All holidays have to end sometime. Anyway, Ruth, how's your mom doing?"

"She's in surgery tomorrow, which means I'll stick around for a week or so, then get back to New York and Bill. It should be straightforward, but I want to be around to make sure she's okay."

Jack wagged his finger at Ruth, saying "Absolutely. And try to get your husband to come over for a visit. If there's no room at your mom's, you could always stay with us. I could give Bill another tour of the island if he likes. You never know, maybe he could give me the inspiration to write my new risk management book."

CHAPTER 2

JETTING OFF

Ruth rushed to the phone, and although she was out of breath, answered quickly.

"Hi."

"Sweetheart, it's me, Bill. How's my sweetheart?"

"Okay."

"Look, darling. I just phoned to say: could you get a message to Jack? I can't get him on the phone, he's never at home. Tell him I'm taking him with me on a trip to London."

There was a slight pause and then Bill heard a low, quizzical voice that he barely recognized as his wife's.

"You call me up, call me darling, knowing that I'm stuck out here with my ma and you're too busy to come over. Then, with the next breath you tell me you're taking Jack to London. Okay. Let's take this slowly. . . . I'll slam down the phone and you can think about what you just said."

For the second time that day Bill forced his brain into creative activity and quickly said, "No, sweetheart. Hold the line, it's not like that at all. I need Jack to work with me on an important business project, in London. Just for a week. When you come home, I'll be home too."

Bill grimaced and held the phone away from his ear just in case there was a small explosion. Nothing. Bill prayed—was he safe?

His prayers were answered to some extent as his wife muttered something along the lines that he had a way with words that verged between being terrible to poor and he was just not romantic enough. A girl needs a little romance. . . .

Sensing success, Bill relayed the words from a song that lingered in the back of his mind, "You're sweet, as sweet as candy," and his marriage lived to fight another day.

Bill's e-mail to Jack was short and informative. The text expressed the importance of getting this job done and that he had a tight deadline to get a paper on risk management to the board in three weeks' time. Jack would receive expenses and a reasonable rate for services provided in supporting these efforts. Would this suit? And if so, Bill would get the CEO's assistant to e-mail an itinerary that would include travel plans and a meeting at a good London hotel. Better still, he would go and see the assistant, Trish, and get her to make up the itinerary for him too.

Bill marched down the corridor and stood in front of Trish, a middle-aged lady with short brown hair that framed a wide, motherly smile.

"Hi. Have you had any luck creating the itinerary?" said Bill, forgoing any opening remarks.

"Absolutely. It's done. Tickets, itinerary, and an expenses budget. You know Georgina has spent a lot of time organizing your conference. It's weird."

Bill took the file and smiled, "Thanks, Trish. You're totally there as usual."

To Bill's amazement Trish stopped giving out her usual good-natured smile, quickly looked around to make sure no one was nearby, and whispered, "Watch out for Lance Strongbow! He'll be at the conference. Okay?"

"Yeah, okay, Trish . . I'll say hello to him."

"No. What I mean is, watch out for him. He's a bully."

Bill checked his watch and wondered if this day was going to get any more confusing. He scratched his chin and said very slowly, "Who's Lance Strongbow?"

"He's Georgina's ex-husband. The story goes that Georgina used to be a stay-at-home wife but then decided to start up this company. When it grew to a success, Lance couldn't take it and became jealous and destructive. He's no good—you know."

Trish's eyes were now wide open and flickering as she launched into high-speed gossip mode.

"He calls her sometimes but she rarely speaks to him. He called her last week and asked her why no one from this company was attending the ERM conference. Then he offered to set up an ERM process for her. He's some big-shot consultant with one of the big accounting firms."

"How do you know all of this, Trish?"

"I've got to monitor the calls. You know that."

"But not after someone takes the call. You are naughty. . ."

"Anyway, listen to this." Trish leaned forward and went on in a hushed voice, "He started teasing her about the conference and Georgina said she was going to send someone. And he shut up. She said she'd send her best man on ERM and he said 'Best at what?' and she said, 'Better than you, anyway.' And he said, 'What—is he your new lover?' And she banged down the phone."

Bill looked at Trish, trying to take it all in as his head started to throb. Trish gave a triumphant smile as this hot piece of gossip had Bill totally enthralled. Bill finally said, confused, "Who's this ERM expert? You know, the fellow Georgina was going to send to the conference?"

"It's you, silly." Trish went into spasms of laughter and Bill started to scratch his head vigorously.

"Trish. Got to go," Bill said as he moved backwards.

Trish waved a hand, "Just watch him. He's horrible. Oh, and he thinks he's going to be a workshop leader."

Bill shrugged, "Thanks, then. Bye. . . ."

Jeeze, he told himself. *I'm supposed to be an expert and I don't know anything about ERM. What next?*

Later that day, Bill sat on the train sweeping him toward his home on Long Island. He would have to see his dad and make sure he was okay. He almost sprinted home, took a quick shower, and jumped into his convertible. He pulled down the top, and after half an hour on the road with the wind whipping through his long black hair, pulled up at his dad's house, his old family home. His father was sitting out front, and since it was a warm June evening, he was enjoying the late-setting sunshine.

"Hello, boy," Bill senior shouted as Bill approached. Bill grasped the bony hand that was offered and in his mind flashed a thought that his dad used to kiss him on the cheek whenever he saw him. But since his wife died two years ago, Bill senior had become so much more reserved. Bill grabbed an empty glass and poured some of the fresh orange juice that sat on the table. He sat down and carefully explained that he would be away for a week and that he would get a helper in. The same person who usually comes—that overweight teenage girl who was always singing Beach Boys songs. Anyway, Dad would be fine and he would call on the phone from London. . . .

"London?" grunted Bill senior, who appeared to be ignoring most of what Bill was saying. "Did you say London?"

"Yes, Dad. I'm off next week."

Bill senior snorted and then pursed his lips. "Slow down son, I need to tell you something. You think that we're all alone. That we don't have any living relatives. Well, that's not true. Your mom had a sister. You know you're mother was originally from England. Well, she left a sister behind and they lost touch. Or had a quarrel, or something like that. Well, your mom wanted Maud, that's her sister, to have one of her rings when she dies. When it happened . . ." he stopped and swallowed before going on, "I didn't know how to contact her and that was that." Bill senior took a short break to stretch the side of his neck up and down, a few times. He continued.

"Where was I? Hold on . . . ."

Bill senior slowly got up out of his chair and wandered into the house, and Bill was not sure whether to follow. The old man was starting to slow down, thought Bill. Getting old and bandy legged. A sudden sadness swept over him as he looked at the garage door where, as a kid, every time he scored a goal by hitting the door when they played soccer one-on-one, his dad would lift him up and kiss him on his cheeks. Bill senior returned, sat down slowly, and handed Bill a shiny gold ring containing a large green emerald, and a creased letter poking out of a torn envelope.

"Here," he said, staring at the ring, "I didn't want to bother you before. I know you're always so busy at work and I know you don't have time for distractions like family things and such. But since you're going off there anyway, please give this ring to Maud. The ring was hers and she gave it to your mother before she left for the States, and now it should go back to the rightful owner. Here—this letter came from Maud last year and it has her address on it. No phone number, just an address in England. She found my address through the Internet. God knows how."

Bill thought that his dad had never really asked him for anything before.

"No worries, Pa. I'll see that she gets it. Gotta go."

Bill jumped up and took the hand that was offered for a farewell shake. He shook his dad's hand and bent down and suddenly gave him a kiss on his stubbly cheek.

"Bye, Dad," shouted Bill as he walked toward his car.

"She don't know," shouted Bill senior.

"Know what?" "Maud doesn't know Mom's gone. Please tell her."

"Okay, Dad. Bye," and Bill jumped in his car and sped off toward home.

That night, Bill twisted around in bed as he slept in fits and swept between vivid dreams and vague images. He recalled his dad, looking tired and frail. His mom singing to herself while baking bread in the kitchen. He conjured up an image of Lance Strongbow—a huge aggressive man with giant tattooed arms. He saw Georgina looking totally confused as he tried to explain his vision of ERM. And all along he kept remembering his wife saying, "A girl needs a little romance. . . ." It got so bad that he woke up, drank a cup of hot chocolate, and spent 10 minutes making a list of all the things he needed to sort out to have a nice and peaceful life. He tucked the list inside his wallet and went back to bed and eventually slept more easily.

CHAPTER 3

THE WARMUP

Jack looked at Bill, sitting opposite him in the hotel lobby, and said, "Okay. You're worried about this monster guy, Lance Whatshisname. We're into risk management, so let's do a risk assessment. What is the risk here? That he'll rip my head off?"

"Right. And how do you assess this risk?"

"Very likely and it'll hurt a lot. High impact, especially on my head."

"Right. Okay, Bill, you seem to like your head the way it is. But how do we mitigate this risk?"

"Search me."

Jack made a cutting motion using his right hand to draw a line under his neck before saying, "I'll take him out. Risk gone. . . ."

Bill looked shocked and shook his head, "That's not risk management. It's physical assault."

"Same thing."

"No, Jack. You'd get in trouble and, more importantly, so would I."

"It would be reasonable cause. This clown threatens you. I take him out."

"No. It could only be reasonable if I defended myself from an imminent attack. He goes for me. I duck and back him up, then that's okay. Thing is, I've never actually hit anyone before in my life."

"Easy." Jack got up out of his chair. "I'll teach you. Meet me at the gym, say eight tonight, and we'll go through a few moves."

Bill nodded rather reluctantly and wondered what he was letting himself in for. "You're on," he said, as he too rose from his chair and headed off for his room.

Bill stood in front of the full-length mirror in his hotel suite, dressed in a black tracksuit and gym shoes. He was not in such bad shape. He worked out at his local gym at least once a week, although he found the equipment boring. He jogged, or he used to jog before he found it was hurting his knees. He was tall, well proportioned if a little on the slim side; he was okay.

He walked closer to the mirror and tried a full-on grimace, "Don't mess with me!" he snarled. "You don't know who you're messing with. Okay, you. . . ." He paused when he suddenly realized that his bad-boy image from the mirror reminded him of a crazy cartoon character. It was not working. He looked more like a comedian than a serious threat. *Hmmm,* thought Bill. He would play it cool and dangerous. That might work better. Then, giving up on the acting, he zipped up his jogging suit and took the elevator to the basement gym. He was a little early and he slowly walked past all the sweating bodies and beefed up Jocks working on various machines and found a quiet place at the back of the gym with mats and a huge mirror that had been set aside as a practice area. Bill engaged in his version of a warmup routine. This involved flapping around like a wounded bird and a rather clumsy attempt at jogging on the spot. Jack appeared shortly after, wearing jogging pants and a blue vest, and assumed a military attitude with straight back, commanding voice, and serious outlook.

"Right, Bill! Let's warm up. Stand beside me in front of the mirror and do what I do."

At that, Jack engaged in a series of skipping exercises in time with the fast dance music that was floating through speakers placed throughout the gym. Jack's legs skipped forward and backward in a skiing action, and with each movement he thrust a fist forward, punching in the air, using first his left fist, then his right hand, in a rapid movement. Each punch was quickly delivered and just as quickly snapped back. Bill copied this motion. The punching action was replaced with alternate front kicks again, left then right foot, that started with jerking the knee up, then snapping a foot out and back at what would be the groin level of an invisible opponent. "One, two, one, two . . ." Jack said, urging Bill on, "One, two . . . you're attacking some punk in front of you. Focus Bill . . . one, two, one two . . ."

This went on for some 15 minutes with kicks and punches being varied to knife thrusts, knee attacks, uppercuts, and a wide assortment of violent-looking attacking movements. Jack moved quickly and his thrusts split the air and snapped forward and back in a most aggressive manner.

Jack stopped and wiped off the sweat from his now shirtless body. His firm muscles glistened from the activity. "Let's go!" he instructed, as he dropped down to the mat and started doing pressups, situps, and a variety of rapid body thrusts and squats.

"You need to develop your body so that you can apply speed, power, and accuracy to your technique," Jack ordered. Bill was too out of breath to reply, as he tried to keep up with his friend. Jack continued, "There's no point doing too much stamina work and exercises today as there is not enough time to develop your fitness or strength. This takes weeks, months, and even years."

Jack jumped up to his feet. "Okay, now we're warmed up, let's do some techniques."

Bill staggered to his feet; this so-called warmup felt like a full-blown workout to him and he could hardly stand up, he was so tired.

"Great, Jack. . . ." Bill sucked in some air, and spluttered out, "Yes. We can have a go, . . ." more air being rapidly sucked in, "say tomorrow."

Jack laughed. "No, my friend. There's no time like the present. Stand in front of me and throw a punch. And remember what my old Hungarian master told me—Master Lajos Jakab—speed, power, and accuracy. He was and still is the best in the self-defense business."

Bill pushed his hand in Jack's general direction and Jack stopped it dead.

"No, Bill. Throw a punch. Like this . . ."

Jack took Bill through a punching sequence that involved aiming an assortment of different punches and attacking moves at an imaginary foe. When Bill was able to throw a decent punch, he aimed one at Jack. Jack blocked this punch and placed his hand behind Bill's neck, dropped to one knee taking Bill with him, and flipped Bill onto his back. Bill bounced on the mat and lay flat as if to signal the end of the workout. "Sorry, Bill," Jack said in a sincere voice, "I should have shown you how to do break falls." Jack explained that he was showing Bill re-straining techniques rather than attacking ones so that he could block Strongbow and stop him rather than attack and cause injury. After a hellish half hour for Bill, Jack was satisfied that he had shown Bill some basic techniques that could be applied if he were attacked. Putting on his shirt, Jack slapped Bill on his back and said, "That's all for now. If Strongbow behaves really badly I'll step in and end it."

Bill was trying to get his breath back and signaled "no" with his waving hands, until he could utter, "No, Jack. I don't want you to get in trouble. I know what you are capable of. Okay! I'm going to catch a quick shower. See you in the bar in, say, half an hour?"

Jack bumped into Bill at the elevator at five to nine and together they went up toward the lounge bar on the top floor of the hotel. They swept through the double doors and were pleasantly impressed with the deep-red decor, huge silver chandeliers, and wide windows that looked down onto a sparkling London night. The lights on either side of the River Thames glimmered as they had been sprinkled by the light rain earlier that evening.

"Nice place," remarked Jack as he slid onto a bar stool and looked around.

Bill nodded, "Not bad. I bet most of the people in here are going to be at the ERM conference tomorrow. That's why it's good to check into the hotel that accommodates the conference.

The quiet clinking of glasses sprinkled through the light conversation that was being held by small groups of well-dressed people gathered around their tables, each table with a shaded light and a single red rose in a long-stem glass. The ambience was slightly disturbed by one short, stocky fellow in a tight-fitting suit and with a huge bald head, whose penetrating voice sounded as if he was lecturing to his audience of mainly young women in a booth at the far end of the bar.

A slim, middle-aged Englishman dressed in a dark suit slid up to them from behind the counter and said, "I'm Silverton; what can I get you two gentlemen?"

After a futile attempt by Jack to secure a glass of Jamaican rum from the famous Wrey and Nephew distillery, Jack settled for a scotch and Bill tried to order an English beer. Silverton straightened his back, brushed some imaginary fluff off his tie and explained that beer over here is different from lager and recommended a pint of John Smiths beer from the barrel. As Silverton brought their drinks to where Bill and Jack propped up the bar, a huge middle-aged man, way over six feet tall, with a bristling white beard, staggered out of a door marked "Gentle-men" and eased his bulk onto his bar stool next to Bill, taking a crumpled paper from his pocket and reading it carefully.

Bill said, "Okay, Jack. You'd better tune me in to this ERM stuff. Give me a head start. What's it all about? ERM, that is?"

"What?" Jack replied, sipping his drink and trying to assess its strength.

"ERM. Tell me what it is. Please."

"Don't ask me, Bill. It's about Enterprise Risk Management. That's all I got so far."

Bill scratched his left ear to check he was hearing right. *Okay, Bill*, he told himself. Slow down. Jack's being funny. He tapped Jack's arm.

"You're writing a book on ERM. That is, risk management. So I asked you to help me set up our systems. So far so good?"

Jack nodded and sipped his drink again.

"So," continued Bill. "It makes sense that you know a bit about the topic."

Jack agreed and looked as if he was searching for the right words before saying, "I've not done my research yet. You know how it works, Bill. We get ideas. Play around with different views and, just like last time, I get my book and you get something for your workplace. Don't worry. It'll work out. How's your drink?"

Bill shrugged and gave up.

"Yep. Drink's good. Everything's good. You know, getting zapped by Georgina's ex, and coming back to work with zilch is not a problem. Oh, and telling my aunt her sister's dead. Yep, the beer's fine, so that should be just about dandy. Another drink?"

Jack looked a little uneasy and said he would use the bathroom and then they could order some more booze.

As Jack moved off, the giant sitting next to Bill leaned over and touched Bill's arm. "Hello, sir. Test me on this, would you?"

And with that, he shoved a crumpled paper into Bill's hand. Bill looked down at some handwritten scribble on this torn piece of paper.

"Forgive me," the giant said with a drunken sway, realizing he was imposing on Bill. "I'm Professor Van Dufos from Sweden. I'm here for the ERM conference, which I presume you are, too. Now test me please."

The professor then proceeded to recite word for word the note on the paper that Bill was reading. He cleared his throat, his red cheeks shining, and without pausing said, "Risk management is applied by formulating a clear but iterative framework such as that used in the COSO model, but it may also underpin a type of process-driven dynamic that appears in the Australian/New Zealand standards, even if this is slightly inconsistent with the UK's IRM guidance and less integrated perhaps than the Institute of Internal Auditors' own format."

"Wow," said Bill. "Well done, sir. What does it mean?"

The professor's eyes were glazing over from too much drink but he looked really pleased. He replied, "You know I spent six months researching risk management issues and this note is the final conclusion of this research."

"But what does it mean?" Bill insisted.

"I presented this to the United Nations' Executive Council and they loved it. I met all the top dogs, and they all said that this position would form the basis of their ten-year international development strategy. They paid me so much in bonuses that I retired and now live in California. Are you from California?"

"No. But tell me, what does it actually mean? Your conclusion."

"Well, it doesn't really mean anything much in particular. It just sounds good. It's like a good song. You hum it and it makes you feel good."

At this the professor started humming a waltz, and shifting his bulk off his stool he stood up to conduct an imaginary orchestra. The professor leaned forward so far that he almost fell on Bill and shouted, "I need another drink. Now!"

Jack was returning from the bathroom and saw the huge man grabbing his friend and he sprung into instant action. He mumbled to himself, "It's that Strongbow guy attacking Bill." Running toward them he shouted, "Watch out, Bill!" Then he spun the man around, pinning down his huge arms, and was about to launch into a head-butt when the man fell forward and took Jack with him. Jack fell under the big man, who then rolled over and ended up under the table.

The professor was surprisingly light on his feet and soon rolled himself upright, brushed his trousers, and remarked to the amazement of the rest of the people in the bar, "Thank you very much, sir. I know I have had enough to drink. A hint is a hint. So I'll say goodnight." And with that he swayed through the double doors and left the bar.

Bill stared at Jack and said, "Thanks, bud. But I don't think that was Strongbow."

Meanwhile, Silverton leaned over to the two guys and whispered,

"Many thanks, gentlemen. But in future I would ask you not to take on anyone who has had a little too much to drink. In England we simply take them to one side and gently suggest that they may have had enough for the night."

Bill and Jack nodded in turn, thinking that they had got off lightly.

"Good," Silverton said as he shook his head and returned to his work.

Bill looked through the window and considered the twinkling lights below. He turned to Jack and shrugged, "You know we need to have a quiet drink and unwind a little."

Jack agreed, and they turned their backs toward the other drinkers as if to signal that the show was over. After a few minutes of calm reflection, a shadow appeared behind them and a loud voice boomed, "I'm Mr. Strongbow. Which one of you is Bill?"

They both turned around to see the short, smartly dressed man, slightly chubby with the large bald head, standing over them with a smirk on his face. He looked down at Bill's identity badge with his first name stamped on it.

"It is Bill Reynolds, isn't it?"

Bill nodded while Jack judged how quickly he could take this man out if need be.

"I'm Strongbow; you may have heard of me." He stretched out his right hand and held Bill's hand while he added, "Bit young, are you not, for an expert? See you at my workshop. You are coming, aren't you? I do hope very much that you have done your homework, Reynolds."

With that he gave a short nod, spun on his heel, and walked out accompanied by an attractive blond who looked 20 years his junior.

Jack snorted, "Don't look very tough."

Bill caught the eye of the barman who had come over as if expecting another fight at the OK Corral. Silverton came forward and said, "Don't be fooled. He is tough. Someone told me that he made a grown man cry at last year's conference."

When Silverton had gone, Bill said he'd better go back to the gym and practice some more.

Jack held up his open palm and stopped him. "No point, Bill. Alcohol and workouts do not mix. Do your workout and drink after, not before. Sorry."

Bill looked worried and watched as a well-dressed oriental-looking lady walked straight toward him. She was of medium height with long, flowing black hair and fine, attractive features, and as she reached Bill she said, "Hi. I'm Helen Choi. What did that man say?"

Bill looked surprised. "Which one?"

"Old big head."

"Nothing much. He just said 'See you at the workshop.'"

"Oh, dear. You're going to be his next victim."

Jack came in, "I don't understand how a man can go around assaulting people and get away with it."

"You mean insulting people," Helen added.

Bill frowned and joined in, "You know, in my country we arrest people like that and they go away for a long time."

Helen laughed and her green eyes sparkled with delight.

"You cannot be serious. I'm from Hong Kong and I don't know anywhere where you get arrested for insulting someone."

Jack held up his hand again in a stop sign, "This guy. Strongbow. He hurts people, right?"

"No." Helen said, surprised. "Yes . . he does, but emotionally. He's a bully. But he would not know how to punch his way out of a tissue. He puts people down."

Bill slumped down on the bar and for the first time in ages laughed out loud. When he had recovered, Jack said to Helen, "You mean he's rude to people. Bill's a New Yorker. He don't take nuttin' from nobody!"

They all laughed and then ordered drinks. Bill, looking most relaxed, said to Helen, "What do you mean—I'm his next victim?"

"Oh, nothing. It's just that if you don't know much about a topic and Strongbow takes a dislike to you, he tries to make fun of you. He can be really rough."

"Not a problem." Bill patted Jack's arm, "I brought my expert with me. Eh, Jack? You can handle anything he asks about ERM."

Helen looked so impressed that Jack got up on his feet and made a short bow. Helen smiled and said, "What you need to do is focus on tomorrow's conference. Absorb the knowledge and make sure you can handle Strongbow. That's what risk management is all about. Knowing your risks and preparing for them."

Jack laughed, "We had Strongbow down as a risk but we forgot to do our research and assess the real nature of the risk."

Helen looked interested and asked, "This is good. What exactly was your risk management strategy?"

Jack replied, "If Strongbow gave trouble, Bill was going to slap him in his mouth. Like I taught him. If you launch a hooking punch just below the ear you can break a man's jaw and stop him talking for at least a month."

Bill frowned, "No good. Strongbow says something smart and I run down to him and smack him in his mouth. No. No good at all."

Jack said, "I'll do it."

Helen jumped in. "Start at the top. ERM is about making sure you achieve your objectives. Which are?"

Bill said, "To bone up on ERM, talk it through with my expert consultant here, and then present a paper to the board on ways forward. Oh, and visit my auntie. She lives on the island."

"What island?" Helen asked.

"Here. England."

"England's not an island. There is Wales and Scotland attached to England. But the entire UK is surrounded by loads of islands. You had better check your facts. Okay, you want to get to grips with ERM. If Strongbow distracts you, then this will not help. Solution—do not attend his workshop. Let Jack go alone."

Bill thought about this and said, "I can't let it go. I shouldn't have to hide. I've paid for the conference and the workshop so I need to go."

"Okay," Helen said, "Go for a win-win and use Strongbow's nonsense to make you concentrate on the conference. Look guys, I gotta go."

She shook hands with both men. As Helen started to leave, Bill picked up a set of keys on the table called out to her, "Helen, your keys."

She turned back and thanked Bill, saying, "I'm all the threes. Room 333," and with that she was gone.

"What a gal," Jack said, dreamily.

Silverton seemed to have attached himself to the two men, presumably in case he needed to quell a new outbreak of trouble. He leaned toward Bill and Jack and said, "That young lady is a world expert in her field. ERM, right? I heard that she works for a mega-huge bank in Hong Kong. And every year the organizers beg her to present a session and every year she refuses and attends as a delegate."

The rest of the evening was pretty quiet in comparison with the early part. Bill and Jack bought Silverton several drinks and he refused the third, arguing that he did not want Jack to use the technique he applied to drunks on him. As it started getting late, Bill eventually broke things up, telling Silverton they had better get going as they had a lot of learning to do tomorrow.

Back at his room Bill reflected on an eventful day. He needed a period of calm to settle himself down. Just as he was thinking about turning the TV on, there was a knock at his door and he got up to see who it was. He opened the door and saw no one. Closing the door he returned to his armchair and studied the TV remote control once again. After flicking through several channels he decided to hit the sack, and just then he heard the knocking sound again. Just like last time there was no one behind the door, and this time he poked his head out and checked the corridor. It was fairly well lit and he could see to the far end and it was empty. Feeling uneasy he called Jack on his room-to-room and explained that there was something strange going on.

Jack said, "It's Strongbow using psychological warfare. Tell the front desk."

Bill replied, "That'll sound odd. I mean, I have no proof that it's him."

"Right. Tell you what, Bill. Next time it happens rush out, spot him, and then tell the desk. This guy's presenting a risk to you. Spoiling your chances of getting some sleep and focusing on the conference tomorrow, and we need a strategy to address it. Okay?"

"I guess so. See you at breakfast."

Bill decided on a long shower to get rid of the day's tension and took time to soak himself in a powerful stream of hot water. Just as he had covered himself in soap he heard an extra-loud knock on his door.

CHAPTER 4

THE CONFERENCE DAY

Helen and Jack sat around their table in the restaurant full of conference delegates and ordered a good breakfast. As they started on their meal, Bill sauntered into the room and sat at the third seat at their table.

"Morning, Bill," Jack said, and Helen added, "Good night's sleep?"

Bill looked upward with a hunted look on his face and Jack frowned, "What happened with the knocking last night? Did you see that Strongbow guy?"

Bill ordered his meal and mumbled, "No. The knocks were from an open window outside my room. The wind was flapping the window and every now and again it made a knocking sound." He looked to Helen in a rather stern manner, "I thought you were 333."

"What?" Helen asked.

"You made a joke about being all the threes and explained that your room number was 333."

"Oh, yes it was." Helen finally caught on. "Yes, I was in room 333 but I swapped with my friend, Maria Abimbola. She's Nigerian, but she lives and works in Canada. Do you know she's done lots of research into the success of ERM in helping organizations tackle the global marketplace? And now she's working on an important new ERM software project. She so reminded me of my uncle that we've become instant friends."

"Your uncle?" enquired Jack.

"It's hard to explain. Anyway she's a lovely person and when she saw my room she really liked it, so I swapped with her. She's in 333 now."

"I know," said Bill, "I met her last night."

Both Helen and Jack stared at Bill who was now eating toast and taking sips of hot coffee. Bill realized the group had fallen silent and sat back saying, "Okay, I may as well explain what happened. Now this is all very confidential. Just between us, okay? So, I was taking my shower last night and I heard another knock on the door. You know, I told you about these knocks, Jack. After we had spoken I was taking a shower when I heard what I thought was a knock. Anyway, taking Jack's good advice I jumped out of the shower, grabbed a towel, and launched myself through the door to catch the culprit. So I'm outside my bedroom door, the wind blows and the door slams shut behind me, and just then I realize I got a hand towel, not the bath towel. I tried to wrap it around my waist but it was just too small. So there I was more or less naked and locked out of my room. I panicked and grabbed a bunch of flowers from a vase on a table outside my room and held it in front of my body. I was in a real fix and I started to panic. Jack, your room is on another floor, and I couldn't go to reception like I was. Then I remembered what you, Helen, had said about 333, which is on my floor, and I took a chance and found the door. The soap was starting to dry on my skin and it felt really itchy and uncomfortable. So I held the flowers in front of my . . . uh . . . in front of me. I knocked and the door opened, and standing in front of me is a large African lady, in her early fifties, in a big white bra and flowing red dressing gown. Before I can say anything, she looks at me, naked and holding a bunch of roses in front of myself, and she shouts out, 'I'm not one for quick flings—now get away!' and slams the door. Anyway, I turned around and Silverton's standing behind me and escorts me back to my room. He tells me he saw me on the closed-circuit TV at the front desk and grabbed a door pass and came up. He lets me in and I'm still in shock and can't find anything to say and then he lets himself out."

Helen and Jack stared wide-eyed with their mouths hanging open. Jack's hand was held tight to his mouth to hold in the laugh that was dying to explode. Bill continued, his face becoming even redder, "That's not all. Silverton phones me up five minutes later and says he's spoken to the African lady and she will not be making a complaint. But then he says that the lady suggests I spend a little more time romancing her before taking the direct approach. And I swear I heard him giggle before he said goodnight and put the phone down."

"Wow!" Jack exclaimed through a gap in his hand, which he still held over his mouth.

Helen opened her mouth and closed it again without speaking. Before anyone could say anything more, a loudspeaker announcement sounded and muttered something along the lines that conference delegates should assemble in the main conference room; they each got up and followed the crowd as they shuffled in that direction.

CHAPTER 5

CONFERENCE
SESSION ONE

They walked into a huge conference arena with plush chairs laid out in ever-decreasing rows forming semicircles around a large front stage. The lighting was subdued, with bright lights on stage, a darkened screen up front, and softer lighting for the audience, who had started to find their seats. Classical music played in the background and this merged with the gentle murmur of hundreds of people as they settled down in their cushioned seats with individual arm rests. Bill, Jack, and Helen managed to get seats together, and they sat with their large folders, containing copies of presentation slides and writing paper, sitting on a tray built into the back of each chair that flapped down in front of each person. The classical music increased in volume and Bill recognized it as a Schubert symphony. He turned to Jack to ask whether Jack recognized the movement and changed his mind as he looked at Jack's frowning face and broad sloping forehead, shimmering with a light sweat. Better not embarrass the man, thought Bill. Now Helen would probably know it, he surmised, as he turned his head and studied her elegant neckline and delicate features in profile as she looked down at the file in front of her. The quiet murmur of hushed voices continued for a while as the auditorium filled up and people flapped open their files and got themselves ready for the big show. Bill placed his notepaper in front of him and took out his pen, determined to write down as much as he could as he sensed that he was about to start a new journey, but this time through the world of ERM.

After a few more minutes the music stopped and a tall man dressed in a smart black business suit strode on stage and placed himself up behind the lectern with a large microphone positioned just below his mouth:

"Good morning and welcome, ladies and gentlemen. Welcome to the annual ERM conference, here in London, England. My name is William Dudsman, and I will be your chairman over the next few days. The conference planning committee is a collective of like-minded people who have a deep interest in ERM and we are pleased to present our latest perspectives on the growing debate about risk management and governance across all types of organizations and as a global concept. I travel around the world and I have found that we are all speaking in a united voice about risk, and the way risk can be mastered in a more dynamic way than was the case in the past. We are the masters of our destiny and, even though there are aspects of uncertainty that mean nothing we do can ever be perfect, there is still some degree of control that we can exercise over our world. And this idea empowers us in a way that is hard to describe. But, back to the conference. We, that is, the planning committee, have invited a range of speakers to talk to you about their vision of ERM and special aspects that they have a particular interest in. You will hear from people who have differing views and differing ideas of what makes ERM important. But, these views are brought together by a common belief that ERM is important, both now and in the future. My own view is that enterprise risk management will evolve into global risk management in a way that impacts people, governments, and entire international programs to make the world a better place, even if we are entering into times of less and less certainty. You have two days of presentations and then a workshop on the third day. We have a large audience and I would ask that you forgive me if I say that there is limited scope to provide interactive sessions and breakout groups as we have done in past years. This year's event will consist of presentations and we ask that questions are left for the morning and then the afternoon panel so that we can keep to a very tight timetable. Anyway, I wish you a good conference and I hope that the sessions will help consolidate your understanding of risk management and perhaps introduce a few new ideas. Now I want you to do something for me. Please push your hand deep into your pocket or purse and fiddle around a bit. Many thanks. Now I want you to take out your mobile phone and turn it off. You may remove your hand from your pocket or purse once you have done that. That was fun. Now, we will start off with some of the basics of risk management and then move into more specific aspects over the two days. Let me introduce our first speaker, professor Byron Holsky. You

SLIDE 5.1   *ERM Definition*

ERM Conference – London

COSO ERM – An Integrated Framework

Professor Byron Holsky

ERM:

A process, effected by an entity's board of directors, management, and other personnel, applied in strategy setting and across the enterprise, designed to identify potential events that may affect the entity, and manage risks to be within its appetite, to provide reasonable assurance regarding the achievement of entity objectives.

will find his bio in your file and it only leaves me to say, I wish you an interesting and rewarding conference."

"Good morning ladies and gentlemen [*displays Slide 5.1*]. My name is Byron Holsky, and today I will be dealing with an important document that emerged in September 2004 from COSO, the Committee of Sponsoring Organizations of the Treadway Commission. This guidance is commonly referred to as COSO ERM, or some call it COSO 2 to distinguish it from the internal control framework that COSO prepared some time ago. COSO ERM defines ERM in the words above. Pretty neat, eh? But I see a question on your faces: What does this really mean? My presentation would be pretty short if I just gave you the definition and left it at that. But I am not going to stray away from our set definition. My session is based on making clear the meaning of ERM established by COSO but using my own interpretation of the words in question. I have decided to break the words down so that we can analyze each aspect. Then after we have done that, we can have a go at putting them together again. COSO is an important organization that consists of various bodies that have come together to help set guidance in important areas of corporate life. Information on COSO, including the executive summary of COSO ERM, can be found on their web site, www.coso.org. Remember that I do not work for COSO so this is my own take on their definition.

"We start with the idea that ERM is a process [*displays Slide 5.2*]. This is important. A process is something that runs across the organization. It is not a fad, or a basic tool, or even a concept. It is a process that works at all levels in an organization and brings together the business, back office, and top strategic layers in an integrated manner. By definition, a process is immersed in the business and does not sit outside of the real work like a separate department that has its own secret goals. ERM is not about setting up a new team to do ERM. It is about getting a process that feeds into the main business lines to add value and make a meaningful contribution to the bottom line, including one's reporting obligations. So far, so good. Let's move on.

SLIDE 5.2   *ERM (A process . . .)*

ERM Conference – London

COSO ERM – An Integrated Framework

Professor Byron Holsky

ERM:

A Process,

"Unfortunately, some organizations employ an ERM consultant and say, 'We've done it' [*displays Slide 5.3*]. ERM that is. We've done ERM—or more correctly, the consultants are doing ERM. Wrong. You can't just install a piece of risk management software and tell staff to input their risks and controls and report them upward to more senior management. My reading of COSO is that ERM is an initiative that is made by the board and through management, driven down into the organization. This means the board has decided to assume a risk-managed approach to their business, where they seek to understand the risks that impact their high-level objectives and want to make sure this approach is applied throughout the organization at all levels. Implicit in this is an understanding of ERM and how it can be used to best effect. And explicit in this is the message that says people must be clear about their

SLIDE 5.3   *ERM (. . . effected by . . .)*

ERM Conference – London

COSO ERM – An Integrated Framework
Professor Byron Holsky

ERM:

*effected by an entity's
board of directors,
management, and other
personnel,*

---

responsibilities and how they have addressed threats and opportunities in a way that sits well with senior executives and the rest of the board. You must make the board, CEO, and senior executives responsible for ERM and not just delegate it down through the business. That is why some of the top people in industry are starting to get to grips with their risk portfolios and working out where to locate their organization now and in the future. More than anything, ERM is about the way people work and the way they relate to the growth and direction of the business—basically, how they focus on and deliver their objectives in a way that is neither reckless nor for that matter too lame. We have said that top management have to rally 'round the ERM banner and we build on this theme in the next slide.

"In the past, risk management was seen as relating mainly to matters of safety and security [*displays Slide 5.4*]. For example, it was important in railway companies to ensure trains did not crash and it was important in mining operations where management wanted to make sure their people were protected at all times. What ERM does is take the basic concept of safety risk management and locate the idea of identifying and managing risk at the heart of an organization. That is, the way it sets its overall strategy and its future direction. If risk is built into the equation when setting strategy for the entire business and not just physical safety, then risk management can become a holistic process that starts at the top and filters its way down through the enterprise. That is not to say that safety is not important. It is and always will be. A rich company cannot say it earns tons of money but unfortunately tends to lose people on a regular basis due to site accidents and major safety breaches.

SLIDE 5.4   *ERM (. . . applied in . . .)*

ERM Conference – London

COSO ERM – An Integrated Framework
Professor Byron Holsky

ERM:

applied in strategy setting and across the enterprise,

That will not do. Nothing a company does can justify risking the lives and welfare of innocent people. What is more sensible is for organizations to use an understanding of risk to drive the way they work, and rather than confine this to narrow interpretations—as in the past—they are now taking a broad view of risk as starting with the overall strategy that gives their organization its identity.

"But strategy has a surreal feel to it. It may well float above an organization in published brochures that do not always reach the hopes and aspirations of the workforce or get driven down into real-life operational issues. We will also need to make sure risk assessment and therefore risk management makes it through to the front line of our business.

"This is an interesting part of ERM [*displays Slide 5.5*]. The best organizations position themselves such that they can seize the future. Risks that materialize become lessons to learn from. Looking at all the

SLIDE 5.5   *ERM (. . . designed to . . .)*

ERM Conference – London

COSO ERM – An Integrated Framework
Professor Byron Holsky

ERM:

*designed to identify
potential events that
may affect the entity,*

things that have gone wrong can help you tighten up your business to make sure these problems are not repeated. This is good, but at the same time is still a narrow view of risk management. Some people go further and make sure they anticipate problems and develop comprehensive contingency plans that swing into action when necessary. Again, this is good, but we need to keep looking ahead and watch for risk so that we can position our organization to best address the implications. Good ERM is forward looking and looks at potential events and tries to handle the concept of uncertainty. Where the event may, or may not, affect the entity. It is this challenge of working out the 'potential' and the 'may' that is so important. That is not to say it can be done with precision. It's just that successful companies have a better grip on this uncertainty than those that are inward looking and too frightened to step outside their comfort zone. All joint ventures are difficult to manage— but where they work, there can be great rewards. Understanding these risks makes it easier to manage them as well as possible. Appreciating the concept of uncertainty makes a business much more flexible as it is able to respond quickly where something breaks or something breaks down. But embracing risk is different from being a risk freak. And that depends on the risk appetite that is applied, which is what we turn to next.

"You know, I'm not going to say too much about risk appetite [*displays Slide 5.6*]. This is being dealt with in a separate session later on in the conference. All I can say is that this idea of risk appetite poses real problems. The theory is simple. The CEO and board set a risk appetite agreed with the key stakeholders. That is, whether they want to grow the business quickly and reach out for new ventures at the drop of a hat, or whether the organization is happy to keep ticking along and resists all partnering offers and new ideas so that it maintains the status quo, or whether it watches the core business very carefully but has an eye on new opportunities so long as they stack up well. As I say, the theory is great but real life mixes in so many different complexities that at times it is pointless talking about risk appetite when the organization is made

SLIDE 5.6   *ERM (. . . and manage . . .)*

ERM Conference – London

COSO ERM – An Integrated Framework

Professor Byron Holsky

ERM:

and manage risks to be within its risk appetite,

---

up of hundreds of parts that work pretty well in isolation. It is the dialogue that is important rather than arriving at some concrete final figure or position. The dialogue opens up debate about what people expect from each other and how they can best pull together to work better and achieve more. That's all on that. As I said, we have someone here who will be having a go at this topic later on. And good luck to them—they're gonna need it. My next slide completes the COSO definition.

"We're at the end now [*displays Slide 5.7*]. This last bit is really very powerful. In fact it's so big that I need to break it down a bit:

- **Provide reasonable assurances**—ERM is about containing bad risks and exploiting new challenges to good effect. It means doing things properly and taking chances only when it makes sense and

SLIDE 5.7   *ERM (. . . to provide . . .)*

ERM Conference – London

COSO ERM – An Integrated Framework
Professor Byron Holsky

ERM:

*to provide reasonable
assurance regarding
the achievement of
entity objectives.*

---

we've checked out the odds. Pretty simple stuff. But ERM cannot ensure that all things will go well all the time. It can only ensure that most things will go well most of the time. But an insignificant matter could jump up and bite so hard it hurts. We might have a policy that customer complaints should be contained to a reasonable level—month on month. But one complaint that a senior manager sexually abused a customer and then another manager tried to cover it up may be blown sky high and make the company look really bad. But with ERM we will have a handle on those areas that could blow and we are able to inform others that we have taken all reasonable steps to guard against problems. Ensuring something happens is not always possible but giving assurances is different.

That is about saying to all parties that our considered view is that all is well because we've checked things out or that where there are problems, they are under control.

- **Achievement of entity objectives** is simply that. All ERM activity needs to be related to achieving our aims. And so long as our aims are wide enough to reflect the needs of all key stakeholders, then this makes ERM a potent force in driving the business in the right direction. If risks cannot be related to our objectives, then they are irrelevant, so long as our objectives are broad enough to take into account all interested parties.

"We can now return to our full definition of ERM, and using the issues that we have raised today it is clear that for ERM to exist there needs to be in place several components [*displays Slide 5.8*]:

SLIDE 5.8   *ERM (A process . . .)*

ERM Conference – London

COSO ERM – An Integrated Framework
Professor Byron Holsky

ERM:

A process, effected by an entity's board of directors, management, and other personnel, applied in strategy setting and across the enterprise, designed to identify potential events that may affect the entity, and manage risks to be within its appetite, to provide reasonable assurance regarding the achievement of entity objectives.

- ERM is seen to be part of the entire business.
- It is led by the board and then through management and the workforce and associates.
- It is part of high-level strategy setting.
- And looks to the future welfare of the business.
- Risk is handled to the extent that is seen as right and proper.
- The realities of all organizational contexts are understood, which means we can never be certain of achieving all our goals.

"But we can assure others that we understand the risks to our business and are taking all reasonable steps to handle the risk of not being successful.

"In short, ERM is a way of living up to our responsibilities and making real decisions in a real world full of threats and opportunities that,

SLIDE 5.9   *ERM (In short)*

ERM Conference – London

COSO ERM – An Integrated Framework

Professor Byron Holsky

ERM:

A process, effected by an entity's board of directors, management, and other personnel, applied in strategy setting and across the enterprise, designed to identify potential events that may affect the entity, and manage risks to be within its appetite, to provide reasonable assurance regarding the achievement of entity objectives.

in the end, make a difference to whether we might be successful or not [*displays Slide 5.9*]. There is nothing in the ERM process that is completely new; it's just that we now have a framework to ensure that what we should be doing happens, at least for most of the time. Thank you, ladies and gentlemen, for listening to me, and I think we will have time for questions at the end of this morning's sessions. Thank you."

CHAPTER 6

CONFERENCE SESSION TWO

"I extend my thanks to Professor Holsky, who has given us a solid start to the conference. It is important that we have a clear position on exactly what ERM is and what it is about. The COSO framework does that and there is no better place to start than a formal definition of ERM. If we are happy with this description of ERM, then we can move on and get into more detail. We turn next to Sarrinda Khan, who will take us through some of the basic ideas behind ERM, again so as to set the context for our conference. Sarrinda sits on our planning committee and she will explain why we need to go back to basics before we launch into specific aspects of ERM in later sessions. Ladies and gentlemen, I give you Sarrinda Khan."

"Many thanks, Chair [*displays Slide 6.1*]. Good morning, everyone. Welcome to the annual ERM conference, here in London, England.

"Let me give you a little background to my short presentation. Last year, we held a similar conference in Montreal, and we launched straight into a new piece of risk management software with several on-line demonstrations and diagrams of complex reporting structures. While some delegates enjoyed this session, we had a lot of feedback from those delegates who had limited knowledge of risk management and felt that they were thrown into things a bit too quickly. We decided

SLIDE 6.1   *Risk Management*

ERM Conference – London

Risk Management – The Basics
Sarrinda Khan

Risk Management

The Basics

---

that in the future, an overview session on risk management would be a good idea to get some of the basics out of the way before other speakers explore specific aspects of ERM. Since it was my idea and since I am on the annual ERM conference-planning forum, I am here before you today. So here it is, a short session on some of the essential elements of risk management.

"We have come up with a basic definition of risk as being about uncertainty, which affects one's objectives [*displays Slide 6.2*]. This means we all have to live with some degree of uncertainty, but it just depends on how much we can control and how much we have to put up with. Moreover, we measure risk by considering how significant the event may be and how probable it is without putting in controls. That is gross risk or what we call inherent risk before controls.

SLIDE 6.2   *Risk*

ERM Conference – London

Risk Management – The Basics

Sarrinda Khan

Risk:

Any uncertainty about future events that impact an organization's ability to achieve its objectives.

Risk is measured in terms of its impact and the likelihood that it materializes.

"The basic impact/likelihood criterion is pretty much accepted worldwide, where we can plot the implication of a risk by locating it on a grid [*displays Slide 6.3*]. Low-impact and low-likelihood risks become green risks and so cause no real concerns to top management, while the further you go toward the top right hand of the grid the scarier it gets. High-impact risks that shift one's ability to succeed and that will probably occur need to be pinned down. Top management will want frequent reports on these running issues. A pending legal case that may open the door to a significant class action may make the organization look highly incompetent. This may be seen as a red risk and it will need to be carefully managed at all stages of its progress. A slower part of the business, say the company payroll that has been running well for years under good management, may be seen as a low risk. Now if the man-

SLIDE 6.3   *Risk Assessed*

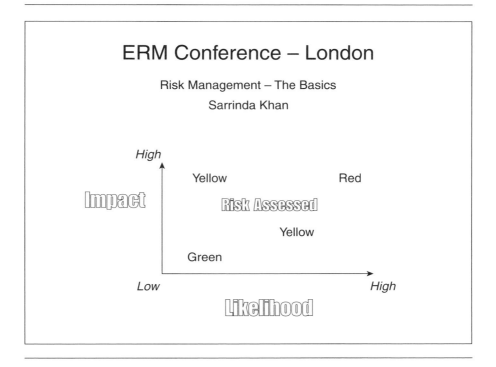

agement in this slow area leaves, this may change things a lot. It may become a yellow risk that starts to get onto the executives' agenda as they need to keep an eye on it. Moreover, if a whole new set of rules come into play concerning the payroll, say on staff deductions, then again this may mean the area becomes riskier. The first example means controls in the form of experienced management change, and the risk that the payroll may fall over therefore increases. The second example is about payroll being inherently more risky because of new laws or regulations, even where the experienced management has been pretty good so far.

"One matter that needs to be clearly understood is the risk cycle [*displays Slide 6.4*]. This is in our slide here. Going quickly through the basics, we start with objectives. This is important because risk cannot float around with its own identity. Risk is only present where it impacts

SLIDE 6.4   *Risk Appetite*

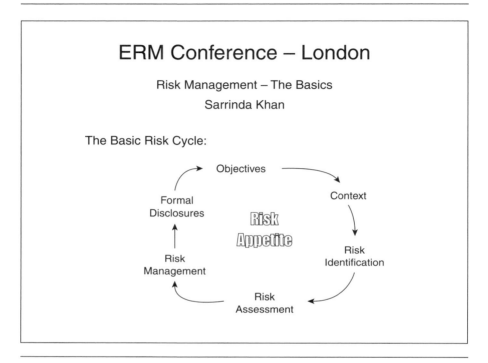

our business and that means it touches our objectives. Context comes next and this is there because we will want to have in place a risk management framework that determines how we deal with risk. The context covers our risk policy and the way risk is defined and captured in the business, including respective roles and responsibilities of auditors, executives, managers, associates, work teams, and so on. Risk identification is the process of spotting risks to our objectives, and this means there needs to be a proactive mechanism in place throughout the organization that enables us to know about new and changing risks that come our way. The risk of terrorist attacks or industrial espionage, or for that matter significant employee fraud may come about because of changes in the way we do business, for example, more web-based business or a new marketing strategy based on penetrating overseas markets in volatile countries.

Risk assessment is the impact/likelihood stuff that we have covered already. We need a way of weighing up risk that allows us to give it a perspective in terms of the extent to which it can damage our business, and this assessment can be applied by work teams to get an agreed-upon position. When we have rated our risks we can then determine the best way forward in terms of a risk management strategy. New risks will need to be sorted out by specially prepared arrangements or action plans, while more general risks may be addressed through our normal internal control systems. There is a final part of the cycle for disclosures as the pressure is now on to report publicly about our arrangements, as internal controls can only be reviewed where we have made an assessment of risk and made sure that our controls are up to the job of managing these risks. Listed companies have to make sure they report on their internal control over accounting systems, and in reality this means they will need to consider controls in the wider sense, and this is where the holistic concept that is ERM comes into play.

"COSO ERM came out in September 2004, and this landmark document has set standards in risk management that will last for many years to come [*displays Slide 6.5*]. It contains many useful ideas, concepts, and examples. It is called the Committee of Sponsoring Organizations, Enterprise Risk Management, Executive Summary, September 2004. But one thing that has come out of COSO is a three-dimensional model that brings together many of the main ideas. One side appears as a version of the risk cycle in terms of setting objectives to start the whole thing off. If the objectives that are used to guide operations and services are poor, then ERM cannot work.

- Risk identification comes next as a way of capturing risk to objectives.
- Risk assessment, as we have said, weighs up the size and probability of relevant risk so we can focus on significant ones.
- Risk response is about the way we react to risks once we have judged them.
- Control activities means specific internal controls.

SLIDE 6.5   *COSO ERM*

ERM Conference – London

Risk Management – The Basics
Sarrinda Khan

COSO ERM:

Risk Identification

Risk Assessment

Risk Response

Control Activities

Information and

Communication

Monitoring

- Information and communication is an important part of the enterprise as this allows a shared understanding of risk and what is acceptable.
- Monitoring is about keeping things under review so that risk management is dynamic and worthwhile.

"COSO ERM argues that risk management is something that impacts the entire organization, and so the second dimension of their model is about risk as it affects subsidiaries, business units, divisions, and the overall entity itself. The final dimension of their model says that ERM is about four main considerations that mean an enterprise views risk at a strategic level, within its operations, with full consideration of corporate reporting obligations and also the entire field of compliance with laws, regulations, and procedures. Where these matters are not properly managed there will be risks that will impair an enterprise's ability to deliver and sustain its future. COSO ERM has brought risk management to a higher level and it is clear that it affects all parts of a business and not just specialist areas, as was the view in the past.

"This risk standard is based on the need to ensure that the cost of reducing risk is less than the cost of the risk itself [*displays Slide 6.6*]. The full title of the standard is the Australian/New Zealand Standard: Risk Management AS/NZS 4360:2004. The main elements of the risk management process are:

- Establish the context
- Identify risks
- Analyze risks
- Evaluate risks
- Then treat them

SLIDE 6.6   *Australian/New Zealand Standard*

ERM Conference – London

Risk Management – The Basics
Sarrinda Khan

COSO ERM:

Establish the
context

Identify risks

Analyze risks

Evaluate risks

Treat them

"This cycle is set within the need to communicate and consult about risk across the organization and also monitor and review the effects. The standard gives further details of actions and considerations for all parts of the risk cycle; for example, within the identify risk part we would need to consider what can happen and how it can happen. There is a further model in the risk treatment process that brings into play the risk appetite by asking whether the risk, once evaluated, is acceptable. And there are available options depending on the answer to this question as various treatments are applied. The risk standard goes into sources of risk and ways of classifying these sources. The impact and likelihood measures are given scales that can be used to assign a risk to the appropriate place. So likelihood can go from almost certain through to being rare. And impact can range from catastrophic to insignificant. Moreover, in this risk standard there is a focus on good documentation and risk action plans to deal with unacceptable levels of risk. You can check the Australian Standard risk management portal at their web site, www.riskmanagement.au/, for further information on this standard.

"Another interesting risk standard from right here in England comes from a collaboration of risk management organizations in the UK [*displays Slide 6.7*]. These organizations include the Institute of Risk Management, the Association of Insurance and Risk Managers, and the National Forum for Risk Management in the Public Sector. This document was released back in 2002, and it breaks risk down into internally driven risks, which are seen as financial and strategic risks, and externally driven risks, which are described as operational and hazard risks. Their risk cycle covers:

- The organization's strategic objectives
- Risk assessment
- Risk analysis
- Risk evaluation
- Risk reporting
- Decision
- Risk treatment
- Residual risk reporting
- Monitoring

ERM Conference – London

Risk Management – The Basics
Sarrinda Khan

Institute of Risk Management:

The organization's strategic objectives

Risk assessment

Risk analysis

Risk evaluation

Residual risk reporting

Monitoring

"All of these are discussed in the standard. One interesting part of the document is about respective roles of the risk management policy, the board, business units, risk management function, and internal audit. The board is seen as responsible for creating the environment and structures for risk management to operate effectively. There is also a section on monitoring, and the standard argues that monitoring should provide assurances that there are appropriate controls in place for the organization's activities and that the procedures are understood and are being followed. The relevant web site can be found at www.theirm.org.

"Basel 2 applies to the banking sector and, although not really a risk management standard, it does contain some useful material on risk [*displays Slide 6.8*]. Banks are now required to have a better understanding of risk profiles when they credit rate a customer. Moreover, banks

ERM Conference – London

Risk Management – The Basics
Sarrinda Khan

Other Risk-Based Guidance:

- BASEL 2

- SOX

- UK's Combined Code

- And Much More

affected by Basel must have a suitable risk management model in place to ensure they have sufficient funds to meet their commitments.

"Over in the States, Sarbanes-Oxley has made inroads into the governance debate by making listed companies sit up and pay attention to the regulators as they strive to protect investors from unscrupulous practices. The rules on external audit, internal controls certifications, board independence, audit committees, and ethical standards all lead to a raft of new risks to the company that fails to respond in a positive manner. As we know, sound internal control is based firmly on the ability of a corporation to deal with risk.

"Here in the UK, listed companies use the London Stock Exchange's combined code to ensure they meet high standards of corporate governance. While there is a lot of material in this code on topics such as the role of executive and nonexecutive directors, the board, and the audit committee, there is also a focus on risk management and the way internal controls should respond to different types of risks.

"There is much, much more. Most government organizations, not-for-profit entities, and special-purpose agencies adhere to standards that incorporate the risk management angle. Risk management and ERM are everywhere. The concepts are seen as universally applicable to running any entity that has objectives and resources applied to achieving these objectives. Even worldwide guidance such as the corporate governance principles issued by the Organisation for Economic Co-operation and Development, while concentrating on the rights of shareholders (and stakeholders), suggests that disclosures should be made regarding material risk and whether companies have put systems for monitoring risk in place.

"I put this slide in to illustrate my view that risk management occurs throughout all types of organizations and in all types of work areas [*displays Slide 6.9*]. Just glancing through my list we can note that there are a few other topics that need to be briefly mentioned in our debate on the basics of risk management:

- **Projects.** In all larger projects there needs to be a careful assessment of risk to ensure that the project runs smoothly and delivers. Risk logs are familiar to all project managers and there is a need to ensure that all projects are based around risk and ways that it can be managed.

- **Information Systems.** We are arriving at a stage where information systems that report using a risk-based approach are everywhere. People are starting to measure risk and report upward where there are items that hit the high-impact, high-probability agenda. Some software consultants are developing pretty tight database systems that record and report risk in a way that gives one company a head start over another that has not got this facility. Most of the information and reports are based around risk registers and we will be mentioning this device in the next slide.

ERM Conference – London

Risk Management – The Basics
Sarrinda Khan

Common Theme

- Projects

- Information Systems

- Upside/Downside Risk

- Workshops

- Chief Risk Officers

- **Upside/Downside Risk.** In the past we have seen risk as threats that hurt our organizations, but nowadays things have moved on. Many see risk not in terms of building bunkers around the business to protect it, but see risk as being too slow or too careful to respond to big opportunities. That is the upside risk: being too bunkered-down to grab new business where it appears. So this new thinking turns risk on its head and suggests that excellent companies know where to take risk that lesser companies fail to go for.

- **Workshops.** Risk workshops is on our list because this is one way of getting people together to discuss risks to their business and ways to move forward armed with this shared knowledge. Really good organizations get their staff to spend time together discussing important issues that affect their business.

- **Chief Risk Officers.** This is last on our slide as it is clear that many organizations are turning to experts to get things going on the ERM front and not leaving things up to chance. Good risk officers seek to spread the word and promote useful tools across the organization rather than try to take charge of the risk management process themselves.

"Most of these things should be decided on via the corporate risk policy.

"I have put up a basic specimen risk register just to show you some of the ways that people capture and deal with risk and ensure that these risks are documented properly [*displays Slide 6.10*]. Flicking through the columns we can see that risks can be noted and assessed so that an appropriate risk management strategy can be adopted as part of a formal

SLIDE 6.10   *Risk Registers*

ERM Conference – London

Risk Management – The Basics
Sarrinda Khan

Risk Registers:

    Objectives:...

    Managers..

Risks	Impact	%	Score	Risk Mitigations	Action	Assigned to

SLIDE 6.11   *Enterprise Risk Management*

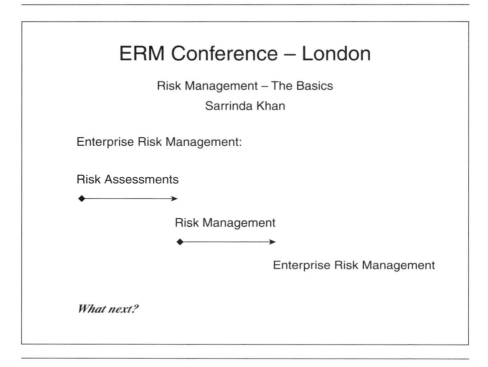

action plan. All of this is set within the context of the objectives for the part of the organization in question. Simple but pretty neat, eh?

"We are getting to the end of our presentation [*displays Slide 6.11*]. Our conference is about ERM and I suggest that the risk assessments that were common in the past turned into risk management where assessments were placed within a formal and standardized process. ERM comes next, where we try to embed risk management into the organization and within all parts of it—including customer-facing operations. What comes next is a question that I would ask you to pose to my fellow speakers; you will hear many varied viewpoints, which I feel enriches the debate more than having people simply say we have discussed things and arrived at one simple solution. ERM is full of dilemmas and inconsistencies and it is this fact that makes it such an interesting topic. ERM is about being successful, and there are many different approaches and perspectives for different organizations and even within the same organization or work team.

"Before I leave, I would like to return to my first slide [*displays Slide 6.12*]. Whatever you hear over the conference and however complicated it gets, just remember that risk is about dealing with uncertainty and getting to your goals. All the rest is subsidiary to these basic concepts.

"I hope that I have given you some idea of the background to ERM, and I wish you a fruitful and interesting conference. Back to you, Chair."

SLIDE 6.12   *Risk*

ERM Conference – London

Risk Management – The Basics

Sarrinda Khan

Risk:

Any uncertainty about the future events that impact an organization's ability to achieve its objectives.

Risk is measured in terms of its impact and the likelihood that it materializes.

CHAPTER 7

CONFERENCE SESSION THREE

"Excellent, Sarrinda. It's always good to talk through some of the foundations of ERM so that we can use these ideas as a platform for the rest of the conference. ERM is in fact pretty straightforward. The principles are simple and logical. In one sense we know that these principles are right. But it is the way we take principles and apply them to complex work environments that is the hard part. People can switch overnight. A fast-food chain can be the ideal model for the world, renowned for speedy service, a nice menu, and a universally reliable product that reaches millions of people throughout the developed and developing world. But, a quick change in pace can occur where fast food is seen as the root of all evil that leads to obesity, chemical additives, and world domination by a select few companies. And the product starts to struggle. But these trends can be anticipated and a good company puts in place a healthy eating program, not as a response to pressures but as a dynamic strategy that anticipates changes in eating fashions. We have said that ERM is evolving from a basic set of ideas to a powerful dynamic for getting organizations fully focused on what matters most. But these changes do not occur overnight and I have asked the final speaker for this morning's program to talk about these changes. Stuart Holiday's bio is in your file. Stuart will present his version of the growth in ERM, and I suggest you sit back and decide where

SLIDE **7.1**   *ERM Levels*

ERM Conference – London

ERM – Tracking the Birth and Growth of ERM
Stuart Holiday

Levels:

1 - Pre-Start

2 - Ad Hoc

3 - Themes Issues

4 - Basic Integration

5 - Board Agenda

6 - Immersed in the Business

Where are you?

---

you and your organization stand in all of this. Ask yourself; How far have we gotten and how much further do we need to go?"

"Well, Mister Chairman. I will have a go at putting some substance to the idea that ERM is an emerging tool [*displays Slide 7.1*].

"Good day, everyone. I'm Stuart Holiday, and for the last five years I have been the chief risk officer for a large international hotel group that has hotels across the world, with more coming on-line as we speak. Before that, I was happily chugging along as the hotel auditor, but I had always been interested in the emerging risk management debate and made it my task to encourage the hotel group to recruit a risk manager and get something going on the ERM front. Well, this recommendation appeared in one of my audit reports and suddenly my operations director tells me that I had been chosen. And as quick as a flash, I get my own office, an expense budget, and the new title, Chief Risk Officer. After a few days of blue-sky thinking and, would you believe it, attending a risk management conference, I finally developed a strategy for getting ERM up and running in my company.

"Now, rather than go through the detailed approach that we used and perhaps bore you with too many specifics about my industry and the way we work, I have put together a presentation that is more general and that deals with this idea of risk management maturity. Taking my experiences, I have developed six levels of maturity as you can see in my first slide. What I would like to do is take you through these levels, and although they are based around my experience, you might see some parallels in your own organizations. If so, I would ask you to consider the question posed by our conference chair: Where are you? And then I guess you might ask: How much farther do you need to go? My view is that ERM represents a manager's journey that keeps on going. It's a bit like your business; it does not have an end in sight but simply keeps developing and evolving as markets change and customers' expectations rise more and more.

"I call this first level the Pre-Start stage [*displays Slide 7.2*]. This is where risk management just does not happen. It's where events break and management reacts in what I call a fire-fighting mode. In fact, the worst-run organizations employ macho fire-fighters who stomp around the office shouting orders as each new crisis breaks. The problem is that their high salaries are based on the existence of lots of big corporate problems and it is in their interests to have these problems happen on a regular basis, so they can swing into action and sort them out. As a career auditor I have seen this happen, not in my current company but in one where everyone was high on adrenaline and fighting fires. The fire-fighting approach is based around three elements:

1. A rapid response to problems where managers expect what should be avoidable problems to happen and have a poor appreciation of preventive controls and do not understand the need for a good control culture.

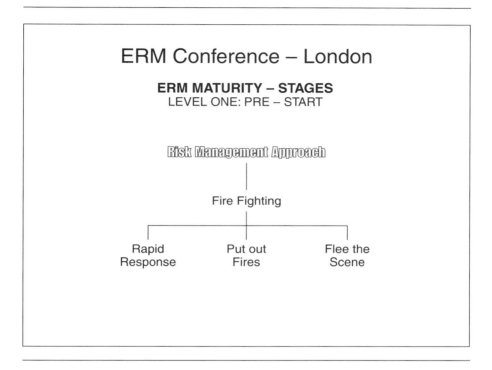

2. Teams that spend most of their time putting out fires around the organization and that are pretty good at crisis management.

3. A 'flee-the-scene' culture, where most managers have a personal escape plan in the event that a fire gets out of control. Some have personal links with competitors who would take them on. Others make sure the trail did not come back to them and there was a fallguy in place. While others still have some leverage or inside information on wrongdoing where they could negotiate a payoff to keep silent if they need to go.

"This stage of ERM maturity is negative in that these types of organizations have no idea what risks could hit them and how these risks could be mitigated. They tend to hold tons of internal investigations and spend their time firing people and clearing up the mess. These organizations do not provide any time to sit back and think long term about building a sound and well-controlled business. As such, they have not really made a start on their ERM process apart from being really good at crisis management.

"My next level is ad hoc risk management [*displays Slide 7.3*]. Here I've noticed that some organizations have started to employ specialists who are trained and equipped in their area of expertise. Some of these specialist teams employ risk assessment as part of their work and so there are pockets of risk management activity in use throughout the organization. But only in some narrow areas of work; some CEOs when asked about their ERM process point to these small teams and argue that risk management is applied where it is appropriate and that there are parts of the support side of the organization where it happens. The 'pockets of risk management' approach has the following features:

SLIDE 7.3   *ERM Level 2*

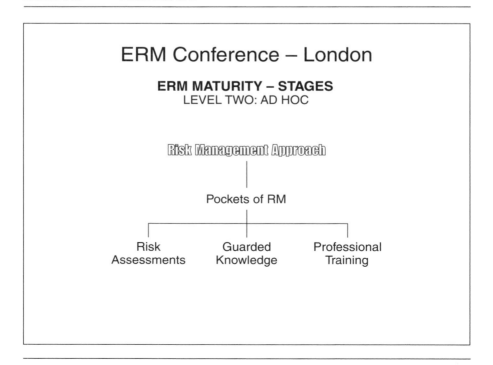

- Risks assessments do happen in, say, the insurance team or the IT security people, but this is only applied so that various back office activities can focus their efforts.
- The use of risk management is generally seen as specialist knowledge and some specialists guard their detailed tools and techniques because they are paid extra for their knowledge.
- Much of the risk-based activity is obtained from the professional training programs that the specialists, such as myself as an ex-auditor, undergo. Risk management is not supported by the organization, as the tools and techniques are mainly learned in the classroom.

"Level two can be dangerous. That is, the CEO and board may point to the few teams that employ risk activity in their work and fail to appreciate the need to spread good practice across the entire business. It can also be dangerous where knowledgeable teams feel that risk management is their tool and something that they do not really want to share with other nonspecialists. In this unhealthy environment, any key messages from the CEO on risk management are not well received by specialists who have a lead on the topic, as it is seen as too basic and patronizing. But the front-line businesspeople can also fail to appreciate these messages because they have been told that risk management is something that is done by back office teams such as the health and safety and the contingency planning people.

"Level three is interesting as it moves risk management away from people and toward activities [*displays Slide 7.4*]. Managers realize that there are issues that have to be risk assessed that run across their business and therefore their zones of responsibility. This new mindset is important as it means that rather than risk-based teams, there are risk themes that run across teams and departments. This risk management approach is based on running themes that people just cannot ignore and has a number of elements:

- Health and safety issues can expose an organization to huge costs if not properly managed. And it is not just the responsibility of the safety experts to get it right, but it is the role of operations management to make sure risks to their people and resources are mitigated.

- Another major issue or running theme relates to new threats from terrorists, and from natural catastrophes such as hurricanes, storms, floods, and fire. Criminal gangs can try to hit a company, and compensation claims can pop up where a customer or employee is not treated properly or loses money on a deal.
- Contingency planning relates a lot to the previous point about threats, and most organizations are starting to realize that everyone needs to understand the physical risks that might hit their business and what to do, as and when one materializes.

"The running themes approach to risk management creates an awareness of risk identification and risk assessment in many people who have never had to bother about these issues; level-three organizations start to develop a risk language even if based mainly on a narrow interpretation

SLIDE 7.4   *ERM Level 3*

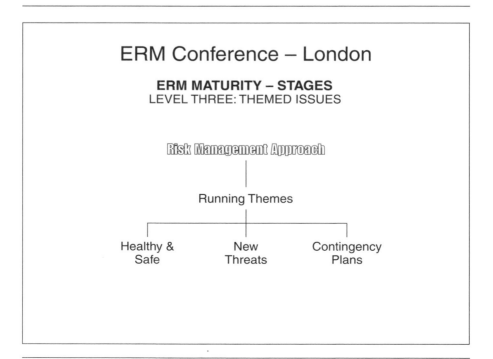

ERM Conference – London

ERM MATURITY – STAGES
LEVEL THREE: THEMED ISSUES

Risk Management Approach

Running Themes

Healthy & Safe   New Threats   Contingency Plans

of risk as being mostly about physical threats and how to deal with them when they hit.

"An organization starts to mature when it appreciates the need to integrate some of the risk activity that is happening across the business [*displays Slide 7.5*]. Basic integration is promoted when the risk management policy approach is drafted and, in my mind, there are three elements that come to the fore:

1. The risk management cycle becomes recognized by most of the senior parts of the workforce as they know they need to set objectives, capture risks to these objectives, assess which risks are significant ones—you know, using the usual impact/likelihood grids—and then go on to develop a suitable risk management strategy.

SLIDE 7.5   *ERM Level 4*

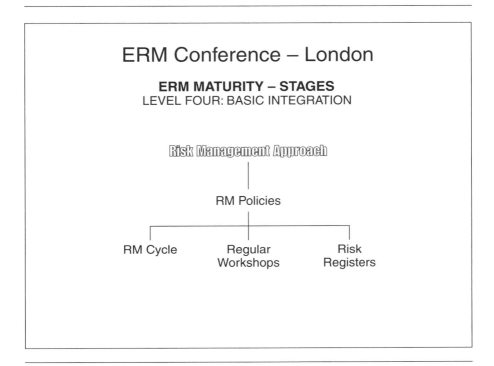

2. Dealing with the risk management cycle that we have already mentioned tends to lead to risk workshops that start to develop in many parts of the organization, as staffs try to grapple with their risks and ways that these risks might be mitigated.

3. The final element of level four is risk registers, or risk logs. Here managers and work teams realize that risk management is not just a chance to talk through key issues, but it also means that people need to develop risk logs and action plans. What happens is that software is bought or designed to create risk databases and reporting systems as people record their risk assessments, and the information is documented and significant issues reported upward. It may be that the so-called high-impact/high-likelihood red risks go up the line to top management and people start to talk about their risks and how they are being managed mainly through mitigation and set internal control procedures. Here there is a sudden influx of reports and spreadsheets that talk about risks and controls and these reports flap around the organization as problems are reported upward and managers start to ask their teams how they are addressing risk. At times the basic integration leads to an overload of information that can become tiresome as people report their risks in ways that are not always consistent or understandable. If we're not careful, risk registers abound and there is just too much information being produced.

"Level-five organizations have moved beyond basic integration to make sure the top table, that is, the board, drives the ERM process and is able to set standards in this respect [*displays Slide 7.6*]. Rather than risk-based reports popping up from all parts of the organization, the CEO builds a sensible process that is driven from the top and sets directions and standards on issues such as risk appetite, accelerated reporting, uniform use of software packages and databases, and how risk can be categorized so that it makes sense to everyone. This driven and directed approach has its own three elements:

SLIDE 7.6   *ERM Level 5*

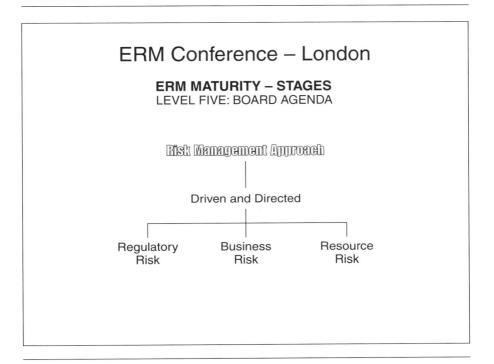

1. Regulatory risk is addressed where the executives and audit committee make clear how they see compliance issues and the expectations of stakeholders and the main regulators. So messages are
sent down about governance and how ERM can help promote a
transparent and well-run business as well as adhering to industry-
wide regulations along with federal and state laws.
2. Business risk also comes onto the agenda. Here line management
is told that ERM is supported by the regulators but it is not just
about keeping them happy. ERM is about making a better business and has real benefits above mere compliance issues.
3. The final element reinforces management's role in protecting the
corporate resources from waste and loss. Although ERM helps a
business prosper, it's still an important part of protecting assets

and having a way of putting problems right as well as dealing with a major crisis.

"Many see level five as the pinnacle in that the CEO, chief finance officer, board, and audit committee have a handle on their ERM process and are able to set standards and get everyone involved in making for a successful business. But is there more to it than that?

"I thought about this idea of maturity a lot before I built this new level, level six [*displays Slide 7.7*]. Here I feel that a really excellent organization kind of moves backward in some ways in that they move away from an obsession with risk. These organizations have started to see their role as setting strategy and then making things happen in a positive way. They deal with problems as and when they arise and, better still, they tend to anticipate and head off problems before they occur. But more than that, they see their role as driving forward and making progress and the risk of not surging ahead is seen as their biggest challenge, rather than concentrating only on those threats that happen on a day-to-day basis. This approach to ERM, which revolves around strategic positioning, has, like the other levels, its three elements:

1. Horizon scanning becomes a way of life where, say, a ship's captain stomps around the deck shouting orders, but listens carefully to messages from the radar technicians about what's on the horizon and feeds these messages into the corporate strategy. The captain may also position a lookout with a powerful pair of binoculars to look far out away from the daily activity on deck.

2. A mature ERM process is geared into reaching forward and growing the business in a dynamic manner. Risks are assessed and, rather than build more controls whenever there is a sign of risk materializing, the approach is more about discarding controls where they have no commercial or regulatory value.

3. More than anything, level-six organizations see ERM as implicit to the change process as they adapt, evolve, and progress to become world-class outfits, or at least strive to become so.

SLIDE 7.7 *ERM Level 6*

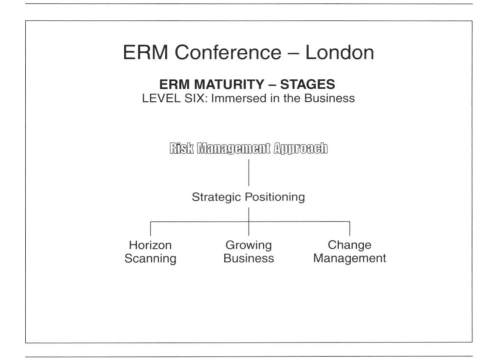

ERM Conference – London

ERM MATURITY – STAGES
LEVEL SIX: Immersed in the Business

Risk Management Approach

Strategic Positioning

Horizon
Scanning

Growing
Business

Change
Management

"Well-defined strategy, in these more developed organizations, is crucial and there is less talk about risk and more talk about making good progress. ERM is just a way of working that is embedded into the business, not as a separate element but as part of the corporate values that underpin the way people work, report performance, and make decisions.

"That's my six levels, and I feel that if I were to come back next year I would probably have another level to talk about [*displays Slide 7.8*]. That is the nature of ERM as it pops up as an issue, then becomes a living thing in its own right, and eventually sits within the business as part of the culture of managing with both zest and care. In one sense I do not know what the future holds for ERM. I don't think that public and private sector organizations will simply march through levels one to six and

SLIDE 7.8 *ERM Maturity—The Future*

ERM Conference – London

ERM MATURITY – THE FUTURE?

then check the 'been there, done that' box on their governance checklist. I feel that the future of ERM depends on the future of corporate life. In my world, ERM simply shadows the business but it does not lead it. The question should be: What does the future hold for public and private sector enterprises? Which means I can duck this one by saying that, once we have answered this question, then, and only then, can we assess where ERM can help in promoting these changes.

"My experience will be different from your own perspectives [*displays Slide 7.9*]. I asked you to consider where you stood in terms of risk management maturity at the start of my presentation. I don't think you can take my risk maturity model and make a guess at where you are located on it. It's much better if you develop your own maturity model and then plot your progress over the coming months and years. Whatever

SLIDE **7.9** *To Close*

ERM Conference – London

To Close:

---

works best for you. I have shown you my approach and I wholly recommend that you develop one that suits your business. One word of advice: When you design your maturity model, get the CEO involved and suggest that it is their model rather than yours. The worst-case scenario is where the chief risk officer is seen to own the ERM process and the executive team stays out of the action. No number of risk maturity models will work where the process is not owned and directed by the top corporate team. Now I defer back to our conference chair before we close in a well-deserved lunch break."

"Right. A great presentation. Many thanks, Stuart. I agree that it's one thing to say onward and upward with ERM, but these become just empty words if there is no real way of measuring such progress. We have a few minutes before lunch for questions from this morning's panel of speakers."

Bill squirmed in his seat as he continued his speed writing, trying to get down all the points raised by the speakers as they went though their slides. Bill's copies of the slides were crammed full of notes and jottings that he had made during the sessions. Helen looked around and a polite quietness spread across the arena as each person waited for someone to raise a question. A round, middle-aged man in a light-gray suit pushed up his hand and almost grabbed the mike as it was passed over to him by a young man who rushed between the chairs with it. The man tapped the mike a few times and placed his lips so close to the device that his words boomed around the room.

"I'm Frank Fransome from Denver, Colorado. Is this ERM thing just another buzzword that we hear so much about and that will sink in a year or so?"

The Chair seemed pleased to hear the question and looked across at the morning's speakers for a volunteer. Sarrinda nodded and leaned forward to the mike in front of her as the Chair flanked by his speakers sat in a row facing the audience. The Chair pounced and said, "Would you like to have a go at this one, Sarrinda?"

Sarrinda, in her late thirties, small and compact in a trouser suit, said in a confident voice, "Thank you, Chair. You know, it's hard to say. There are many helpful tools that present themselves to management and then get replaced by newer and perhaps more helpful approaches as we strive to develop better ways of managing our affairs. In one sense ERM is new to many people, but in another way it is as old as the hills. This desire to take hold of fate and try to work out how and to what extent we can adapt to best suit the circumstances is something that has always been part of human nature. ERM is just an extension of this desire. We may call it something else in years to come but its essence remains. I think ERM is important and the sentiment that underpins the way risk can be gauged and responded to before an event occurs will not disappear. But the shape and form of the way we see risk and the way we respond may well alter in the future. Right here in the UK, the British government has issued guidance on strategic risk management. They call it the Orange Book and it recognizes the importance of understanding risk and innovation. The European Union has published guidance on risk management and internal control. And most countries have their own version of risk management with various guidance, standards, and best practice publications. It's not really going to go away. Just the opposite; people are getting more and more interested in the topic. But you do raise an interesting question. Someone once told me that nothing stays the same but the more it changes, the more it remains pretty much the essence of what it already was."

As Sarrinda spoke, the Chair carefully slid his watch toward him so that he could see the time and glanced at the fellow speakers. A quick mental calculation was all he needed to work out that he could not let each speaker answer each question, and with skill he moved things forward. "Time waits for no one, so we must push on. I see another hand over there . . ."

Pointing to a hand held up toward the back of the room and ignoring three hands held up in the front rows, the roving mike was rushed to the back and in no time it was shoved under the nose of a large, older man who looked as if he had changed his mind about asking a question. After looking at the mike for a few seconds as if it were a loaded weapon, he finally said, "If a company were only at the start of the maturity model, does that mean it will collapse?"

Stuart needed no prompts to recognize that this was his session that was being referred to and nodded to the Chair before he replied, "Not necessarily. ERM codifies what a good organization is doing. If you have not gone through a risk maturity process, then it is hard to tell whether you are doing things well or not. That is the organization. But it may be that instinctively risks are being mitigated and chances taken but in a careful manner, and people may not call this ERM at all. But risk maturity is a chance to benchmark intuitive decision making and tell the world how you work. More importantly, it is a chance to tell your staff how things should be working, and the fact is that business is under pressure to be more open. Communism has all but disappeared across the world but we have a form of cultured capitalism where big business is being held accountable for its actions and ERM is part of this drive to reveal how we work and how we deal with risk. Does that answer your question?"

A quick nod from the questioner closed that discussion.

Again, the Chair considered opening up the question to the other speakers but realized that lunch was fast approaching. He looked at the few hands that remained upright and said in a firm tone, "We have time for one last question. Over here please," pointing to a young lady near the front. She stood up and, using an impressive range of hand gestures, asked, "How can one set a risk appetite, if it's so hard to do?"

The Chair stood up, relieved that this called for a short answer. "Not a problem. We have a separate session on that so we'll leave that question in the air if you don't mind. See you back here at two."

The audience engaged in a combined shuffle in their seats as they spotted the large clock behind the speakers move on to the appointed lunch time. The Chair, still standing, made a sweeping gesture with his hands and said, "Before we go for lunch through the marked doors on my left, I feel we should thank the speakers in the usual manner."

A loud round of applause spread across the arena and tired limbs climbed out of comfortable chairs and the crowd shuffled their way to the large green sign that read "Restaurant," as the Chair, smiling broadly, shook each speakers' hand in turn.

Bill, Jack, and Helen joined the crowd and soon found themselves a table, although they had to split up and sit next to others who were already seated. The noise levels meant it was difficult to conduct a conversation with anyone other than an immediate neighbor. As the hotel staff set about their task of serving the set meal to the hundreds of delegates, a short, tanned-looking man next to Bill, in his late thirties and sporting a light brown suit, turned to Bill, "My name is Enrico Mendez, from South America. How are you enjoying the conference?"

"Hi. Name's Bill, from the States. Really good. I'm new to all of this and I guess I'm at level one in terms of maturity. That is, my company has not yet really looked at ERM seriously."

Bill looked across the table and saw Helen in an animated conversation with a younger man who seemed enthralled at her words. Enrico coughed slightly to attract Bill's attention, and said, "Okay. That's interesting. It's quite basic so far. But that's what they said they would do to start. My global board has sent me on a mission."

"What's that?" asked Bill politely.

"To tell them how they set the risk appetite for the group and our operating companies. Each one is different. And they cover the whole of South America, the States, and Canada."

Bill looked at Enrico, whose raised eyebrows suggested that a suitable response was required. Bill bit his bottom lip and searched for something to say about risk appetites. But before he could display his complete lack of knowledge, an attractive woman with flowing blond hair touched Bill on his arm and said in a sleepy voice, "Could I ask you to pour me a glass of water?"

Bill obliged and replied, "This here is Enrico. I'm Bill Reynolds, and you are?"

"Oh. Just call me Sherry. You from Texas?"

Bill laughed and said, "Funny you should say that. I'm a New Yorker. But my family is from Texas. In fact, I was born in Dallas but moved north soon after. Enrico was asking about risk appetite. Right?"

Enrico put down his fork midway from his mouth and studied his food as if deciding whether he should talk or get stuck into his meal. Looking at Sherry, he abandoned his food and assumed his most earnest gaze, gesturing with his hands as if caressing a football. "Yes, my dear Sherry. I am interested in risk appetite. Don't you think it is a most interesting topic?"

The absent look on Enrico's face suggested he would much rather talk about something a bit more intimate with this attractive lady. Sherry laughed and Bill and Enrico seemed to fall into a trance-like state looking at her. She said in a musical voice, "Absolutely. Risk appetite. It is a hard concept to get hold of and some say once you have a great appetite, it gets harder and harder to get satisfied."

Bill looked at Enrico and the silence that ensued reflected the difficulty they had in focusing on the topic in the presence of a beautiful woman. Before one of them could answer, Sherry got up and said, "Well, boys. That's my two cents. See you later." She turned to walk away, displaying a short skirt and long legs set in black high-heel shoes.

Enrico got up, shook Bill's hand, and said, "I've got to, uh . . . get going. Goodbye, Bill . . ." He quickly marched in the direction that Sherry took, following her strong perfume as she occasionally fell out of sight amid the crowd.

Jack moved across to Bill and asked, "Who's she?"

"Sherry something. Anyway, what about the conference? Like it so far?"

"Not bad. It's a bit hard to concentrate on the speeches. But I understand why the organizers have had to use this format. There are too many people here to make it a question-and-answer approach. I get bored at conferences, as it's hard to listen to someone at length. But I guess there's no other way to get the message across. You taking lots of notes?"

"Oh, yes." Bill glanced down at the file that he had taken with him for safekeeping. "Lots. Anyway, how about we rescue Helen from that guy over there and get a coffee? There's not too much time left until we resume."

CHAPTER 8

CONFERENCE SESSION FOUR

"Welcome back. I trust you had a good lunch and are raring to go. I remember asking my accountant how much tax I would need to pay this year. It seemed a straightforward question and he looked at my file, smiled, and replied, 'How much tax would you like to pay?' But seriously, folks: The public perception of big business is on the decline. We have had so many scandals over the years and it seems that back in the States, here in the UK, and almost anywhere you can think of, there is a regular flow of corporate scandals, along with a constant stream of government debacles. We, and I mean all of us here, need to think about the future for large multinationals as well as government and nongovernmental organizations. We need to think about the medium-sized concerns, the startup ventures, the share issues, and the way finance is raised. I think ERM has come at the right time, not just as another management tool, but a way of thinking about risk and telling others how you see it and how you are dealing with uncertainty.

We all know that some things happen and it's no one's fault. But we also know that people get paid to look for these problems and they get paid to sort them out. Sensible people get paid to take a lead in areas where others fear to tread. It always amazes me that some of the most important world resources sit in some of the most hostile places around the world. And this means we have to take risks to simply survive. Anyway, I hope that I have warmed you up for our next speaker. You can see from your files and the bios that Alfred Regina has been a senior figure in public sector risk management for many years and he will be talking about risk registers. Again we have asked our speakers to stick to the basics so that we might all be part of this journey through ERM and not just those of us who have more experience. Over to you, Alfred."

"Thank you, Chairman [*displays Slide 8.1*]. Good afternoon. I asked my accountant how much tax I will pay this year and he said that the good news was that he had the bill under control, but the bad news was that this was easy since I hardly earned any money. I am going to talk to you about risk registers. I know that many of you will be okay with this concept, but that others may not have come across the widespread

SLIDE **8.1**   *The Basics*

ERM Conference – London

Risk Registers

The Basics

use of risk registers as such. I do not have much time, so I'll get straight into it.

"What I have found is that people have different ideas of what is a risk register, and it is a good idea for each company or public body to define what registers mean to them and how they will be used. I'm going to stick to the basics and not get into too much detail. But what I can say is that no matter what type of organization and what type of business sector, from retail to building to insurance to investment to media to manufacturing, there will always be risks that need to be managed. And there will always need to be some way of capturing these risks on a formal document. Moreover, this basic concept applies equally to all public sector organizations.

"This is my formal definition of risk registers [*displays Slide 8.2*]. The registers form part of the ERM framework, but more than that, they form

SLIDE **8.2** *Risk Registers*

ERM Conference – London

Risk Registers

The Risk Register:

A record of risks, risk assessments, risk mitigations, and action plans prepared by the responsible parties that help support the overall ERM and controls disclosure reporting process

---

part of the accountability regime that applies to all but the smallest family-run and -owned company. So ERM means risks are understood and managed. Controls reporting means that we need a formal record of what is happening and how internal controls are being reviewed. This is an important point. Many organizations manage their risks instinctively, but there is no formal record of decisions, actions, and ways that issues are prioritized at both strategic and operational levels. We are now living in a claims society. As they say: "Where there's blame, there's a claim." It's funny how many leading politicians are trained as lawyers, and a cynic might argue that lawyers tend to promote a society based around lots of laws, lot of claims, and lots of legal actions. The corporate world is running scared. Executives and nonexecutives can be sued or even go to jail if they mess up. Don't get me wrong. They are paid big bucks for these responsibilities but they need to build safeguards into their business and make sure their managers are accountable for their decisions. Executives can take as many risks as they like so long as they make clear their position to investors and they take all reasonable steps to mitigate risk where possible and practicable. Documented ERM to my mind is a must. We need to get into the habit of explaining our decisions and ensuring they fit with the appropriate risk appetite. I guess this is a bit of the downside to ERM in that we have to construct some kind of process that can live up to external scrutiny. And this is where the risk register comes into its own—as a record of risks and risk management decisions and a way of reviewing underlying internal controls.

"I am not going to spend much time on this slide [*displays Slide 8.3*]. It is a basic risk register with columns or data fields for all the relevant bits of the risk management process. It ends with an action plan. There are many variations of this basic format, and a database approach means we can record sources of risk, how risk was assessed, the parties involved, recent control reviews and when last checked, record of issues regarding controls and recent changes to procedures, and so on. It's really up to you. You put in whatever information you feel is right to ensure significant risks are understood, captured, and addressed. I've put in Key Performance Indicators (KPIs) in the end column because if there are

SLIDE **8.3** *Objective*

ERM Conference – London

Risk Registers

Objective

REF	RISK	IMPACT	%	SCORE	RISK MITIGATIONS	BY	DATE	REVIEW KPI

---

action points arising from the risk assessment, then it is a good idea to locate KPIs so that these actions can be monitored. If, for example, a call center's main risk relates to high rates of customer complaints, it may be that the center staff are inefficient and the supervisors need to tighten up on the way staff use the customer information system. This strategy has to be set as a target, and the management need to be able to monitor progress, say by falling complaint rates or regular performance reports on center staff. It is better to set out customer complaints as a risk to be managed, rather than sit back and wait for a large number of complaints and then respond. Some people do not complain; they just stop using the service. This is where ERM comes in; to anticipate, and act, rather than sit back and hope for the best. Even where there are still some customer complaints, the management team can use their risk register to help explain the strategy for dealing with this matter. And the strategy can be endorsed by more senior people. Anyway, I do not want to get into too much detail, only to say that risk registers simply help codify and document the way a business is being managed.

"Risk registers are real versatile [*displays Slide 8.4*]. They can be used in many ways on many different aspects of corporate life. They can be used to record risk assessments in operational work teams, large contracts, new ventures, a manager's workload, financial systems, security arrangements, international marketing strategies, organizing a large conference, buying a new business, downsizing the workforce, and anything else you can think of. One important area is in project management. Many organizations run their business as a series of new projects. These businesses and public sector bodies may well have some core operations, but they spend a great deal of time, energy, and money on developing new systems or launching into new markets or products or services. These

SLIDE 8.4   *Project Objectives*

ERM Conference – London
Risk Registers
Project Objectives: Give all local and international office staff Internet access

REF	RISK	IMPACT	%	SCORE	RISK MITIGATIONS	BY	DATE	REVIEW KPI
8 June	Lack of operational capacity	H	M	80	Capacity planning exercise	FO	20 July	Report
25 June	Misuse by staff	H	H	92	Awareness training & blocking procedures	LD	19 Sept	Training days review
15 June	Excessive help desk use	M	M	55	Web site info & help phone service	FN	8 Aug.	Recruit new help desk staff
15 July	Inefficient staff surfing web	H	L	40	Supervisors interventions	SW	When live	When live
9 July	Project misses deadline	H	H	95	Project Milestones and sponsor	FT	On-going	Weekly reports
18 July	No commercial benefit	H	L	50	Business case reviews	SW	August	Project board reports
1 July	Poor support from operations staff	H	M	80	Staff seminars & web site news	SW	End Sept.	Monthly Attitude surveys
3 July	Security breaches	H	M	79	Security office review	GO	Aug.	Security report to project board
19 June	Poor procurement decisions	H	H	96	Use specialist procurement staff	LD	August	Procurement reports and costings
17 July	Frequent changes delaying project	M	M	60	Request for change system	FN	30 July	Procedure approve forms

matters can be swept into the generic concept of projects that need to be managed as such. Good projects incorporate the idea of ongoing risk assessments and good projects maintain dynamic risk registers to help ease the progress of the project. In the past, project risk assessment was a one-off exercise done at the start of the project, but things have moved on from here. I want to take you through a simple example of project risk assessment as a way of illustrating the way risk registers can be used. This register records some of the big risks to the project that were identified by the project team and stakeholders at a formal workshop. The risks were assessed and scored before being entered onto the register, and the project manager and key sponsor would review each one on a weekly basis. All progress reports to the project board included an up-to-date risk register that was always discussed as an agenda item. Let me take just one item from the register—excessive help desk use. The project team felt that this could mean a disrupted service and problems with poor response from the help desk and frustration from users. The mitigations were quite involved but in the main involved lots of training, web site help lines, and a lead person for each section who would have received extra training at the start of the process. The project budget also included an extra staff member for the help desk team and the recruitment of such a person was seen as a main target.

"One interesting side product from the risk register was a lessons-learned program. Here all of the issues that proved difficult were filed in a lessons-learned database and the company spent a great deal of time reviewing these lessons and holding web-based and face-to-face seminars on the points raised for future projects and programs. In fact, all new projects had to start with a review of the lessons-learned data, and this was seen as a really important step. Lessons learned tended to come from risks that had materialized because they were either not anticipated or just had not been dealt with properly. As such, a lot of information came from reviewing risk registers and ensuring that all the items were addressed and planned actions followed. The theme used in this organization was that risks should be tackled before they became live issues that hurt the business.

SLIDE 8.5   *Control Analysis*

"Okay [*displays Slide 8.5*]. It's all very well using a basic risk register on a project, but we need to stand back a bit and look at other implications. The thrust of corporate life is based around internal controls and ensuring that these controls are robust. Investors for private companies, and we the public for public service organizations, have a right to know whether an organization that we have a stake in is well controlled. That's to say whether our investment is safe, notwithstanding the level of risk that is involved. If we invest in a high-risk dot-com company, we expect great returns, but we are prepared to live with the volatile nature of this investment, which may well go bust. This is not a problem. 'You pays your money, and takes your chances.' What is important is that the level of control we expect, whatever the risk appetite, is actually achieved. That is, controls do what they are supposed to do.

This slide takes on the control dimension by getting into more detail. The risk register has a small column that I have called 'mitigations,' which is really about controls. Using the database rather than the spreadsheet approach, we can put in more data fields and drill down into things. For risk mitigations in identified controls we can go to the next schedule and examine the controls in some detail. We can check whether the controls are being complied with, since they are so important to managing significant risk. If, for example, one big risk in our payroll system is an internal firewall where payroll staff cannot access their own payroll account, then we may want to see whether this control is both robust and working as planned. The payroll manager may want to run regular checks over this control and keep it under constant review. If payroll staff can get into their own employee account, then this is obviously dangerous. The residual risk can be assessed as the risk left over after having put in suitable controls. These controls will need to be assessed to see how good they are in managing risk and then checked to see if they are being used as prescribed and are not bypassed at all. It is after weighing these issues and doing the necessary checks that a manager can say that controls have been reviewed and that risks have been managed down to fit the corporate risk appetite. This analysis will come out of the unit's risk register. I have put in the word 'evidence,' as the manager will want to be able to demonstrate that key controls have been checked and that there is good evidence to this effect.

"Our next issue is to work out how the risk register fits with the overall ERM process [*displays Slide 8.6*]. The risk assessments that should be an ongoing part of business life are based around assessing the impact and the likelihood of identified risks. This is in our x-y graph at the top right of the slide. When staff or managers are making this assessment, or periodic reassessments, the results should be recorded in the risk register as I have already suggested. But we can take this a step further and place the review KPI into the circle at the bottom right of the slide. The KPIs should be slotted into the overall performance profile that is applied in your organization. My version of this performance profile is about basic

SLIDE 8.6   *Impact—Likelihood*

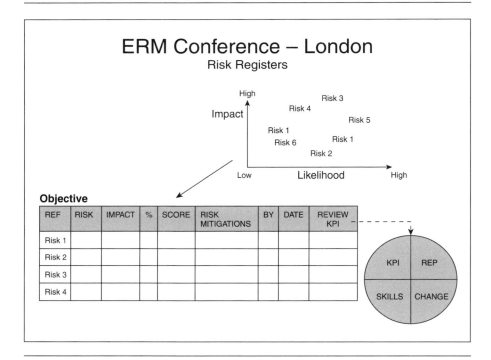

KPIs such as output measures, along with the development of skills that underpin performance. The other two items I use are change issues where staff are encouraged to get involved in the projects and improvements that are a feature of our workplace, and the final item is 'Rep.' This is the overall reputation of the work unit and how it is seen both by outsiders and within the organization. If we set the outputs from the risk register into our overall performance profiles, then ERM becomes part of the way services and resources are managed, rather than a separate concept that stays outside the main business. In fact, we can go further and build the concept of performance, employee skills, change issues, and reputation into our risk assessments and consider the risk of not achieving these ideals, along with normal business risk in our documented risk assessments.

SLIDE **8.7** *Detailed Assessment*

ERM Conference – London
Risk Registers

1. Detailed assessment

REF	RISK	IMPACT	%	SCORE	RISK MITIGATIONS	RO	DATE	REVIEW KPI

2. Summary assessment

REF	RISK	SCORE	RISK MITIGATIONS	RO	DATE	REVIEW KPI

3. High-level assessment

REF	RISK	RO	REVIEW KPI

"We need to take the risk register approach further [*displays Slide 8.7*]. One drawback of ERM is that there may be an abundance of risk registers popping up all over the organization. There's a register for everything that moves, breathes, and lives. People get swamped with paperwork and ERM starts to flop. It is seen as tons of bureaucracy that is all about form filling. This is the regulator's nightmare—no real business value, just lots of random documentation. My solution is to secure a hierarchical approach to risk registers and provide detailed registers at the sharp end of the business, summary registers for management levels, and high-level assessments for executives. Where we focus these reports on significant risk, where there is a high residual risk, then the logic is that high-level reports will be about crucial issues that suit the degree of seniority of those receiving the reports and making or endorsing relevant decisions. You really need to think through this hierarchical design and make sure it suits the way you do business.

"Let me work through this idea of organizational reporting systems [*displays Slide 8.8*]. Each part of the organization will have its own risk register, but these registers will be set out in a way that fits a predefined corporate standard. The registers will be made up for projects, new ventures, business units, operating outfits, and so on, as I described a few minutes ago. We will then need to aggregate the registers into middle management registers that run across, say, a whole department or subsidiary. Control disclosure reports come from the risk mitigation parts, as we have already mentioned, and these in turn are aggregated into a high-level report that feeds directly into the formal chief executive officer/principal finance officer's quarterly and annual control

SLIDE 8.8   *Department System*

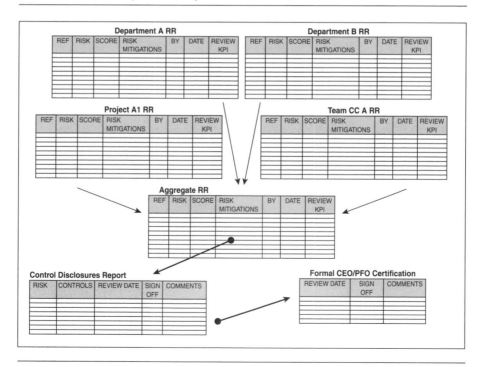

certifications. Does this sound simple? It can be, but the infrastructure needs to be sensible and respond to changes in the organization as it is restructured, changed, redesigned, and so on. In this way ERM, along with the internal audit and external auditors' reviews, feeds into internal control certifications in a reliable and meaningful way. But more than this, the registers feed into performance targets that drive the business so that it can be better and more efficient. I know of several organizations that have used registers to drive their business reporting system, but remember: Garbage in/garbage out. Risk registers are only as good as the material that goes into them and whether the risk assessments are carried out in a meaningful manner. There are no shortcuts. If staffs do not really believe in the risk assessments and action plans that result from these assessments as a main part of their

SLIDE **8.9**   *The Risk Register*

ERM Conference – London

Risk Registers

The Risk Register:

A way of making everyone feel part of the journey
that forms a reliable record of what's good
and what needs improving.

---

work, then this approach and the way that it fits with their reporting structure, the whole ERM process, will not stack up in the long run. But if staff can buy into meaningful ERM, then we can make good progress.

"I want to finish with my new and more powerful definition of the risk register [*displays Slide 8.9*]. Do you like it? Many thanks, and that's all from me."

CHAPTER 9

CONFERENCE SESSION FIVE

"Super presentation. Many thanks, Alfred. I know the feeling when a whole raft of risk logs gets reported in such detail that it gives no overall impression. I also sat on an audit committee that went through years of receiving overkill reports that went into far too much detail. We wanted the high-level picture, but we also wanted to know that we could get someone to drill down into detail if there was an issue that needed exploring properly. I recall seeing some red risks flagged up on a report about staff disciplinary action and that controls were poor. Anyway, we picked up on this and asked for detailed reports that went into the causes. Eventually we found that management in one operating company was paying off staff when they fell foul of the disciplinary procedures, as they felt it was too expensive to launch an enquiry and hold a disciplinary hearing. The upshot was that people who wanted to leave the company misbehaved, got paid off, and went to their new job—a very worrying situation. Our next speaker is going to have a go at this idea of risk appetite. If you look at your file, you will see that Dan Blocker has a great deal of experience in a whole range of different organizations and we are lucky to have him here to talk about his perspective on risk appetites."

"Hello. I'm Dan Blocker and I work as a freelance risk management consultant [*displays Slide 9.1*]. Sounds good, doesn't it? It basically means I help keep company directors out of jail, wherever possible. Anyway, I need to tell you the background to my presentation at this international ERM conference here in London. Just under a year ago, I made a presentation to the board of a small private company on ERM and how it could be used to create a business advantage in a highly competitive environment. During the presentation, one of the directors asked what was the difference between risk appetite and risk tolerance, and I said they were much the same—that is, how much risk a company was prepared to take to stay ahead and survive in the long term. Later that night I thought about this point and felt that I had misled the board and that appetite and tolerance were not really the same at all. Anyway, over

SLIDE 9.1   *Risk Appetite—Coverage*

ERM Conference – London

Risk Appetite – Making Sense of It All
Dan Blocker

Coverage

1. Why Risk Appetite?

2. Appetite and Tolerance.

3. Four V Model.

4. Ways Forward.

the last six months I have worked with many different clients and I have made a bit of a study of this idea of risk appetite. It is the results of my somewhat limited work that I wish to share with you today. I want to discuss why risk appetite is important, and the difference between that and tolerance. I want also to mention a model I found in a book that I recently came across, and to close, I want to think about moving forward with ERM.

"I first pose the question: Why is risk appetite so important [*displays Slide 9.2*]? To me the concept of risk appetite seems to drive the whole ERM process. We can put four top managers around a table and ask them to develop new ideas for our business services. Whether to reinforce the main brand, or diversify into new but suitable areas, or whether to set up loads of new projects or, say, streamline our procedures. We could

SLIDE **9.2**   *Why Risk Appetite?*

ERM Conference – London

Risk Appetite – Making Sense of It All
Dan Blocker

1. Why Risk Appetite?

perhaps focus on customer needs and try to build them into our business systems so that we become leaders in giving a hassle-free service. But the proposals that come up from these four managers depend on their perspective, or in my language, their risk appetite. I know one manager who got poached by another competitor because he was surging ahead with ideas for dynamic new web-based services but his company did not want to move so quickly. A competitor spotted his frustration and explained that they support rapid innovation, and he jumped ship. The new company's high-risk appetite suited this person much more than the existing company's more sedate approach. If our people do not speak the same language in terms of what is seen as risky and what is seen as good business, then our four managers pictured in the slide will have a hard time agreeing to ways forward. The problem with risk appetite is that people do not bother to challenge the concept and find out where the top executives, or for that matter, where the shareholders stand in this matter. I think that the challenge for ERM in the future will be based around the idea of risk appetite and all that this entails.

"I told you that I felt I misinformed a client about appetites and tolerance [*displays Slide 9.3*]. The model I use here is fairly basic. It simply says that inherent risk is what faces the organization as it operates in the business climate in question. An international oil company operating in unstable parts of the world may have a lot of inherent risk, while a well-established spare-parts supply company may run a basic operation that is quite straightforward and have low inherent risk. But all organizations face some kind of risk and therefore controls need to be put in place to reduce this risk to what we call residual risk. That is the level of risk that is left when we have established mitigations. An oil company may have a huge security procedure to ensure that staff working in volatile sites overseas are properly protected and that the operation runs smoothly, while our supply company may have a robust inventory control system to ensure the right goods get to the right place. The residual risk that is left over will be low, high, or somewhere in between.

SLIDE **9.3**   *Making Sense*

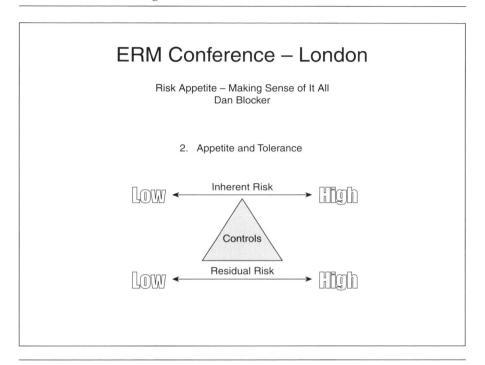

"Okay, we move now into our discussion of appetite and tolerance [*displays Slide 9.4*]. They are not the same. Risk appetite in my book is the level of risk that the organization is attracted to, to carry out its business and develop its future strategies, which will vary between the two extremes—low and high. Our supply company may be very aggressive and want to break into new markets by taking over existing companies or winning new contracts and have a high risk appetite. The oil company may not bother about new explorations or breaking into new sites that are hard to get to because it has a low risk appetite. It depends on the board and what it needs to deliver to the shareholders and investors. Much the same applies to the public sector, where government organizations may want to keep a low profile and stay out of trouble. Or, they may want to try out new things and get their services out to the public in innovative ways. Whatever the appetite, risk tolerance is different because it is based

SLIDE **9.4**   *Appetite and Tolerance*

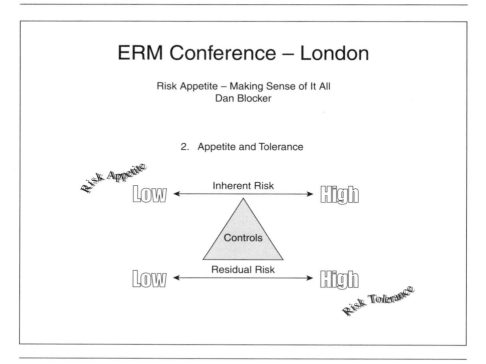

on the type of controls that the organization installs to guard against risk. That is, it depends on the level of residual risk that the organization sees as acceptable. A company in a high-risk environment may install many levels of control because it has a low tolerance for residual risk. Another company may give its people loads of space to go out and explore new ideas with little controls in place over their activities because it has a more reckless approach to making quick wins. Controls cost money and they tend to slow things down, so they are only put in where they are needed. And this depends on the risk tolerance levels that rule in an organization. That's the difference between risk appetite and risk tolerance.

"I need to put one further spin on my model, literally [*displays Slide 9.5*]. That is, rather than appear as a pyramid that leads to low or high risk tolerance, the control component should be spun around. In our model it is skewed to mean that more controls are located at high-risk

SLIDE 9.5   *Appetite and Tolerance, with a Spin*

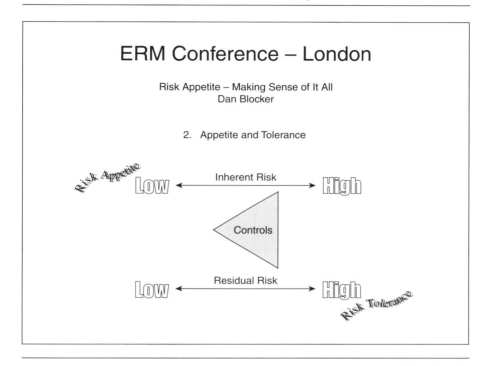

aspects of the business, where there is a high inherent risk, and fewer controls at the low-risk aspects of the business. In this way we can suggest that rather than see risk tolerance as low or high, we can aim at a low risk tolerance at all times. That is, we take risks and are attracted to businesses that have high inherent risks but we ensure that this is not reckless by installing controls to get the residual risk to an acceptable level. We take risks, but only where it makes sense and it does not expose us too much. We aim at considered risk taking by making sure our controls fit the bill.

"We all know about the risk grid [*displays Slide 9.6*]. That is the Impact and Probability grid where you measure the impact of a risk if it were to materialize and the likelihood of such a risk arising. The grid then allows managers to focus on high-impact/high-likelihood risks and ensure that these areas of the business are kept under control. Reports of red

SLIDE 9.6   *Four V Model*

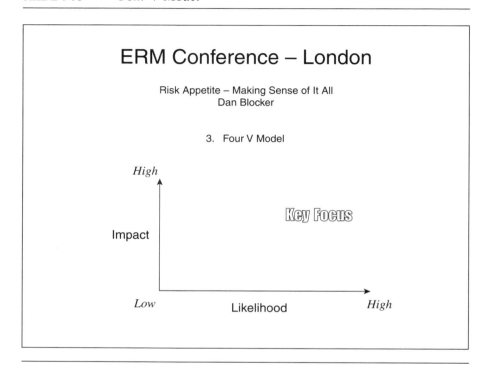

risks at the top right of the grid will be accelerated upward throughout the organization. Great; then let's move on.

"I came across an interesting model as I looked into this question of risk appetite [*displays Slide 9.7*]. This is in a book published by John Wiley and Sons called *Auditing for Managers: The Ultimate Risk Management Tool*. Its ISBN number is 0-470-09098-7. Although the book does go on a bit, there is some useful stuff on risk appetites. It suggests that instead of trying to get a final figure or fixed view on risk appetite, we could set out a framework within which we set tolerances of what is acceptable and what is not. The book suggests we widen the view of business objectives to bring in the needs of key stakeholders, including regulators, users of published accounts, and investors who want to know that their investment is protected in these uncertain times. The four V model says that there are four considerations when thinking about risk levels:

SLIDE 9.7   *Four V Model—Auditing for Managers*

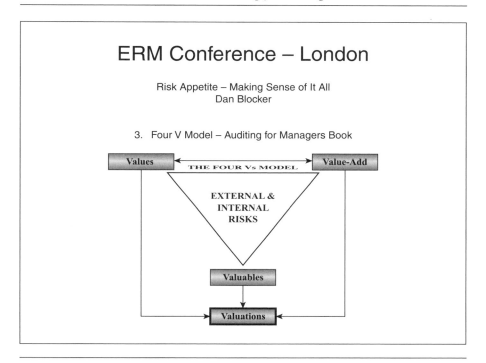

1. **Valuables.** This is the resources, assets, people, and intellectual heart of the business and ways that we can protect it from external attack, fraud, accidents, waste, and loss. The board can set tolerances on what it accepts as natural waste and what it sees as unacceptable exposures.

2. **Values.** These are the core principles that underpin the organization, and the board may suggest that these are nonnegotiable. In this case, there is zero tolerance for any behavior that undermines the corporate values of the organization.

3. **Valuation.** This is how the organization is presented to the outside world, including the published accounts. In the past we have seen tremendous problems where companies have tried to massage their figures, accounting policies, and performance ratios to

keep investors happy. Again, the board may allow only a small margin or discretion for any sharp practices.

4. **Value add.** This is the final criterion and this is what the organization does. It is the business part of the equation. Here there may be quite a high tolerance for risk, where managers are encouraged to go out and explore new ventures, new ideas, and new markets. But where there is a conflict between retaining core values, say on wider social responsibility, protecting the resource base, or reporting the results (that is, valuation), then the CEO and board should set rules to deal with any significant inconsistencies.

"The Four V model uses this basic principle and compiles a four-dimensional grid to reflect the four Vs that we have discussed [*displays*

SLIDE **9.8**   *Auditing for Managers Book*

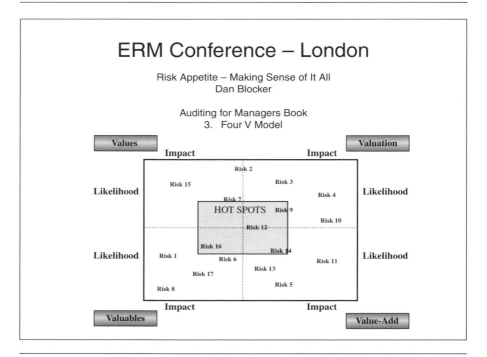

Slide 9.8]. In this way, senior management can focus on the middle box where high-impact/high-likelihood matters that impact any of the four Vs can be isolated and considered. These high-priority risks are referred to above as Hot Spots. Quite a useful approach, don't you think?

"I have looked at risk appetite and some of the theory behind this concept [*displays Slide 9.9*]. But we can't really come up with definitive answers. An investor cannot look at a table of companies and see a figure for their risk appetite and say, 'I'll go with this one as it suits my profile.' The investment industry does have a basic view on different stocks and whether they are volatile with potentially big returns or whether they are steady stocks that are less exciting but with much less risk attached to them. This equation is well understood by most investors. What we don't have is a generic index that says this is a reckless company that states that

SLIDE **9.9**   *Ways Forward*

ERM Conference – London

Risk Appetite – Making Sense of It All
Dan Blocker

4. Ways Forward

it may collapse or break through in a big way and this other company publishes a different risk index that reflects its own risk appetite. Risk appetite differs in industries, organizations, within different parts of an organization, and between different people who may work on the same team. Ways forward is really about making sure each organization is able to develop a worthwhile framework that makes sense to its people and its stakeholders, and then goes on to develop policies that are derived from their framework and that make it different from other organizations than may be in the same basic business. Not an easy process; but this approach is better than just ignoring ERM and not bothering to think about the ideas that underpin the concepts of risk appetite and risk tolerance.

"We have had a quick look at why risk appetite is important in ERM and how, using the idea of controls and residual risk after controls have been employed, appetite can be seen as different from tolerance [*displays*

SLIDE **9.10**   *Back to Coverage*

ERM Conference – London

Risk Appetite – Making Sense of It All
Dan Blocker

Back to Coverage:

1. Why Risk Appetite?

2. Appetite and Tolerance.

3. Four V Model.

4. Ways Forward.

Slide 9.10]. We have had a quick look at the four V model as one way of viewing the issues behind the risk debate and we have considered ways forward. Each of you will have your own view on how ERM can be used to work for you and each of you will have your own interpretation of risk appetite. I find it is a fascinating subject and one that will be subject to much debate and discussion for many years to come. Well, that's all from me, folks, and I thank you for your time."

CHAPTER 10

CONFERENCE SESSION SIX

"Well, Dan, we've all been waiting for the risk appetite session and that was great. I endorse your view that it is for each organization to decide where it is going with risk appetite and that there is no quick fix here. The best-run companies give boundaries to their people and then let them loose. If you don't do this, then you will not be letting them loose but you will be letting them lose. Our final speaker for the day is Solomon Propos. As you can see from the file, Solomon has traveled far to bring us his messages on ERM. But the focus here is on fraud risk management. I have heard Solomon speak before and he is on a mission to convert us nonbelievers. So be prepared to be challenged. Ladies and gentlemen, Solomon Propos."

"Good afternoon [*displays Slide 10.1*]. I have to say, Chair, that I'm not sure I can challenge anyone here today and I'm only five-foot-five and quite a peaceful man, most of the time. But I feel you are right; our messages should be challenging and ERM is a great vehicle to bring forth important matters. What matters most will feature in an assessment of risk, and I don't care what banner I fly under, so long as I can have a chance to tell you about my concerns as we move further into the new millennium. I want to take you through my personal view on fraud risk management. I've been around a bit and seen the risk

SLIDE **10.1**   *Fraud Center Stage*

ERM Conference – London

Fraud Risk Management

Solomon Propos

Let's Put Fraud Center Stage

in

Risk Management

---

management machine on the march. Most companies are pretty okay with their basic risk management and are starting to get to grips with the new ERM thing. But I have some issues that I want to share with you today. Mainly this is about the failure of many managers to put fraud inside the ERM frame. I say it's just not good enough. Over the last year or so, I've been on a mission to put this right, that is, to put fraud center stage when thinking about risk and risk management. A lot of what I will go through today is based around the presentations that I deliver across various private and public sector organizations that invite me to speak to them. I have quite a few slides to go through, so we will need to make this a short, sharp presentation. So, hold on to your seats and off we go.

SLIDE 10.2   *The Risks*

ERM Conference – London

Fraud Risk Management
Solomon Propos

The Risks:

- **ACFE study covered 508 cases of occupational fraud totaling over $761 million in losses.**

- **Organizations suffer tremendous costs as a result of occupational fraud and abuse – estimated the typical U.S. organization loses 6% of its annual revenues to fraud.**

- **Applied to the US Gross Domestic Product for 2003, this translates to approximately $660 billion in total losses.**

ACFE Report to the Nation 2004

"We need go no further than the ACFE, the Association of Certified Fraud Examiners, for a view of fraud in the United States [*displays Slide 10.2*]. The one figure that jumps out at me is that organizations are losing some 6% of their annual revenue. This is real scary. More than that, it's a real cause for concern. Why is this happening? And what can we do about it? I do not have the answers but it seems to me that if we can put fraud into the ERM framework, then we can at least make a start. I do not mean to lecture to you and I'm sure that many of you are doing a good job. It's just that I've worked with quite a few organizations and seen quite a lot of poor practices in terms of dealing with, or more correctly, failing to deal with employee fraud.

"I guess it's always a good idea to start with a definition of occupational fraud [*displays Slide 10.3*]. We can turn again to the ACFE for

SLIDE **10.3**   *ACFE Report to the Nation*

ERM Conference – London

Fraud Risk Management

ACFE Report to the Nation 2004:

Defining "occupational fraud":

"The use of one's occupation for personal enrichment through the deliberate misuse or misapplication of the employing organization's resources or assets."

---

their views. Most people work for a fair day's pay. But there are some that are there for their own personal gain over and above this equation. Where this gain is deliberately secured in the sense that it involves the misuse or misapplication of resources, we enter the murky waters of employee fraud.

"When I deliver fraud awareness seminars, I tend to use imagery to help get the audience to rally round a simple concept [*displays Slide 10.4*]. Most risk management concepts use red to indicate where something is bad. Red risks mean danger, and these are dealt with by the responsible manager and should also get reported upward. But in my world, we need to turn things on their head. Red means a red stoplight for potential fraudsters. Green gives the go-ahead to the fraudster to take on your company. Remember, fraud can be carried out by employees, or outsiders, including criminal gangs, or a real dangerous scenario where an insider colludes with external parties to get into your systems.

"In my experience, organizations that present a clear red light to fraudsters are better placed than those that do not bother to take this risk seriously. Where management can't be bothered, the light remains green and you will be vulnerable. A significant fraud may never happen, but good fraud risk management makes it much more likely that you can stay in the clear, one step ahead of the fraudster. Be very clear about this. Fraud is big business and some of the characters out there are pretty scary. In one organization a cashier was approached by a shady young man as she left work and was quietly taken to one side and told that her teenage son's leg would get broken if she did not provide her system identification and password. In another case I worked on, a

SLIDE 10.4   *What Are We Saying?*

ERM Conference – London

Fraud Risk Management

What are we saying to the prospective fraudster?

temporary staff member was taken on in a sensitive job and we found that he was actually part of a well-known criminal gang involved in company credit card fraud. If you do not build a stoplight for these people, anything could happen.

"Before we move away too far from the ERM agenda, let me tie some of this fraud stuff into the conference theme [*displays Slide 10.5*]. Risk is about things that affect your objectives, good and bad things. Management has got to understand these risks and each manager is responsible for dealing with risks that affect their work. Fraud is one risk that, when it breaks, can cause a great deal of embarrassment. It can also be quite unpleasant as it may challenge some of the long-held beliefs that all your colleagues at work are okay and not evil. But unlike most risks, fraud involves a deliberate attempt to deceive and mislead. And more

SLIDE **10.5**   *Special Factors*

ERM Conference – London

Fraud Risk Management

Special factors on fraud risk management:

1. **Risk - chance of an event that impacts on your objectives**
2. **Management's responsibility to manage risk**
3. **Fraud causes loss, exposure, and public embarrassment**
4. **Deliberate nature of fraud**
5. **The best planned frauds are invisible**
6. **Fraudsters attack areas where there are weak controls**

than this, frauds can happen without anyone knowing that they have been hit. Complex frauds can involve concealment where it is not clear that there has been a loss and that someone has abused your systems.

"The final point to note is the close link between fraud risk and controls. Good controls can guard against fraud, but these days we have to be firmer and say that where controls are not robust, the likelihood of fraud increases. In fact, some fraudsters are so sophisticated that they know which companies are lax in their controls and they know which law enforcement agencies are understaffed and which parts of the country suffer from lack of police resources. These fraudsters have done their own risk assessment. So fraud is a risk that has several peculiarities that can make it more difficult to spot and manage. I examined one simple fraud where a finance staff member added $300 dollars to staff expense claims hundreds of times and made up vouchers to the extra value. He paid out the correct amount on the claims and pocketed the difference. But the vouchers looked authentic and the auditors checked them off for several years before someone spotted the trend where standard round sums were included in the claims. I was told about another case right here in the UK, where a government legal agency sent out an inspector to visit the house of deceased persons to look for a will. The inspector started making up fraudulent wills, making the estate payable to his associates; this went on for over five years before it was found out. These types of fraud can be hard to uncover, and in both cases the losses were pretty much absorbed and not entirely obvious.

"This is one of my favorite slides [*displays Slide 10.6*]. I call it the four-star failure syndrome. I have found that many people at work and at all levels of management just do not understand the risk that fraud presents, and I have pinned this down as due to four main issues.

"Many managers cannot see the link between controls and fraud. They operate a workplace that has weak controls and feel this is okay so long as the performance targets are hit. What they do not realize is that poor controls may not affect performance but they can lead to losses, waste, and abuse.

SLIDE **10.6** *A Four-Star Failure*

ERM Conference – London

Fraud Risk Management

A four-star failure:

Weak Controls

Dishonest Employees

Negligent Managers

Unprotected Resources

"The next item is negligent managers. Some people do not like to report fraud or expose it in some way, as they feel that they in turn will be exposed. Some companies fire a fraudulent employee and do not want to do any more. If it were to go public, management would then be faced with the prospect of being implicated as negligent or simply mixed up in it all. I have seen this many times where senior people just want the problem to go away as they may face tough questions about their failure to stop it happening. Or, they may be seen as failing to be on guard to the warning signs that there was something wrong.

"The next issue relates to organizations that do not make clear who is responsible for which resources. They set tight targets for their management team that encourage them to turn a blind eye to how their staff achieve these targets and what shortcuts happen. Some finance companies like to lend monies at high interest rates and do not check on what their salespeople are doing to close deals. So long as the number of approved loans is rising, anything goes. These same managers do not always understand their responsibility to protect the company's resources and reputation in the marketplace.

"The final part of the jigsaw relates to the idea of dishonest employees. Many organizations find it hard to accept that their people may not be all they appear to be. It is a fact that the more senior and more experienced people can do more damage simply because they have more access to systems and decision making and simply because they tend to have a great deal of knowledge about the procedures and how they work in practice. Some more senior managers can override standard procedures and they rule over their staff, making it hard for junior people to ask questions or demand the right paperwork. When a company is hit by a long-standing manager, it can go into shock and want to hide the matter rather than expose it to public glare if it goes through the courts.

"The image I have given to this slide is that when a lone voice preaches about fraud risk management, it can fall on deaf ears because of the four factors that go to make the four-star failure. I've seen some organizations write off losses due to fraud as part of business life rather than take it seriously and go to court, recover funds, and face up to the reality of poor controls and secretive management. Fraudsters and people involved in scams and abuse tend to flourish in this type of environment. What's more, management actually runs the business on behalf of the stakeholders and they must take all reasonable steps to both protect and promote that business. An ERM process that does not have this ethos built into the way it is established will be poor.

"Returning to the fraud theme, I want to mention four ingredients of fraud [*displays Slide 10.7*]. First, there has to be one or more persons who are equipped and willing to carry out fraud and abuse, that is, dishonest people who feel that it is okay to get involved in criminality. We will be returning to this point later on. Second, there must be assets or interests that are at risk. This could be cash, attractive items, information, or

SLIDE **10.7**   *Four Basic Elements*

ERM Conference – London

Fraud Risk Management

Four Basic Elements:

1. People to carry out fraud
2. Assets to acquire
3. Intent
4. Opportunity

Present and Correct = Fraud

---

anything that has a value to someone. Third, there must be intent to commit fraud. There is no point assuming everyone is dishonest and firing anyone who makes a mistake or loses something on the assumption that it must be fraud. In any investigation, one of the first questions to pose is, Could the loss be quite accidental? We will need to show that there was an intention to deceive rather than just an unfortunate incident that caused loss to the organization. The final point is that there needs to be an opportunity for fraud to arise, that is, in my book, a failing in control that means someone can breach our systems and get away with something of value. The interesting thing with good fraud risk management is that rather than say these four things need to be in place for fraud to happen, we can take a different stance. We can say that if these four elements come together, then there will be fraud. And if we do not take steps to make sure that these risks are managed, then we will be falling down on the job.

"I told you that I spend my time going around the country and talking to organizations about fraud and the dangers of poor fraud risk management [*displays Slide 10.8*]. But I'm often flying solo in that there are many strong forces that make it hard to get people to take the risk of fraud seriously. Let's run through them quickly:

- **General lack of awareness.** People may just not appreciate that fraud and the chance that fraud will arise is an ever-present threat. If someone phones through and says they need to log onto the system and cannot recall their password, a lot of people will just give them this sensitive piece of information. They do not understand that this information could be used to cause a lot of damage.

SLIDE 10.8   *Reasons Not to Bother*

ERM Conference – London

Fraud Risk Management

REASONS NOT TO BOTHER:

General lack of awareness	Not seen as a personal threat
No real victims	Business before security
Not understanding fraud and controls	Not seen as high risk
Security = doorman issue	Pressure of work
Less experienced managers	Face-value assumptions
Less time for procedures	Rely on insurance cover
Perks are just perks	Undetected fraud is OK
Only happens in chaotic organizations	We need to trust our people
Board agenda crammed	

- **Not seen as a personal threat.** Another problem is where fraud is not seen as a real issue. I've seen shop security staff sitting around and failing to watch suspicious customers because it is too much bother.
- **No real victims.** There is one school of thought that fraud does not affect real people. It is just a small dent in the huge money that big business makes. Some fraudsters feel that their needs are greater and no one will miss a few thousand dollars.
- **Business before security.** Demanding targets drive business and many employees want to sell stuff or make stuff available without bothering to make sure the assets are secure. A corner shop may display its goods out on the street and feel that even if they are at risk of theft, it is worth it to get the exposure for their goods.

"Many organizations have a tremendous range of assets and personal information that needs to be kept secure but delegate securing this information to low-paid security staff who have little understanding of the value of what they are guarding. A night watchman may be given a dozen CCTV monitors to study that he more or less ignores most of the time.

"Pressures of work may mean that checks and questions are not always asked as people are just too busy. A series of complicated low-value invoices may just not be checked, but the aggregate value of payments may become quite large. Temporary staff may work whatever hours they want and put in inflated claims because people are just too busy to check them properly.

"I am not going to go over the other factors on the slide, but it is clear that people can do more work when they don't ask tough questions and just accept that nothing can go wrong or, if it does, it is not really their responsibility—or someone else can take the blame. The sad thing is that there are many organizations that have a culture where people are lax and procedures hazy, which can lead not only to fraud, but also to coverups, and make it really hard to investigate and work out what should be the correct procedure in use. I will pick out one important factor called 'perks and just perks.' This is where teams get used to abusing the system as a way of life. These low-level scams can add up to a great deal of money and can also escalate into bigger things. Moreover, once managers accept small scams they may be blackmailed into silence as they become culpable if it gets out of control. In some cases these supervisors also get involved because whichever way it breaks, they would be in trouble if the scam were to come to light.

"There are lots of reasons why people do not see corporate fraud as an issue [*displays Slide 10.9*]. But there are also many reasons why both big and smaller organizations are starting to take more of an interest. The cost of fraud at what we said could be up to 6% is significant. The laxer the attitude, the greater the risk and the costs involved. This also impacts

SLIDE **10.9**   *Reasons to Bother*

ERM Conference – London

Fraud Risk Management

REASONS TO BOTHER:
- Financial costs
- Business reputation
- Protect resources
- Culpability
- Company accountability
- Stakeholders
- Encourage dishonesty
- Become a target
- New business context

SHOULD WE BOTHER?

on the business reputation. Would you want to trade with an organization that does not take care of your personal data? And who allows this data to get into the hands of criminals who could steal your identity? Would you deal with a company that is rocked by scandal and rumor on a regular basis? Top management must protect the corporate assets and they may be culpable if they have failed to do so. This equation is part of corporate accountability and ways that management should account back to their stakeholders. If there are sound antifraud policies in place, then the organization is better placed to tackle fraud. Taking fraud seriously discourages dishonesty and means that the company may not be as big a target as another one that has not resourced their antifraud efforts. And the new business context means that customers are happy to use a web-based interface or deal with the company over the phone as part of the changing nature of business—but only where they feel the company is in control of all important risks, including fraud. I feel that the reasons to bother about fraud really outweigh the reasons not to. It's just that the CEO, board, and executive management team need to understand this equation. It's not just about being good, but there is a real business driver to think about. My own view is that it is your duty to understand the nature of the risk and to take all reasonable steps to guard against fraud and make sure your staff does likewise. Nothing less than this will do.

"Okay [*displays Slide 10.10*]. Now I've been going on about the need to put fraud on the agenda and ensure it is tackled. But what about you? I know that the standard rules say that you should not ask delegates questions at conferences. But I don't mind breaking the rules if it's for a good cause. Look at your handout packs and have a go at answering this question. A show of hands, please: In your organization, are your people essentially honest all the time? That's a pretty high showing. Nearly all of you feel that your staff is honest. How many are completely dishonest? No hands at all. How many are basically honest, but might go bad depending on the circumstances? That's just three; no, five or six of you. Thanks, ladies and gentlemen, for your efforts. Let's leave it there for now and turn to the next slide.

SLIDE **10.10** *Your View of Honesty*

ERM Conference – London

Fraud Risk Management

Your Views of Honesty:

%

A. Essentially honest all the time

B. Really depends on the circumstances

C. Essentially dishonest most times

100%

"The vast majority of you have just told me that your employees are essentially honest [*displays Slide 10.11*]. That's fine. But I have spent a lot of time investigating the downside, where people go bad. And I can tell you, it happens. People are motivated by different things and some are attracted to material things like crazy. I know one guy who stole like mad and bought a huge beach house in West Palm Beach. He was trying to acquire a light aircraft when we caught up with him. Some people are motivated by need. They have a pressing need that overwhelms them. It becomes the most important thing in their life and may be something they need to do for a close relative or friend. Opportunity is another factor. Some people do bad things because they can. They feel that if the company can't be bothered to tie things down then they might as well pick them up. This is related to the next point on technical

SLIDE **10.11** *Why Does it Happen?*

ERM Conference – London

Fraud Risk Management

Why Does it Happen?:

- **Motivation – greed or need**

- **Opportunity**

- **Technical ability**

- **Risk of discovery**

- **Expectation of discovery**

- **Consequences of discovery**

---

ability. I recall one IT expert who had a back door in the payments system, and he could stop a payments run, change details, and restart the run at any time. This included the ability to change the payee's name and address. Where the risk of discovery is low and if found out the remedy is known to be relatively painless, then some people may think it's worthwhile. There are people around who commit crimes because they know that the fine, if they are found out, is much less than the amount they have gained. Some health care frauds and travel frauds have this flavor. Where a fraudulent employee can just walk away from a problem if found out, then this is not much of a deterrent. What I'm saying is that rational people can weigh the pros and cons of bad behavior and have a go—they kind of do their own risk assessment and then act on the results.

SLIDE **10.12**   *Ingredients*

ERM Conference – London

Fraud Risk Management

INGREDIENTS:

* **Perceived opportunity**

* **Nonshareable pressure**

* **Rationalization**

"We have said that good people can go bad, and the result can be tremendous [*displays Slide 10.12*]. I've seen a hit-and-run crime where a finance staffer diverted a check, changed the amount to near $1 million, banked it over a holiday weekend, withdrew it, and left the country before the alteration had been discovered and acted on. It all depends on timing and knowing the system. Fraud happens where the employee or associate has seen an opportunity to abuse the system, and experiences what some call nonshareable pressure. That is, something bugs them that they cannot talk about and get help on. It may be a financial dilemma due to drug or alcohol abuse, or an addiction to gambling or expensive one-night stands. It may be that they feel demotivated at work and believe that the employer is unfair and exploits them. Whatever the issue, the key is that the employer doesn't have a way of picking up on these problems and providing support or guidance before they get out of hand. Rationalization is a big issue. This means an otherwise-honest person may get involved in fraud because they feel that the reasons why they should outweigh the reasons why they should not. So it becomes less a crime and more of a necessity. A man who has been refused health care coverage because of a technicality may turn to fraud because he feels the system is so unfair that he is not being dishonest, but simply evening the odds. Rationalization is dangerous because an apparently honest person, who has always been trustworthy, can turn, and this risk may not be fully appreciated. This is why tight staff vetting systems when recruiting people is not the only answer. People can go bad after they get into the company.

"I asked you to tell me if people can be dishonest and most of you said everyone they know is honest [*displays Slide 10.13*]. But you cannot build controls based on an assumption of honesty. If this were the case, I would not be going on about fraud risk management, because if everyone is honest, then there is no risk. But the reality is that a lot of people fit into category two in that they are kind of honest but circumstances can change to tempt them. I'm not saying that most organizations employ tons of dishonest staffers. What I am saying is that you have to design internal controls in a pragmatic way and not based on the assumption of complete honesty.

"Okay, with that in mind, let's shoot through the risk management cycle. You have your objectives and I feel they should be reviewed to incorporate the need to adhere to all legal provisions and protect the corporate resource from abuse. Next, you work out which parts of your business could be vulnerable to fraud where there are assets, resources, and personal data under your control. Assess which parts are most at risk and where a fraudster could do most damage and then make sure responsibility is clearly defined for minimizing the risk. Controls should be put in place to protect the resource base, bearing in mind the risks that you have identified, and then these controls should be kept under constant review as the nature of fraud changes as we move into on-line business and empowered supervisors who can make lots of local

SLIDE 10.13   *Fraud*

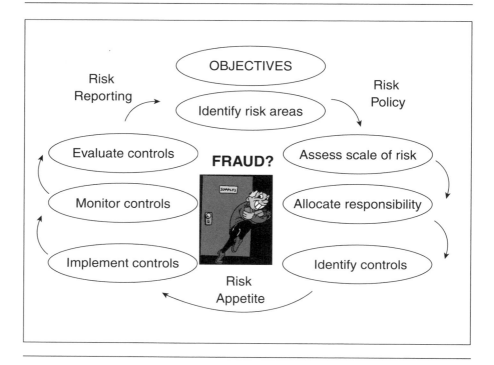

decisions. As such, you need to evaluate your controls regularly and keep up-to-date with fraud issues and new trends and new threats. That is the fraud risk management cycle in shorthand with the overall policy, the level of acceptable risk, that is, the risk appetite, and the final part, which is your duty to report on the way you make sure fraud is understood, assessed, and properly contained. Quite a lot for you to do.

"It's not all bad news [*displays Slide 10.14*]. We can substitute a Four-Star Success model in place of the failure model that I mentioned earlier:

1. Corporate ethics and a sound antifraud policy, where the corporate machine has bothered to make ethics a big deal; this can be used as the engine to drive antifraud measures.
2. Fraud awareness training is important—training in fraud response and what is involved in supporting a formal investigation,

SLIDE **10.14** *A Four-Star Success*

including the rights of suspects and legal provisions regarding evidence and whether it is admissible in the courts.

3. Alert and proactive staff are looking out for problems that indicate that fraud is happening or could happen. This is so important. Many frauds are found out by staff who challenge something that appears odd or inconsistent. It's not as if this is an explicit part of their job but it is just that they look around at what's happening, what people are doing, and where something does not stack up. You know customer complaints can be quite important. They could indicate where goods, cash, assets, or even staff time has been misdirected. Rather than have staff just try to placate the customer where they have a complaint, good antifraud measures may include reviewing complaints to assess

whether this means there has been a breach of procedure, one that is being abused.

4. I've put control self-assessment (CSA) in as the final part of the model because I have seen many control self-assessment workshops, that is, risk workshops, where staff have not put internal and external fraud up as a potential risk. I say, put it up. Have a discussion and ask people to say where systems could be abused—or even where they could abuse resources if they wanted to. Then fix these problems before a real fraud breaks.

"My image on the slide suggests that these measures should be well received by staff and people will want to hear about ways forward in contrast to the negative aspect of fraud issues.

"We have already mentioned ethics and I want to make one more point [*displays Slide 10.15*]. This is that ethics and ethics management where sponsored by the board can be a pivotal part of fraud risk management. The problem is to see this whole thing in context. Society sets standards and this flows down through the corporate chain right down to individuals and how they behave. If your kids come home from school and do their homework in ten minutes, you might care to ask them whether downloading an essay from the World Wide Web is really an ethical way of doing assignments. If our kids grow up with no real understanding of ethical behavior, then when they get into the workplace, how will they behave? The tensions in our slide arise where there are inconsistencies in the ethical chain or people do not trust the messages from above on ethical behavior or where there is pressure to get a result whatever the costs. Companies that themselves behave badly, say in the way they trade with third-world countries, or the way they treat their workers or vendors, may find it hard to convince their people that they take ethics seriously. I guess what I am saying is that fraud risk management starts with analyzing the ethical chain and making sure this makes sense on paper and in real life. And, have a look at any tensions that mean this chain is weak or even broken. I find that this is one of the most difficult things to sort out when I advise organizations on tackling fraud. Top people have to be big enough

SLIDE **10.15** *Board Sponsorship*

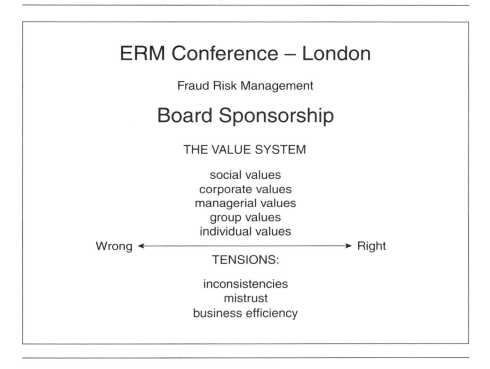

to look at themselves, over and beyond issues like meeting targets and delivering profit forecasts. I can tell you this is not easy. If the top people do not accept this point, then they will find it hard to see risks in issues that they can simply sweep under the table and ignore.

"We are getting to the end of our presentation and there are just a few more things to consider [*displays Slide 10.16*]. So far we have talked about fraud as a personal issue. That is, some people behaving badly and breaking the rules for personal gain and other people taking a lead in making things better. I need to take this concept out of the minor league and put it up as a corporate issue. My slide suggests that business risk management is happening in most larger organizations and that it runs across areas such as projects, operations, financial systems, contracts, and the staffing arrangements. This ERM approach enables the CEO to report on internal controls and issue published accounts that are looked at by the external auditor. Sarbanes-Oxley and all the other regulations that affect different types of organizations sit behind this accountability setup, and these rules demand that risks are properly managed and internal controls are reviewed on a regular basis. What worries me is that while account-ability means that published accounts are fairly stated, are complete, and are accurate, does this mean all is well? If the organization has not set up comprehensive antifraud policies and procedures, then how can this be so? How can the published accounts and control disclosures stack up in this environment? There's no way of knowing for sure. The standard steps for most risk management processes are:

Step 1. Establish business risk management across the enterprise.

Steps 2, 3, and 4. This means the disclosures are okay.

SLIDE **10.16**   *Business Risk Management*

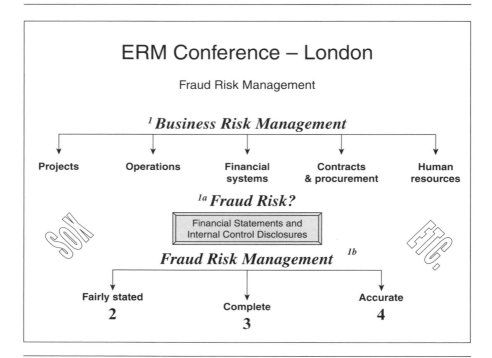

"But I say we also need to work on fraud risks to projects, operations, financial systems, contracts, and the staffing arrangements—and extend ERM to include fraud risk management. It is only then that we can say disclosures are fair, complete, and accurate. I believe this is not always happening in many organizations and this gap needs to be addressed.

"Okay [*displays Slide 10.17*]. My next slide moves us a little deeper into the fraud world and points to a way forward. I have already given you the standard risk management cycle adjusted a little for fraud aspects. What I want to do now is build a more focused cycle that makes fraud a central issue. I start with objectives, as this is what it's all about, performing well and staying completely within the law and being alert to the chance that others may break the law and abuse our resources. The next stage is to carefully assess exactly what is at risk. Which resources are attractive to an internal or external fraudster? We do this by developing a

SLIDE **10.17**   *Fraud Objectives*

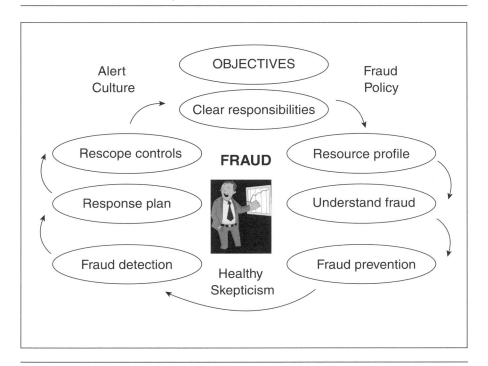

good understanding of fraud, what people are getting up to and what scams are around. The next stage is dedicated to proactive fraud prevention. That is, tight security, good separation of duties, supervision of staff, monitoring work loads, and all those measures designed to make sure people cannot get into our systems, or if they have access that this is controlled properly. An employee debt-counseling service can help stop people slipping into the abyss. This applies to alcohol and drug counseling, and so on.

"But even tight systems can be abused by the dedicated fraudster. Therefore we will need to set up systems that allow us to detect fraud if it is happening, for example, an ongoing program of analyzing our data for odd trends and inconsistencies, or, a whistleblowers hotline so that any suspicions can be reported and acted on. There really is a lot that can be done to uncover fraud, including looking for so-called red flags that tell us something may be wrong. Unreconciled accounts, lost documents, unauthorized payments, and so on are all red flags. Strange behavior from an employee, such as large debt, or for that matter, lots of spare cash, erratic behavior, being excessively territorial, being aggressive, not taking time off work, really close contact with select vendors, and other factors should ring bells, especially if they come together at the same time. Fraud risk management requires a good response plan in place so that people know who to talk to when there is a problem and how to preserve evidence. It should cover what not to do, such as managers carrying out their own investigations or confronting suspect employees or interfering with the suspect's personal computer, and talking to the press and so on.

"The final part of the fraud cycle is to rescope controls so that weaknesses that allowed the fraud to happen can be quickly addressed. The context of the fraud risk management cycle is the corporate antifraud policy, staff who exhibit a healthy skepticism and are happy to ask searching questions where appropriate, and finally an alert culture where fraud is understood and seen as a risk that needs to be carefully handled.

SLIDE **10.18**   *Fraud Center Stage*

ERM Conference – London

Fraud Risk Management

Let's Put Fraud Center Stage in Risk Management

"Okay [*displays Slide 10.18*]. I've got through the slides and hopefully made my point, that fraud should be given center stage as part of the overall risk management process. I've been through the reasons and I've beaten the drum. The rest is up to you. Put it on the corporate agenda. Make it an issue. Resource it properly and keep up the momentum; that is, stay one step ahead of the fraudsters. Some fraudsters are very clever and some are pretty stupid. The problem is that the stupid ones employ clever people to help them get around your systems. This can lead to a very scary future for those organizations that allow themselves to fall behind and fail to show a clear and bright red light to the would-be fraudster. Thank you, ladies and gentlemen."

"Thank you, Solomon. I would like to think that we have all moved a little toward presenting a red light to fraud, abuse, and waste. This seems to be to be an important aspect of ERM, and we are all in some way involved in ensuring the corporate resources and corporate name are preserved. I think you will agree that we have had a very full afternoon, and we have time for a few questions before I will have to wish you all good evening. You sir, in the brown jacket."

"I am Enrico Mendez and my question is for Mr. Blocker; how does the board go about setting its risk appetite?"

"Okay. I feel that the board cannot just set a risk appetite. The board is about setting policy and an appropriate framework. This is really about how it sets policy on the way decisions are made, the way that projects get approved and funded, about the way change is implemented, and more than that, it is about the way strategy is set and delivered. Appetite is inherent in the way messages are given to the customers and the public and whether these suggest an upbeat or cautious approach to existing and new business. It's really about a lot of intangible things. Which is why the four V model that I showed you may be seen as one possible framework that incorporates what may be seen as four key aspects of corporate life. I'm going around the question a bit, but I would say that the short answer is that the board will set its appetite in the same way that it sets its strategic plans and its performance expectations, and that is through a framework that works for the organization and by setting out relevant examples and then telling people what we expect from them."

"Many thanks, Dan. We need to push on. Another question? Lady over there with your hand up, please wait for our roving mike . . ."

"Should fraud as a risk appear on all risk registers?"

"That's one for you, Solomon."

"The answer is yes, absolutely. If this happened, then fraud would be addressed across the entire organization. People sometimes forget that we all have some responsibility to be alert to the risk of external and internal fraud and to ensure it is contained. If it went on risk registers then that would be a great start."

"We only have time for one last question. At the front here."

"I want to know whether this great emphasis on risk appetites means that we will all become much more risk averse? It is a fear I have that the regulators are now running the show and whichever way we turn, we will lose out."

"Solomon?"

"I don't think so. Developing and communicating your views on risk appetite just means that we want to understand our parameters better and when and how they can be extended or brought forward, rather than just make it up as we go along. ERM is about understanding risk, not being too scared to act. The more we understand risk, the more confident we can be, and this means we may well wish to take more chances in competing markets, but only where it makes sense. This is not really about being risk averse. People will always have new ideas and want to run with them. The art of business is to decide whether to support each one as it develops.

"Let me say that years ago a man called Shaw was driving down a dark country lane when he saw a glare that came from a cat that was staring at his car. He went home, thought about it, and invented 'cat's eyes'—devices that are placed in the middle of unlit roads and that reflect the glare from car lights. This is a great way of illustrating the way people take a chance with new ideas, and if we could encourage our staff to do likewise we could stay ahead of the game in all walks of life. Understanding risk and how much risk you are prepared to take does not mean we close people down. In my mind, it means just the opposite. We listen to ideas and only write them off when they are so off the radar that they do not stack up. Going back to this idea of parameters and how we can draw rules for times when we can move outside of them. For some of the four Vs this is rare, but for other aspects there is much more scope for freedom."

"One important job that the Chair has is to ensure we keep to time. And I'm afraid we are now at the end of the first day of the ERM conference. There's a lot to think about and I hope you have enjoyed our speakers. I know that I have. I thank you for your interest and hope you have a pleasant evening. I feel we should close with a round of applause for today's speakers. Goodnight."

Jack suggested that Helen join himself and Bill to go and see a show in town, which Helen declined as she had already agreed to go with her friend Maria, who was visiting relatives who lived in London. Jack decided to hit the gym, while a rather tired Bill felt it best to retire to his hotel room to write up his notes for the day and, for once, get an early night. As they split up to go their respective ways, Bill looked up and saw in front of him a smart-looking short man with a large bald head, who seemed to be studying him as a scientist might study a small insect trapped in a jar.

Lance Strongbow pushed out his jaw, smiled widely at Bill, and said in a soft but sharp voice, "Do you feel that the dashboard approach to risk metrics has more scope than one based on straightforward probability analysis?"

Bill stared at the man and was, for a few seconds, completely lost for words.

Lance lightly gripped Bill's arm and placed his face closer to Bill. He frowned and looked very concerned for his specimen, before he gently said, "Good. Silence is a good cover. Well done to the Reynolds boy. Goodnight."

And at that Lance Strongbow spun around and strolled off in the general direction of the bar, rubbing his hands together as he walked with the air of a man who was king of all he surveyed. Bill looked down at the pile of rough notes on ERM that he was clutching tightly in his hands and experienced a sinking feeling in his stomach.

CHAPTER 11

CONFERENCE SESSION SEVEN

Helen, her hair flowing down, having been freed from its normal ties, was dressed in a white trouser suit and arrived at the conference hall early. She managed to save seats for Bill and Jack. Bill arrived next, followed shortly after by Jack.

"Good morning, ladies and gentlemen. I trust you had a pleasant evening. We set the scene yesterday and we now need to delve into some of the less-well-known aspects of ERM. We have a full program today and our speakers will be giving you their personal views on ERM, which I, for one, am looking forward to. Just let me remind you that we have the workshop session tomorrow morning led by our risk management expert, Lance Strongbow. He has promised me that his session will be most challenging, and I know that you enjoy being put on the spot by Lance. He tells me there will be no hiding place and he wants all attendees to contribute. But . . . back to this morning. I want to introduce you to Steve Manning, who will talk about those much-feared people, internal auditors. Steve tells me that he wants to dispel some of the popular myths surrounding auditors and how they only come out on Halloween or when the moon is full. But let me ask Steve to give you the real deal."

"I thank you, Chair, for inviting me to give this presentation [*displays Slide 11.1*]. Hello, everyone. I am the internal auditor for a large multinational company and I'd like to talk to you today about internal auditing's role in ERM. I recall earlier this year attending a meeting of senior people in my company on ERM and ways forward. Before the meeting, I was drinking coffee with one of our overseas operations managers and he could not understand why I had come along to the meeting. He thought that ERM was about getting systems right and that audit would come along sometime after these systems were refined and check that any financial transactions that went through the system were okay. I said we need to be around at the front end of important new developments. I was then approached by another manager, who said that she was far too busy to be at this meeting and that audit should be in charge of ERM, not her people. In the space of ten minutes it suddenly became clear to me that the audit role was not always properly understood in my organization and probably quite a few other organizations.

SLIDE **11.1**   *What Do You Know?*

ERM Conference – London

What Do You Know About Internal Auditing?

Steve Manning

What Do You Know About Internal Auditing?

Anyway, at this meeting I gave the group a brief overview of the audit role in ERM and it went down pretty well. I have performed this awareness task many times now, and my presentation today is about getting this basic message across.

"To get inside the audit role we need to set out where each of us stands regarding ERM [*displays Slide 11.2*]. I have to keep this a bit general since my view is that ERM affects the private and public sector alike and I don't want this session to focus too much on one detailed business sector.

"Before I start, let me ask a question. Put your hand up if you have had your role clearly defined in respect of the ERM process employed in the organization. That's about half, or no, two-thirds here; not bad. Now let me give you my checklist from the slide.

"The CEO has overall responsibility for designing and implementing ERM and he or she needs to make sure this happens in their organization.

SLIDE **11.2**   *ERM: Respective Roles*

ERM Conference – London

What Do You Know About Internal Auditing?

Steve Manning

ERM: Respective Roles:

- The CEO
- The Board
- Management
- Risk Officer
- Employees Generally
- External Audit
- Others

Internal Auditing?

Short and simple: Not only must the CEO make sure it's happening, but they need also to make sure it is happening in a way that makes sense and works.

"The board sets policy and oversees the way this policy is impacting the business. ERM is a board agenda item and the board in turn needs to understand what it is about and how it fits with strategy. One big issue is this idea of risk appetite, which we have already seen in an earlier presentation. The board sets direction on risk appetite and the CEO refines this in a way that makes sense across the organization. But more than this, the board needs to have in place a mechanism where it can get reports on areas where its risk appetite is being exceeded. You know, where there are big risks that are running wild. The CEO should report on the state of risk management and in turn the board needs to endorse these reports. The board will want to set up an audit committee to oversee ERM, controls, and auditing arrangements and advise the board on whether their arrangements are working.

"We come next to management. Managers are responsible for identifying and managing risks to their business and ensuring there are proper controls to mitigate unacceptable exposures. Managers implement the ERM policy and they are in the sharp end of employing ERM, where it matters on a day-to-day basis. Management may employ a risk officer to take a lead on ERM and ensure it is focused and coordinated across all parts of the business, that is, customer facing and back office parts, and with all key associates and subsidiaries.

"I have listed employees generally on the slide since it is important that ERM touches everyone in some way. I really cannot think of any organization that has employees who do not have objectives and risks that impact these objectives. So everyone needs to be involved in the ERM process. Some staff only have internal customers and serve people who are inside the business. But they still have objectives, and if they do not achieve the required level of service it must affect the overall performance of the organization. You might care to ask whether anyone who sits outside this basic equation needs to be employed, anyway.

"External auditors will want to see ERM in place and will want to see whether internal controls are properly aligned to the risks that the business faces, particularly in respect of financial systems and transactions that feed into the final accounts.

"So there you have it. We all fit into the circle, and others such as partners, stakeholders, vendors, and contract staff need to be part of the ERM process. Now that we have a working model, I can tell you how I see the way that internal audit contributes to the drive to getting ERM in place.

"I need to give you the official definition of internal auditing [*displays Slide 11.3*]. This comes from the Institute of Internal Auditors, who are the leaders in internal auditing across the world. Let me pick out some of the key bits from this definition. Internal audit is independent. ERM

SLIDE **11.3**   *Define Internal Auditing*

ERM Conference – London

What Do You Know About Internal Auditing?

Steve Manning

Defining Internal Auditing:

Internal auditing is an independent, objective assurance and consulting activity designed to add value and improve an organization's operations. It helps an organization accomplish its objectives by bringing a systematic, disciplined approach to evaluate and improve the effectiveness of risk management, control, and governance processes.

is about managing risk and telling stakeholders how this is done. The board needs to have a way of knowing what is happening, and while its business managers can tell them, it is important that there is a validation aspect to the reporting system. The internal auditors have no vested interest in any parts of the business, and their view on ERM and what is working and what needs further attention is impartial. And audit's view of whether significant risks are being hammered down, and whether the risk management process makes sense, should be entirely reliable. This view is objective because it comes from a team that has no conflict of interests in their review, advisory, and reporting role. Let's look at the audit assurance and consulting activity.

"The audit assurance role is about telling the audit committee and board whether controls are sound and whether the ERM process is established in a way that supports sound controls. The audit assurance is independent and is an important source of information for the board and CEO, as they in turn formulate their published reports on internal control. That's the audit review and assurance role. But the consulting role reflects the view that auditors have a long-standing background in risk management and control and can provide advice and support to management in the way they might implement ERM. Consulting is the other arm of auditing and is about helping out in getting things up and running, rather than just reviewing what's been put in place. Internal auditing is one of the few professions that have the concepts of governance, risk management, and control built into their formal definition. These matters drive the audit process and it means that audit staff should have a great deal of expertise in this aspect of corporate life. In some audit outfits, the auditors are the center of expertise in governance, risk, and control issues. These topics are a major part of our training and skills base.

"Let me drill down into this idea of assurance and consulting roles [*displays Slide 11.4*]. You might wonder why the auditors sometimes come in and help you set up your ERM process, that is, the policies, awareness, standards, information systems, and overall integration with the rest of your business processes. And other times the auditors' focus

SLIDE **11.4**   *Consulting and Assurance Work*

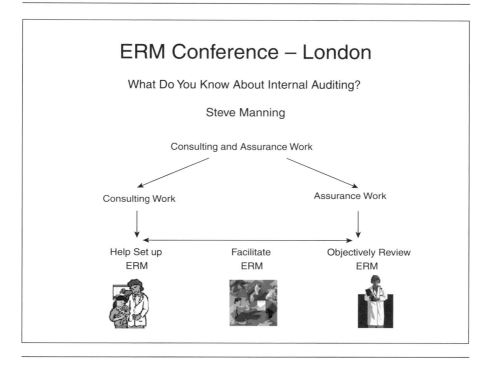

is to assess what you have in place and look for areas for improvements and areas of weaknesses, and also get involved in reviewing specific risks that may be posing problems. This difference in roles is not something that happens by chance, something that we make up as we go along. The type of role we adopt is a reflection on the best way that audit can add value to the business. Value is about doing the right things in the right way, and all auditors understand the need to focus their work on the corporate agenda. I have used a diagram to explain the different roles. Lots of audit consulting work happens where the organization, or parts of the organization, have just started to get ERM going. There is a view that audit adds little value if, when visiting a business unit, they just say that proper ERM is not yet in place. In this scenario, we are better off working alongside management teams to help them set up the necessary arrangements, taking a cue from the relevant corporate standards.

"When some progress has been made we arrive at the central part of the diagram, where auditors help facilitate the ERM process. This may be by working with you on your risk workshops, assisting with risk policy design and implementation, awareness training, assessing risk reporting systems, or just helping spread good examples of what's happening elsewhere in the organization. Auditors are real lucky. Our work runs across the entire business and we tend to have a good idea of what is happening elsewhere and how each unit fits with the bigger corporate picture. Audit work tends to move toward the right of our diagram, as we do more assuring work as the organization starts to get ERM in place. We stand back from on-line consulting engagements and start to go back to what really is our core role. That is giving independent views on whether the ERM arrangements are sound and whether risk is being properly managed. These assurances are for everyone at all levels. But these formal assurances are real important to the board and their audit committee. They, that is, the CEO, chief finance officer, executives, and nonexecutive directors, have a legal responsibility to review and then publish their report on internal controls. They have to have good grounds for saying that all is well, or for that matter where there are significant problems, that is, risks, and any resulting problems are being sorted out. The above range of consulting versus assurance roles is applied differently in different organizations and, more importantly, in different parts of the same organization. My pictures in Slide 11.4 suggest that audit moves from helping the struggling patient, to helping the combined effort of your team, through to formally reviewing your progress on ERM.

"How do we tell whether ERM is in place and working [*displays Slide 11.5*]? Well, there are three main questions that I ask:

1. **Is the process well designed?** If not, audit can help here.
2. **Is the ERM process well understood?** Good systems are both well designed and well understood. People need the right skills to

SLIDE **11.5**   *There Is an ERM in Place*

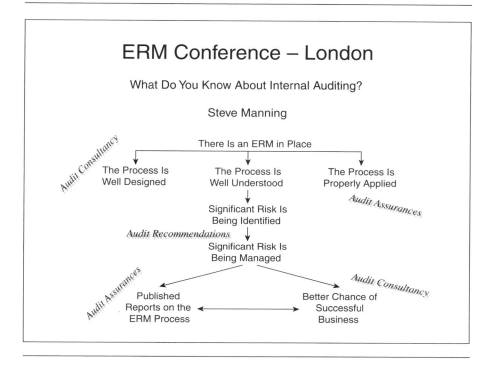

implement new approaches. It is no good saying that all major decisions should be risk assessed before implemented, when you have not told people how this can be achieved. Again, audit can help here.

3. **Is the process properly applied?** The first two questions fit well with our audit consulting work. But the final question means we have to do some careful review work to find out what really happens in practice. Audit gets real concerned where the formal arrangements have been set up and people are trained, but the actual working practices fall short of these standards. We will want to make sure the system works and we will look for evidence that this is happening.

"If the above three questions have been tackled, we can work down through the hierarchy of issues. Next we want to know, since there is a good and reliable system in place, does this mean all significant risk is being managed? Again, this means drilling down into the business, and auditors may need to reexamine some of your risk assessments and mitigating controls to make sure all is well. In my books, ERM has two dimensions. It is about being able to report on controls through an effective ERM process and tell the world that we have good systems in place. The other thing is that good ERM means you are able to handle risks more effectively. That is, you have a way of isolating risk and getting your systems to respond to the fast pace of change that throws up new risks or makes well-known risks much more dangerous. In short, you will have a better chance of running a successful business.

"Let me take you further into the auditor's world [*displays Slide 11.6*]. When we get to a defined part of the organization that's to be audited, we will want to know who owns the process, who has to achieve what objective, and as such, who has to get risks properly managed. I spend a lot of time with management teams on their objectives. If these are vague or inconsistent, then the ERM process falls over. I recall one audit where the management team were in such a mess that we ended up rescoping the audit and running an objective-setting workshop for them. We just could not get past first base, and the director in charge of that unit asked us to help with this task. In the end it was pretty successful as, in agreeing with their objectives, we got the team to better understand their respective roles and work out how they could work together more efficiently.

"Anyway, let's move on. Once we have clear objectives for the area in question, we need to get the risks identified and evaluated. I use a three-pronged approach. Where the manager has a good ERM process in place, I work around their risk profiles for the first four columns of our schedule on the slide. Where the process is not really there, I get the managers and some of the work teams together and facilitate a workshop to get to their risks and their risk assessments before starting the

SLIDE **11.6**   *Audit Risk-Based Evaluation*

ERM Conference – London

What Do You Know About Internal Auditing?

Steve Manning

Audit Risk-Based Evaluation   Sarrinda Khan

Objectives:...

Process Owners...

Risks	Impact	%	Score	Risk Mitigations			Action	Assigned to
				Evaluation	Tests	Opinion		
				Alignment *Improvement* *Evidence*				

audit proper. Where there is no real ERM in place and the manager does not want to get involved, I will then have to perform my own risk assessment by talking to the managers and their staff and work teams. One way or another I get to complete my schedule.

"Turning to the middle columns, I need to evaluate the controls that are in place to tackle big risks and make sure they stack up. And then I test them. I look for evidence of errors, problems, and poor performance due to risks that have no corresponding mitigating controls. I look in parts of the business where there are significant risks but no obvious controls. In one audit I found that the risk of failed projects was huge but there were no real controls to ensure projects delivered and kept to budget. My tests revealed a number of instances where projects had overrun badly and large sums of money were lost on bad decisions. Some projects were pulled before their time and the spending was lost in a corporate holding account that was badly defined. The other type of test is where there are big risks but these risks were meant to be contained by rigorous controls. These tests check that the controls that were so important to the business were actually working and are being applied properly. In one audit I traveled to several overseas sites and found that the antibribery procedures were more or less being ignored by many of the local account managers. This was exposing us to a major threat as international bribery is as much a crime as internal corruption.

"The final two columns are designed to get management involved in setting an action plan to sort out areas where improvement is required as a result of our audit findings. And then assign this action to the right people, bearing in mind our work on defining the process owners at the start of the audit. The audit process is about promoting a better chance of achieving objectives, and I always go back to management's objectives and ask whether the risks to achieving these objectives have been properly addressed. My audit evidence simply shows to what extent this is happening. I have written three other words over my schedule, which I will now go over:

1. **Alignment:** Audit will want to see that the area under review has aligned its ERM to the corporate arrangements and there is a good consistency. What the CEO thinks is happening should be happening in practice.
2. **Improvement:** Where ERM needs to be improved, audit will help identify these improvements and provide recommendations to encourage such remedial action.
3. **Evidence:** This is where audit comes into its own. We form an opinion on what's good and what's not, based on formal evidence and not just hearsay. This means our work is reliable, defensible, and remains outside corporate politics. That's not an easy task.

"We have gone into a bit of detail and I apologize if you are getting tired [*displays Slide 11.7*]. But this is the reality of ERM. It's not just

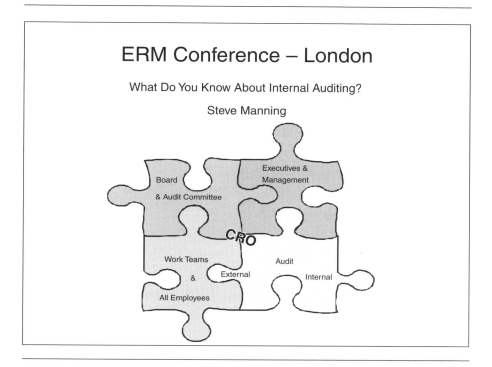

policy and standards. It's real-life business practices. What I would like to say now is that we all fit into the ERM jigsaw, in some way or another: the board and audit committee; executives and their management teams; the entire workforce, and both external and internal audit. The chief risk officer, what I have called CRO on my slide, may well bring these parties together in a shared understanding of what ERM means in the organization. But it is important that we all have a role and discharge our responsibilities in this respect.

"We are getting to the end now. Let me just mention a few summary matters [*displays Slide 11.8*]:

- Internal audit can help you start up ERM—just ask them.
- They can help you get it right.

ERM Conference – London

What Do You Know About Internal Auditing?

Steve Manning

Internal Audit:

- Help you start it up
- Help you get it right
- Suggest improvements
- Review efforts
- Provide an objective opinion

- They can suggest ways of improving your approach, say by better performance information systems that build in this idea of risk and risk assessment.
- They can review your efforts and let you know how you are doing.
- They can give an objective view on your overall process and report this view upward through the organization.

"Let me ask you something as we point a way forward [*displays Slide 11.9*]. After having been so good as to listen to me for a bit, can I ask for a show of hands and ask you whether you have a better understanding of how internal audit can help you in your ERM efforts? Excellent, most of you have put up your hands. I leave you with this message.

SLIDE **11.9** *Now You Know*

"You each have your journey through life at work and ERM can help you stay on the right track. Like the traffic lights, it can tell you when it is best to slow down and when you should actually speed up, that is, to keep within the law but, more importantly, to stay safe and adjust what you do to the ever-changing environment within which you find yourself. Meanwhile, internal audit can certainly help you with this task.

"Goodbye, and I wish you all a safe and pleasant journey through ERM."

"Excellent, Steve. We will never be the same again. Auditors are nice people and although we suspected they were somehow different, in truth they are our friends. I feel it is high time that someone set the record straight on the audit role, even if this is a personal perspective from Steve. Thank you, Steve. Questions at the close before lunch. Let's move on and look at our next session. Gloria Marsh is going to take the audit theme and keep it going for a little longer. Gloria is a consultant who helps organizations assess their risk management arrangements, and she feels that not only do we need to have a sound ERM process in place, but we also need to review that process on a regular basis to make sure it is right. In fact, we need to audit it. And Gloria has some ideas on how we might go about this task. Over to you, Gloria."

CHAPTER 12

CONFERENCE SESSION EIGHT

"Thank you, Chair. Right, then, I'll get straight into it.

"Good afternoon [*displays Slide 12.1*]. My name is Gloria Marshe and my job here today is to give you my version of an integrated enterprise risk management process. Much of what I describe is taken from a John Wiley and Sons publication called *Auditing the Risk Management Process*. Just for the record, the ISBN number is 0-471-69053-8. I was invited here to go through this ERM model because many people talk about ERM as if it is something you can buy in a store. 'A bag of ERM and a beer, please.' We go on and on about ERM and how it is so important for all of us wherever we work, but at times we need to take a step back. We need to be sure about what we mean and how ERM is actually part of our normal business systems. Anyway, let me tell you how we need to play this. I have a holistic model of ERM, taken from the book, that is developed in stages. And I will quickly describe each stage as it is added to the model. But before we do this, I will give you the bottom line right away.

SLIDE **12.1**   *Auditing the Risk Management Process*

ERM Conference – London

Holistic Enterprise Risk Management

Auditing the Risk
Management Process

John Wiley & Sons

"So here it is [*displays Slide 12.2*]. The model's pretty scary, but don't worry, folks. I'm going to take it apart and put it back together again in front of your eyes.

"Let's go through each aspect of the model [*displays Slide 12.3*]:

- **External Global and Market Developments.** Risk is inherent in the way global events shift in the economy, including changing interest rates, international developments, and the fluctuating movement of capital. Meanwhile, markets are constantly changing as consumer demand alters and competitors enter or leave the marketplace. Public sector services are also affected by constant changes in the demands and expectations of society.
- **Statutes, Regulations, Codes, and Guidance.** Governance codes and company legislation can be generic or industry specific, and

SLIDE **12.2** *Risk Appetite*

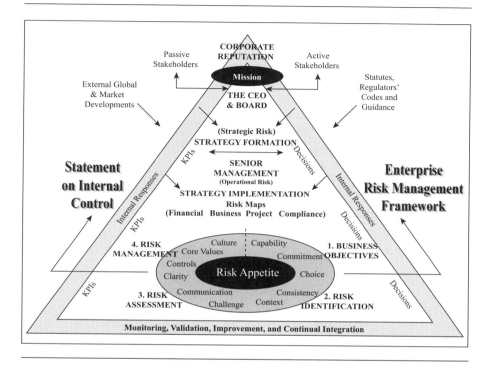

they create additional demands on enterprises, normally in response to heightened expectations from society or as a result of corporate scandals that revealed a need to tighten up on existing regulations. The most famous of the more recent laws arrived several years ago in the form of Sarbanes-Oxley, with the resulting impact on companies listed on the New York Stock Exchange and NASDAQ. There is also an assortment of local state laws that add to the compliance framework within which enterprises must operate.

- **The CEO and Board.** The driving force for the enterprise is the CEO and board of directors. This is where the key decisions are made regarding the strategy that will transform the mission into firm results. The board formulates strategy and employs executives,

SLIDE **12.3**   *The CEO and Board*

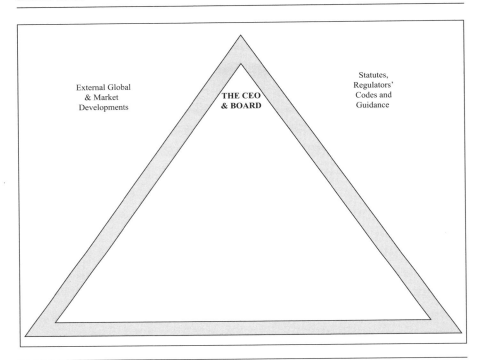

managers, staff, and an appropriate resource to implement this strategy, and the need for sound boards has been a feature of corporate life for some time. Moreover, the board has a key role in overseeing the risk management process, and COSO ERM has provided some direction in helping to clarify this role.

- **The Mission** [*displays Slide 12.4*]. The risk management framework is driven by what the organization is trying to achieve, which, at its highest level, is the overall mission. The reality of private, public sector, and not-for-profit environments means that there can never be total certainty that the mission will always be fully achieved to make the vision a reality. Remember, risk is all about this lack of certainty.
- **Active Stakeholders.** Over the years we have come to accept the role of stakeholders in corporate life. Active stakeholders have a

SLIDE **12.4** *Corporate Reputation*

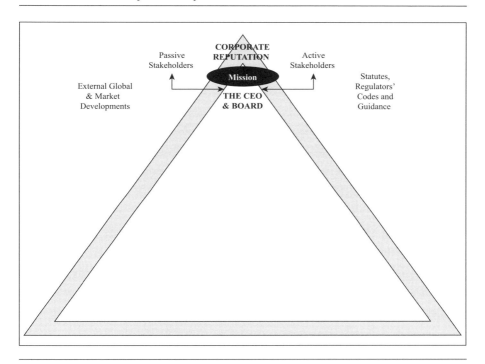

direct influence over an organization, and in incorporated companies, this relates to shareholders who can vote out the board members and decide what they are paid for their services. Investors,
lenders, associates, partners, bankers, employees, and other parties
each have an important impact on the organization. Likewise, in-
stitutional investors have a major role in holding a batch of voting
shares in many large enterprises. Meanwhile, public sector organizations are beholden to their public to ensure they deliver and
deliver well.

- **Passive Stakeholders.** There is a growing band of stakeholders who
sit just outside of direct interfaces with specific enterprises and this
is what I mean by 'passive stakeholders.' Local communities, the
media, religious groups, environmental groups, and people who

are concerned about the behavior of big organizations may have no obvious influence over the board, but do have some collective sway in the way the organization is seen by others. Increasingly, such pressure groups are able to influence businesses that are be-having badly or have not made a full assessment of their impact on local communities. There is an emerging theme based around the concept of corporate social responsibility that is starting to en-hance the importance of all types of stakeholders.

- **Corporate Reputation.** I feel that the extent to which an organiza-tion is able to meet the needs of all stakeholders essentially defines its reputation.
- **Strategy Formation** [*displays Slide 12.5*]. Our model suggests that the context for the development of a formal strategy is found

SLIDE **12.5**   *Corporate Reputation Mission 1*

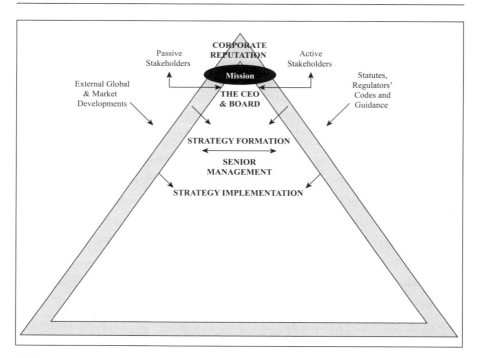

within the global market forces and the relevant regulatory framework for each individual organization.

- **Senior Management.** The next aspect of the model relates to senior management, that is, the people who sit in the firing line to get the job done. The corporate strategy will result in various objectives that will need to be delivered to ensure the organization is successful and the overall mission is achieved. Senior management run the business lines and are responsible for meeting key performance targets.

- **Strategy Implementation.** Managers are responsible for ensuring that their staff, systems, and budgets are applied to delivering the set strategy. They do this by breaking down the longer-term corporate strategy into more manageable shorter-term chunks that are handed out to their workforce and associates. The workforce is in effect the engine room of the organization. Empowering organizations allow people to make decisions at the front line and flex their response to the needs of customers and clients.

- **Strategic Risk** [*displays Slide 12.6*]. Our model places strategic risk firmly on the corporate agenda. The risks from changing markets and the risk of failing to comply with various laws and rules, or to meet the needs of stakeholders, may mean the stated mission will not be achieved. It is the task of strategy to take on board these diverse risks and ensure they are addressed in such a way as to achieve the set objectives. The concept of strategic risk places an emphasis on strategic solutions, and there are several matters that affect all organizations. There are many big risks that confront all sorts of organizations, and global terrorism, rapid technological change, and the availability of good staff cannot always be underwritten by insurers. Many organizations have now moved toward internal insurance arrangements in the form of good risk management systems to reinforce the need for a sustainable business base.

- **Operational Risk.** This should also be mentioned as it has an important effect on the actual operations of an organization.

SLIDE **12.6**   *Corporate Reputation Mission 2*

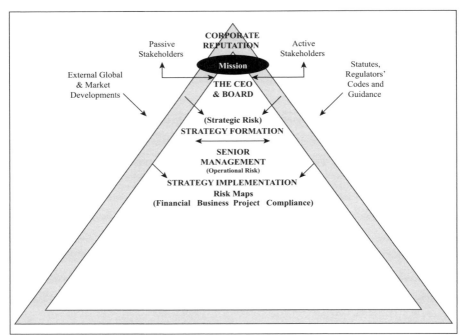

- **Risk Maps (Financial, Business, Project, and Compliance).** The next factor that we need to add to our model relates to the way generic risk is structured to fit the way the organization sees the world. There are many and varied perceptions of risks to an organization. We have broken down risk into various categories of financial, business, project, and compliance risk. In this way, a map can be drawn as to how these different types of risk run up, down, and through the organization. Risk maps attempt to track the way strategic and operational risks affect different parts of an organization.
- **Strategy Implementation.** This is about putting strategy into action across the business and it is the responsibility of management to get it right.

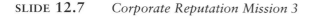

SLIDE **12.7** *Corporate Reputation Mission 3*

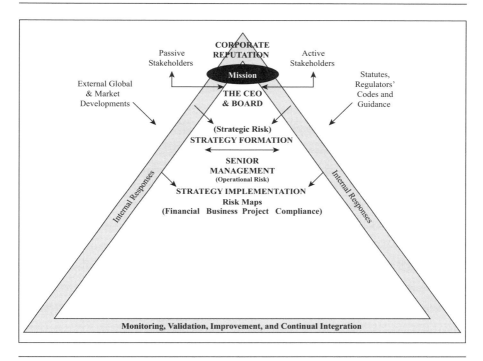

- **Internal Response** [*displays Slide 12.7*]. This is the way each organization responds to its environment in terms of moving forward in meeting its objectives. In short, the entire organization is constantly engaged in responding to risk.
- **Monitoring.** The holistic risk management process must be kept up-to-date and vibrant. It must also be reviewed to ensure it still does the job as intended. This is where this holistic model may be most useful.
- **Validation.** Another aspect of our risk management model is that risk activities need to be done in such a way that they can be validated, if necessary. This means there should be good documentation. Validation enables the board to set a mandate that designates that there will be an effective risk management process in place and

in turn make several firm statements about their risk management policy.

- **Improvement.** Risk management must be set within a learning environment for it to be of any use. As such, our model includes the need to provide continuous improvement to the process for capturing real risks in a meaningful way.

- **Continual Integration.** The final part of this stage of the model captures the need to integrate risk management into the actual business systems and work methods. It is the business that responds to risk, and it does this by incorporating threats and opportunities into the way it works.

- **KPIs** [*displays Slide 12.8*]. Having used risk management to arrive at an action plan to improve controls or refine the way work is

SLIDE **12.8**   *Corporate Reputation Mission 4*

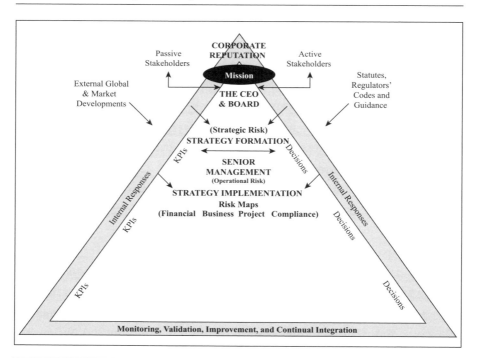

planned and performed, there is a need to consolidate these measures. The model is enriched by adding in the attachment of key performance indicators (KPIs) to action plans, which result from an assessment of risk. The realities of corporate life mean that any actions that are needed to grow the business must feed into personal or team performance targets to have any real chance of happening.

- **Decisions.** Decision making should happen after a consideration of risks that are being addressed and also, and this point is often missed, in response to any new risks that may result from the actual new decisions themselves.

"The basic risk management cycle sits with the holistic model as a central theme and consists of various items that I will now describe [*displays Slide 12.9*]:

- **Business Objectives.** All risk frameworks have the term 'Objectives' set somewhere in their central components. This is a key point. Risk as a vague concept that floats above an organization is often associated with disasters and accidents, that is, things that appear out of the blue and that are largely uncontrollable. In this sense, risk is something that one suffers in silence, and not, as we suggest, something that can be anticipated and managed. We can view risk as anything that impacts our objectives, and in this way we encourage people to take charge of their work by viewing many risks as potentially controllable, or which can at least be minimized.
- **Risk Identification.** Once the need for effective risk management has been recognized, we come to the task of isolating all possible risks. This is before we have weighed each one to determine whether it is substantial. Risk identification is the process of capturing all those risks that impact on the relevant business objectives. This task is included in our model as an important step in promoting better-run organizations.
- **Risk Assessment.** The next part of the risk cycle relates to assessing known risks for their potential impact on an organization's

SLIDE **12.9**   *Corporate Reputation Mission 5*

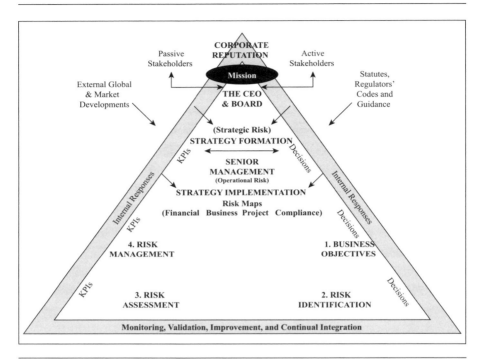

ability to achieve its objectives. The most popular approach to risk assessment is to judge the possible impact of the risk if it materializes, and then judge the extent to which the risk is likely to occur.

- **Risk Management.** Risk management comes into the model, in suggesting that having assessed our risks, we can then determine what steps to take to deal with anything that causes a concern—that is, risk that is significant and likely to arise. There are many possible responses to different types and levels of risk, and the options are found in COSO ERM: avoidance, reduction, sharing, and acceptance. Avoidance and reduction strategies will tend to be associated with high-impact, high-likelihood risks, while sharing fits more with high-impact, low-likelihood risks. Acceptance will tend

SLIDE **12.10**   *Corporate Reputation Mission 6*

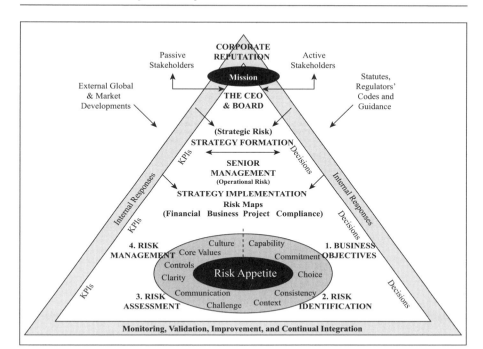

to focus on low-impact, low-likelihood risks, or where the high cost of controls is prohibitive.

"The concept of risk appetite appears next on the model, as it holds a central role in all risk management frameworks [*displays Slide 12.10*]. Here we focus on 11 Cs that are important to understanding the way risk is perceived by an organization:

1. **Capability:** Our first C relates to the capacity within an organization to understand and manage its risks.
2. **Commitment:** The next C concerns the need for people to buy into the risk management concept, that is, a commitment from the top that runs through the workforce.

3. **Choice:** Risk appetite resides in the choices that are made or not made, concerning issues that have a significant impact on the success or otherwise of the business, and is about the level of risk that remains after controls have been put in place.

4. **Consistency:** The next *C* suggests that the organization should apply a consistent approach to the way it manages risk. That is, it fits with the way people behave at work.

5. **Context:** Risk appetite should be seen within the context of the way an organization operates and deals with its customers and other stakeholders. Establishing the right context is therefore a prerequisite to establishing the right risk appetite.

6. **Challenge:** Risk management should not lead to a bunker mentality where people become obsessed with a multitude of risks that have a remote bearing on the business. It should lead to an empowered workforce that is able to take charge of its priorities and decide what works best at the sharp end.

7. **Communication:** The corporate risk appetite can only be understood if people around the organization understand each other and their priorities. If the board has a view on what is acceptable behavior, it will need to paint this image for their stakeholders and employees, to support a common understanding of risk appetite.

8. **Clarity:** Clarity of objectives, clear accountabilities, and clear risk triggers all underpin the way risk is perceived and addressed. In an attempt to clarify risk owners and risk appetite, the way accountabilities are set and applied is important.

9. **Controls:** Controls are an important equation in setting risk appetite. Controls are set against high levels of inherent risk to reduce this risk down to an acceptable level. The extent to which an operation is controlled depends on an organization's perspective of acceptable risk. The greater the focus on risk taking, to enhance market share, the less the emphasis on flexible controls. Controls nowadays are moving toward being more flexible and organic and entirely responsive to changing risks.

10. **Core Values:** Risk appetite is closely aligned to corporate values. When we decide on what is acceptable in the way we work, this requires a value judgment. Acceptability is about appropriateness. That's what fits under the circumstances. An organization that has spent a great deal of time and effort to define its core values has a better chance of defining its risk appetite.

11. **Culture:** The next part of the risk appetite model relates to a matter that has already been alluded to, that of culture. Many commentators view governance as a meeting of performance-driven success criteria and conformance-based constraints. That means delivering the goods, but in a right and proper manner. This balance is affected by the type of corporate culture in place, ranging from 'Gung-Ho' through to 'stickler-for-rules' employee attitudes.

"The final parts of the model can now be included as we turn to the need for formal disclosures from the organization [*displays Slide 12.11*]. Transparency relates to the obligations assumed from corporate accountability.

- **Enterprise Risk Management Framework.** One major aspect of the model is the all-consuming ERM framework that sweeps up all the issues that have appeared so far on the model. Good ERM means that an organization is in a better position to meet its set objectives while also complying with external regulation. It is about strong but sensible business continuity, against all types of problems that result from an uncertain environment. Good risk management is also required by the federal sentencing guidelines along with a system for ensuring compliance and reliable decision making. ERM is a significant business tool that comes into play whenever there is an objective to be met and whenever there is an understanding that there will always be some risk associated with achieving these objectives. Risk is not to be dreaded. Nor is it to be laughed at. The important point to note is that a framework is needed to capture the essence of risk and risk management.

- **The Statement on Internal Control.** Our model suggests that the CEO's Statement on Internal Control is related to the ERM applied by an organization. The equation is fairly straightforward. Risks cause an element of uncertainty in meeting objectives. Controls help guard against risks that threaten an organization's ability to achieve its objectives. A good ERM process incorporates a good system of internal control and a mechanism to update controls as and when risks alter in types, impact, or likelihood. Moreover, any examination of a listed company by the Securities and Exchange Commission into internal controls will start with the risk management system in operation. The bottom line of our model suggests that it is not possible to establish a sound system of

SLIDE **12.11**   *Corporate Reputation Mission 7*

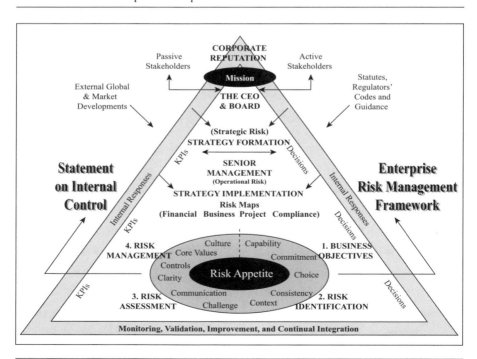

internal control without first establishing an effective enterprise risk management process.

"What I have tried to do today is suggest that ERM is an integrated part of business life and we can develop holistic models to work out how it all fits together [*displays Slide 12.12*]. The model I have described can be used as a benchmark to assess how ERM should be employed, and I suggest that each organization builds its own version of holistic ERM and uses this to ensure ERM is embedded into their systems, to audit the ERM process and to make sure it all makes good business sense. It's really up to you how you do this. I hope I have given you some ideas and that what I have given you has not been too hard to decipher. Many thanks for your attention."

SLIDE **12.12** *Holistic Enterprise Risk Management*

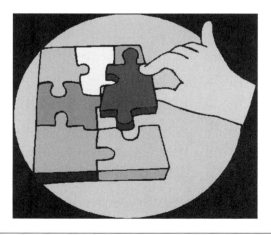

"Wow. I don't think I've ever seen so much information get delivered in so short a time. Well done. It's good that we have heard from someone who has had a go at illustrating ERM in a holistic manner. I guess we will all need to have a close look at the notes after the conference and consider some of the important issues raised in this model. As Gloria says, we all need to develop a template to suit our organization. And I'm sure she has given you a few ideas. I know that is true for me. We've come to our final speaker this morning, and I'd like to introduce Sue Highland, who says that ERM is really about empowering people. Ladies and gentlemen, I give you Sue Highland."

CHAPTER 13

CONFERENCE SESSION NINE

"Good morning, one and all. I have sat here enthralled at our speakers and the way they have developed their theme on ERM. I hope to add to this in my small way.

"I have been the human resources officer for a large pharmaceutical company for many years, and I was pleased to be asked to present my views at your annual conference [*displays Slide 13.1*]. By the way, in case you're wondering, the answer to your question is 'Yes, I am at the right conference.' Many of you may feel that human resource people are not too interested in ERM as we work on only one aspect of the business, that is, the people: how to find them; how to recruit them; how to keep them or get rid of them; and how to keep them focused and on track. But why is this task key to ERM? I want to start my presentation with the concept of *empowerment*, which is about getting people to release their energies, and to take charge of their work and their areas of responsibility. My job involves the physical task of getting the right people in the right place at work. But it's the extent to which people feel involved in their work and confident enough to make good decisions that can make the difference between a good organization and a great one. I believe ERM is mainly about empowering people and I hope to convince you of my proposition this afternoon.

ERM Conference – London

ERM – Power to the People
Sue Highland

ERM = EmpoweRMent

"I want to build a model that takes ERM and the wider context of ERM and relates this to the way people behave at work [*displays Slide 13.2*]. I know that many of you are well up to speed on ERM but I want to start from the basics to illustrate my point. The first level of my model has four main parts:

1. **Stakeholders:** The people, investors, government agencies, employees, local communities, and many others who have a real stake in what an organization does and does not do need to be acknowledged. These groups are affected to a greater or lesser degree by the extent to which corporate objectives are achieved and the implications of what the organization does to survive and grow. The risk management equation starts here, with the needs and expectations of key stakeholders.

SLIDE **13.2**   *ERM: Power to the People 1*

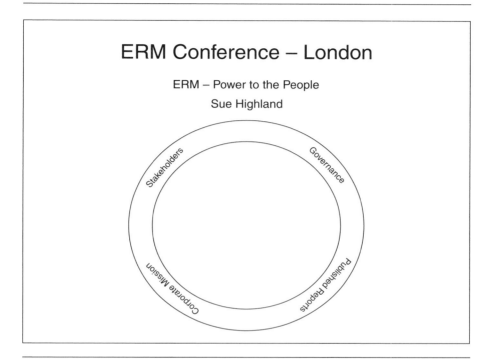

2. **Governance:** In my book, governance is about the way an organization conducts its affairs. Where this conduct is fair, respectable, and organized in a transparent way the organization can be positioned to meet the needs and expectations again of key stakeholders, including regulators and investors. A lot of this is about having a well-understood risk appetite that fits with the reality of how the business operates. An organization can be as risky as it wants so long as it tells people its policies and current position and always keeps within the law.

3. **Corporate mission:** The next item on our contextual agenda is the aims and ambitions of the organization. By the way, I use the word 'organization' instead of 'enterprise' because some people wrongly feel enterprise means profit-making companies and my

ideas relate to all types of organizations. The corporate mission should drive the organization, and it is those risks that impact on the mission that are most important in ERM.

4. **Published reports:** The final piece of the jigsaw is the annual published report. That is, whatever the organization says it does and whatever the organization has actually done should be reported each year, along with the financial accounts that show its performance and balance sheet value. Most organizations are also required to prepare quarterly disclosures where regulations stipulate. It is essential that these reports make sense and reflect the reality of the business so that all those who have a stake in the organization can assess how it has been managed. Remember, in all but the smallest businesses, the management tends not to own the business. And in the public sector you could argue that we, the public, own the organizations that we pay for out of our taxes. Published reports on the finances, risk management process, and state of internal controls are important as part of the accountability regime.

"The second level of my model has a further four main parts [*displayed Slide 13.3*]:

1. **Risk policy:** We have discussed the external environment within which most organizations operate. Now we turn to the way senior management need to respond to these influences. The board should develop a risk policy that says how it will address the risk of not delivering its corporate mission, stakeholder expectations, and the need for good corporate governance arrangements and reliable published statements.

2. **ERM process:** The risk policy is implemented through the ERM process, that is, the process of building risk inside and throughout the way the business works. You will have heard a lot about the ERM process today, so I need not go into any more detail.

3. **Planning process:** ERM should inform the planning process in that the risk of failing to deliver plans should be managed along with the risk of failing to plan properly.

SLIDE **13.3**　　*ERM: Power to the People 2*

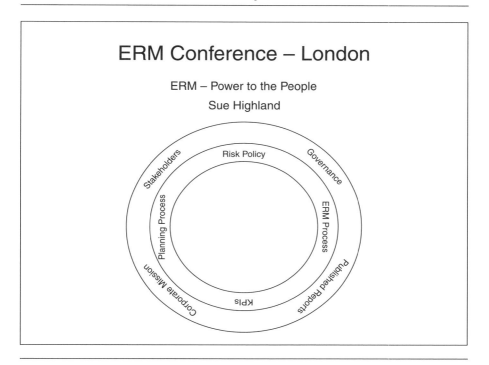

4. **KPIs:** The final aspect of our corporate response to risk is to make sure performance targets are geared into the ability to manage risk. It is clear that any action plans that are devised to mitigate significant risks need to be built into the agreed performance framework and personal targets if there is to be any chance that these action points will be achieved.

"The next level of my model has its own four parts [*displays Slide 13.4*]:

1. **Decision making:** We get into a further level of detail when we argue that the way decisions are made should result from a good understanding of risks that affect our areas of responsibility. These decisions may be strategic, periodic, or even made on a day-to-day basis. But they should all result from the effective risk-based

planning and performance management process that I mentioned earlier.

2. **MIS:** Information is seen by most as the lifeblood of any organization, and details of significant risk and actions needed to address risk appear at this level of our model. Risk registers and red flags should generate quick action to address aspects of the business that may be getting out of control, or highlight parts of the business that are ripe for further development.

3. **Procedures:** I put procedures on the model, as many internal controls arise from procedures that need to be in place to ensure the risks of error, waste, or fraud do not arise. The key is to develop procedures as an aspect within the risk policy and as a result of the ERM process that enables management to identify top risks that must be controlled.

SLIDE **13.4**   *ERM: Power to the People 3*

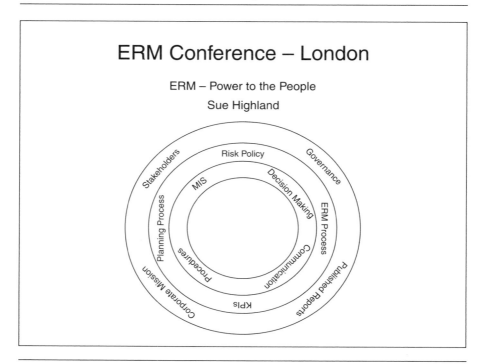

4. **Communications:** This is something that underpins all good business models. A shared understanding of risk and the way we deal with high levels of unacceptable risk is something that should be part of the way people interact at work.

"We move now onto the next level [*displays Slide 13.5*]:

1. **Values:** The obvious things were placed on the previous level but now we turn to the softer and often hidden issues that can make or break a business. Values are important as they guide the way people work and the way they decide between alternative courses of action. Ethical values can promote a reliable ERM process where people are open and honest about their work and make an earnest attempt to improve things.

SLIDE **13.5**   *ERM: Power to the People 4*

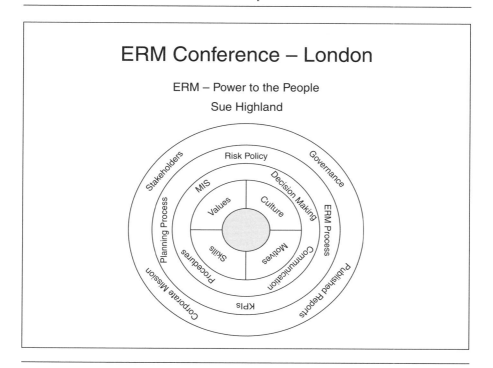

2. **Culture:** The culture of an organization can mean much more than a hundred published reports on risk appetite. Culture dictates the way people behave and whether they are macho, reserved, or out-and-out sharks—or a combination of these things. Corporate culture tends to come about from the recruitment and promotion policies in place and also from the way the top people behave.

3. **Motives:** I put staff motivation in my model as I feel that ERM should be motivating. It should not just be about formal risk management procedures but be more about helping people do a better job at work and not get bogged down in detail as they understand what matters and what does not really make much difference. One line of thought says people are motivated when they are empowered and, as you know, this concept of empowerment is the theme of my presentation. ERM empowers people because it suggests that they can come to understand risk and how to take control and take charge of what affects them at work.

4. **Skills:** The final part of this level is the new skills-sets that are needed to work in a dynamic and changing environment where risk can be embraced to good effect. This idea of new skills based on a good understanding of ERM is an often-overlooked aspect of making risk management work.

"The final level is what I'm most interested in, and that is *people* and their values, skills, level of motivation, and the overall culture in which they operate [*displays Slide 13.6*]. I place people at the heart of my ERM model, because no matter what systems, procedures, and work practices you put in place, it is the people and the way they behave that sets one organization apart from another. I am not going to say much more on this slide, just that by focusing on the people you employ and the way they behave you can reap dividends. When I say people I mean all your staff, and associates, partners, and contract personnel, that is, everyone who is part of the way you do business.

SLIDE **13.6**   *ERM: Power to the People 5*

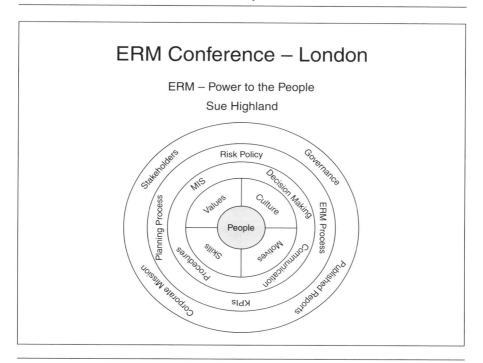

"A firm link can be drawn between your workforce and the contextual elements of ERM [*displays Slide 13.7*]. So we return again to the stakeholders, governance arrangements, formal published disclosures on ERM and internal controls, and the actual mission of the enterprise. If we can get our people to understand these high-level aspects of business life, we can get them to use the ERM process in a dynamic way. It is the way people behave that affects the achievement of the corporate mission, governance issues, reported results, and the extent to which stakeholders feel the organization is a success.

"The reality of making the people factor work is to concentrate on the values of your people in terms of the way they take responsibility for

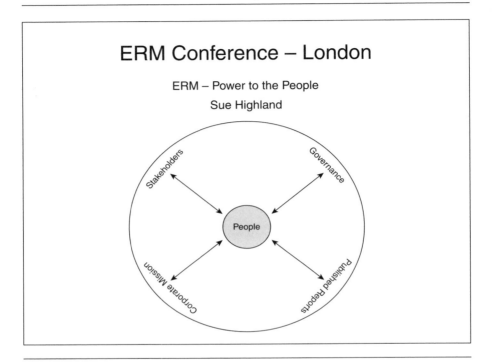

their work and their ethical stance [*displays Slide 13.8*]. Training people in the skills to employ ERM and its wider context is essential and it is here that your human resource staff can be of great help. Managers and teams can be motivated by getting them to understand how they can take charge of their internal controls and make life easier all around. ERM is also about being in control by understanding your risks and how they might be managed. The final aspect of *people power* is the culture where ERM—by identifying, assessing and managing risk, and reporting on controls—is part of the way people behave at work; and this takes us near the end of my presentation.

"What I am saying is that ERM can be seen as a set of policies, procedures, workshops, risk databases, and sophisticated reporting software [*displays Slide 13.9*]. But more than that, ERM is about getting

SLIDE **13.8** *ERM: Power to the People 7*

your people to behave in a way that promotes the achievement of the corporate mission and in a way that fits the expectations of key stakeholders. Where there is a poor fit we will probably have an underperforming business, or worse still, an apparently good performing business that is corrupt. Where there is a good fit the business will be run by people who understand the mission, understand risks that impact this mission, and take proper steps to deliver the goods using this understanding. Many organizations are happy to spend millions on software, consultants, and procedure design but they more or less ignore their front-line and back office staff as an expendable overhead. My proposition is to reverse this trend and spend time and money changing behaviors to make ERM an empowering real-life issue, rather than see ERM as a complex project that does not really reach the front line. As

SLIDE **13.9**   *Empowerment and ERM*

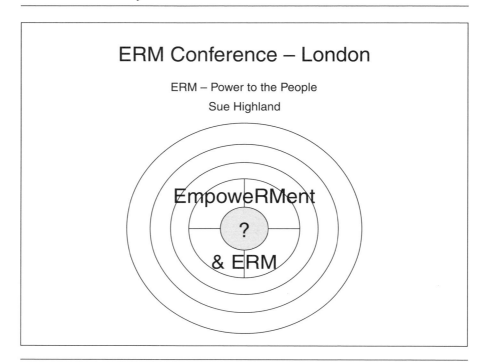

such, dynamic human resource strategies in my world and in my company are a fundamental part of making ERM work. Thank you, ladies and gentlemen; that concludes my presentation."

"Many thanks, Sue. We often overlook the real engine room of our business and that is the people who turn up and give us their all. I think Sue has grabbed ERM back from the regulators and made it an important corporate tool for growing a successful business. We have had an interesting morning of presentations and now it's your chance to ask a few questions. Remember, our speakers are around all day and they have told me that they would be happy to talk to you during the break, and we found that this worked well when people had really specific questions that they wanted to discuss. But here we have an opportunity to deal with a couple of more general issues that may have popped up over the course of the morning. Yes, madam, your question?"

"Steve has made a good case for the auditors. But in my experience our audit people do not have much to say about ERM. They concentrate on our accounting systems. Any views on this?"

"Chair, if I may. I have given you an insight into the way internal audit has developed over the years. When you say auditors, please remember that there are external auditors who have to do a lot of work on the accounts and internal auditors who are more involved across the whole business. All I can say is that the profession of internal auditing has moved on in leaps and bounds over the years and the Institute of Internal Auditors has a lead role in this. Their web site will give you a good idea of what to expect from your internal auditors, which is at www.theiia.org. If your auditors work in a way that bears no resemblance to the sort of things you find on the IIA web site, you might need to rethink the way you resource the audit service."

"Thank you, Steve. Next, please. Sir?"

"With respect, I would like to ask the second speaker why her model is about auditing? I can't see the link."

"Gloria?"

"Right. I see the model as a benchmark for holistic ERM. It's not mine; it's from the book that I referred to at the start of my session. The idea is to use the factors in the model to assess where you stand in terms of the extent to which your ERM process is holistic and integrated within your organization. That means you can audit your setup by comparing what you have with a model that you might care to develop. I use this model and others in the book to judge the state of ERM when I do consulting work."

"Thank you, Gloria. As I have already said, I think your model is something that may take a little time to digest. You know we only have a few minutes to present headline issues at a conference. The idea is to get you thinking about some of the things that are happening out there so that you can revisit your own unique ERM arrangements. Any questions for our last speaker? We need to close for lunch soon, but may I ask Sue a question? How can you really get low-paid workers involved in the ERM drive?"

"Thank you, Chair. I thought I could get away with not having to answer any questions. I can answer this question by describing what I have seen where the workforce is treated as the last and least significant item on an ERM model. One such template contained a complex diagram of ERM metrics, risk policy statement, authority levels, and reporting lines. Right at the bottom right of the diagram was the word 'Employees.' I rewrote the template and placed 'Employees' at the top, in the middle, and at the end. And I started a change management program to get people empowered to take responsibility for their work, and made sure they were skilled up to do this. It's about starting at the right place and moving on from there."

"Well. We have got through a great deal of material this morning and we will have our last formal part after lunch. I have arranged a buffet lunch upstairs and we will be using the dining room for this afternoon's sessions. Please return to the large dining room at two p.m. and find a place around the tables. We want to get you a bit more involved in the sessions wherever possible. See you at two p.m."

CHAPTER 14

CONFERENCE SESSION TEN

Bill, Helen, and Jack followed the crowd to the upstairs buffet room and found themselves standing around a food stand and helping themselves to finger foods and drinks. By the time they got to the food there was little time to do much more than grab something to eat and think about getting back to the conference room. Jack managed to get Helen's attention and asked, "Where's this friend you keep talking about? Marion, was it?"

"No, her name's Maria. She's got to stay with her team. They're working on a new piece of ERM software. It all sounds real interesting. Actually, she wants me to help her, but I'm not sure my boss would like that."

Bill was working his way through a tasty sandwich when a short, olive-skinned man grabbed him by the arm.

"Enrico . . ." Bill sputtered.

"Where is she?" Enrico's eyes were large and he had a worried frown on his face.

"Who?"

"The girl. The girl we saw yesterday. The one with the perfume and legs, who looked like Marilyn Monroe . . ." he looked at Helen and stopped talking.

"We've not seen her, Enrico, sorry," Bill replied, shaking his head.

Enrico sniffed the air, smiled, and quickly walked away, waving a friendly goodbye to the small group he had just interrupted.

Jack laughed out loud, "What a guy!"

Helen was just about to ask what was going on when the speaker boomed out a muffled message that sounded like an order to abandon ship, but was in fact a polite request for the delegates to come to the dining hall for the start of the afternoon sessions.

The delegates shuffled along to the huge dining hall and were greeted with a large number of dining tables, each with around eight to ten chairs set around it, with each chair angled to face the front of the room, where a speakers' platform had been erected. Vivaldi's *Four Seasons* was playing, and on each table sat several keypads, one for each delegate, and in the middle of the table was a computer laptop.

"Welcome, welcome back, one and all. Time for the final sessions. That is, before the workshop tomorrow morning. I know that many of you will not be attending the workshop, so let's make this afternoon a cracker. Without further ado I want to welcome Donald Southwest. You can see from the file that Donald has a wealth of experience and I know that he has been beating the ERM drum to nonbelievers for many years. Donald will be continuing our prelunch theme about the softer side of ERM and how to get people involved. Donald . . ."

"Thank you, and good afternoon, all [*displays Slide 14.1*]. I am glad to be here today and welcome this opportunity to give you my views on this idea of risk management. But I want to get personal and I want you to get involved in this session. Now, are you up for it? Okay, now please stand up and walk around for a few minutes and say hello to at least five people you haven't spoken to yet. And ask each person you meet a question: 'What does risk management mean to you?' I'll give you ten minutes for this."

"Right; time's up. Please return to your table.

"Now, grab hold of the little computer—there's one on each table— and type in some of the things that people have said in terms of what risk management means to them. Look up and you will see that your

SLIDE **14.1** *Let's Get Personal*

comments are now appearing on the screen behind me. Let me read some of them out:

- 'Doing things better.'
- 'Taking care of big risks.'
- 'Getting risks under control.'
- 'Not sure, but this conference will tell me.'
- 'Is that a wig you're wearing?'
- 'It's about taking charge of things.'
- 'Reducing uncertainty and better controls.'
- 'Developing risk management strategies.'
- 'Just a fad; it'll go away after a while.'
- 'Making sure we get the right things right, as far as possible.'

"Great, there are loads more ideas and I thank you for your contributions. I must let you in on a secret. I was asked to speak at this conference and a few weeks ago the conference organizers asked me to send in my presentation. Anyway, I e-mailed back saying I'm just going to talk to you all and that's it. So I get another e-mail asking for my slides and I made up a diagram on one slide and sent it back. Don't laugh, but a third e-mail came, asking for all my slides, and so I bought a whole set of royalty-free clip art, made them into slides, and sent it in. What's all this fuss about slides? I don't want to have you sit through twenty slides and listen to me babbling on about each point on each slide. I want to talk to you and get you to give me your ideas using a few slides as prompts. There is a great deal of combined talent here among you, the delegates, and I want to hear from you. Sound okay? Right, then, my first slide suggests that we are all entering this maze called ERM and we need as much help as possible to work our way through it.

"This is it—my complete diagram [*displays Slide 14.2*]. Do you like it? I want to try to align people's own experiences with the corporate machinery they work for. Don't worry about the detail here, because we will be breaking the thing down and taking each bit in turn. Then it's your turn to get involved. You said to me just a few minutes ago that ERM is about getting risks under control and doing things better.

"Let's start with corporate policy [*displays Slide 14.3*]. Most of you will work in organizations that have started to say, 'Let's get ERM in place.' And then they prepare a corporate policy saying just this.

"Take five minutes at your table to discuss this question: 'Is the ERM policy in your organization working well?'"

"Okay, let's look at some of the comments you have logged on your personal computers:

- 'Pretty much pie in the sky.'
- 'It's okay but could be better.'
- 'Not bad.'

SLIDE **14.2**   *Your Own Risk Reality*

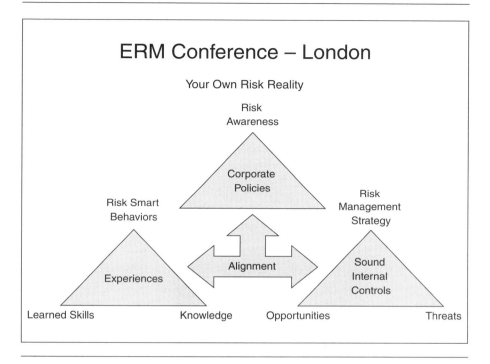

- 'Does not mean much outside of the finance people.'
- 'I think it's okay.'
- 'Do not have one.'
- 'There is one but I have not seen it.'

"I think that some of you are saying that there is room for improvement. I believe that a good ERM policy hinges on three main elements:

1. An awareness of risk and what it means at work
2. An ability to develop a risk management strategy in response to risk to your work product
3. What people are starting to call risk smart behaviors

"It is the 'risk smart behaviors' bit that is most often missing from the way organizations are applying ERM. Pinning the ERM policy up on a

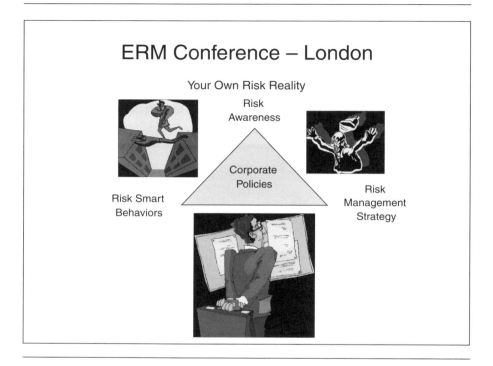

wall or on the intranet doesn't do much, much to the surprise of some senior managers. Real change needs much more than this.

"Let me jump to the next part of our model, internal controls [*displays Slide 14.4*]. My question to you here is: 'Do you feel entirely confident about making a formal statement on the adequacy of internal control in your organization?' Let's take five minutes on this."

"Let me read out some of your comments:

- 'Controls are fine.'
- 'Hard to give formal comments on complex things.'
- 'I think things are good but hard to issue formal statements.'

SLIDE **14.4**   *Your Own Risk Reality: Sound Internal Control*

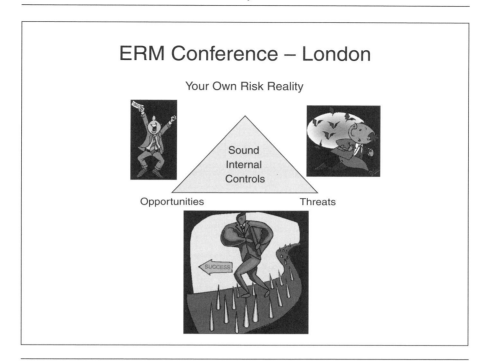

- 'Not been asked.'
- 'It is something we need to think about.'

"Internal control is important and in the future we will all need to think about giving formal statements on our controls as a matter of course. To me control is about managing threats. And it's about making sure opportunities are not missed. But it is also about thinking through your own risk reality, what has happened in your life and how it has affected you. My clip art says that big business is like moving through sharp obstacles at speed—dangerous, but absolutely necessary.

"The next bit of our model is about these personal experiences that we have that make us what we are [*displays Slide 14.5*]. It's what we know about our goals and the ERM process. Lots of this is from the

SLIDE **14.5** *Your Own Risk Reality: Experiences*

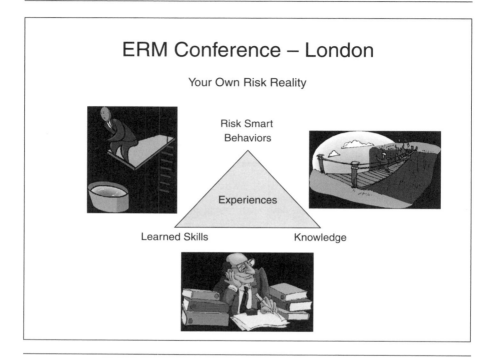

ERM policy and awareness seminars. The next item is learned skills and this is about making the risk cycle work in practice. You will have gone through this in earlier sessions at this conference. The thing I find most interesting is the final item—risk smart behavior. And we will look at this some more in a few moments. But let me ask you upfront: 'What to you is risk smart behavior?' Five minutes please . . ."

"Many thanks. Points are starting to come through:

- 'Being one step ahead of the opposition.'
- 'Being smart—that is it.'
- 'Making sure you are in control at all times.'

- 'Understanding risk and responding to risk.'
- 'Having a clear risk appetite and sticking to it.'
- 'Yes, I'm sure it is a wig.'
- 'Not sure that people are really risk smart at all. Most are just lucky.'

"You can read books on ERM and in fact attend conferences like this one. You can also learn skills and operate new systems that record and report risks. But it's harder to pin down what risk smart behavior is all about. And it's this factor that to me is most important.

"Now what I want to get to is the problem with ERM [*displays Slide 14.6*]. That is aligning different perspectives. Let's go back to my original model. The internal control standards in use may see people as

SLIDE **14.6** *Your Own Risk Reality: Alignment*

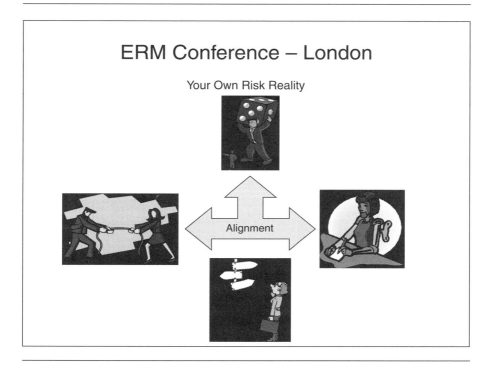

robots that just follow the standard procedures. That is my picture of the lady with a key in her back—like a clockwork mechanism. The corporate risk policy may see risk as fate or chance and many people may be unsure what they can control and what's outside their remit. That's the man with the die above. The couple on the left have completely different perspectives on what that are trying to achieve at work and end up pulling each other over most of the time. They each have a different interpretation of risk and different risk appetites that are in conflict. The character at the bottom is stuck in the middle of these mixed messages.

"Let me ask another question: 'Are you clear about the risk appetite that drives your organization's ERM process?'"

"Right, let's look at some of your comments:

- 'No idea.'
- 'Sort of, I think.'
- 'We have discussed this but it is a complicated concept.'
- 'Not too bad on this—we are risk takers who assess our risks before acting.'
- 'Wig or no wig, I still think you are cute.'
- 'Most people around me are risk averse.'
- 'Do not understand the question.'

"Let's carry on.

"What I am saying is that we need to align our ERM policy with the way controls are applied at work and the way our people behave [*displays Slide 14.7*]. It's about getting our people risk smart and knowing when to take a chance and when to pull back. It also means that our controls reflect this position. They are not too rigid so as to stop any new thinking. But they are not so loose as to mean anything goes. My cartoon says that we need to work together as a team, at least being on the same side to make any real progress. ERM can bring us together in

SLIDE **14.7**   *Your Own Risk Reality: Risk Awareness*

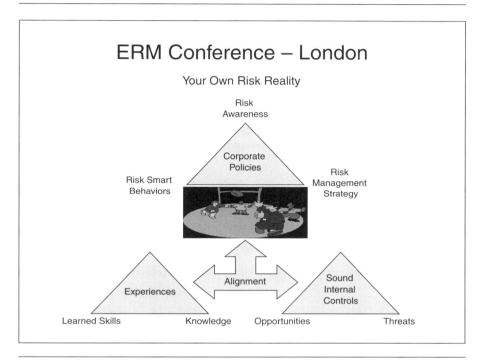

this way but only if it is applied carefully. That is, if it is aligned to our business system and the way we behave in making a success of things.

"Risk smart people who are lined up with the ERM policy and the way controls are applied at work is what we need to aim at [*displays Slide 14.8*]. Now as before I am going to ask you what we need to do. You realize that I am just a facilitator. You here have the combined knowledge to provide more or less all the answers. I just want to get this knowledge out of you. I want now to ask you: 'How can we align ERM and controls to encourage risk smart people in our organization?'

"I want you to get up grab a cup of coffee and ask five people who you have not met yet to come up with their best idea. Twenty minutes and counting."

"Okay [*displays Slide 14.9*]. We're all back. You have worked so hard and you now need to plug your ideas into the keyboard. Remember, everything we have entered onto the system is recorded and we will e-mail your comments to all delegates by the end of the week. To close, then, let's look at some of your ideas:

- 'Hold workshops on risk appetite and get people to think about where they stand and what is expected of them.'
- 'Pick your teams with care and analyze different personality types before they are set to work. Get a good combination of people.'
- 'Develop an ERM policy that has examples of what we expect from our people in terms of decision making, taking responsibility, and accountability.'

SLIDE **14.9** *Risk Smart Behaviors*

- 'Develop a no-blame culture where we accept careful risk taking backed up with risk registers for major decisions and ventures.'
- 'Hold an internal ERM conference and set guidance on what it takes to be successful but responsible.'
- 'Use staff training programs to develop new skills.'
- 'Appoint leaders and role models from people who have got it right.'
- 'What are you doing tonight?'
- 'Develop a set of values that incorporates risk smart thinking.'
- 'Make ERM an important standard that is applied by all managers and work teams.'
- 'Ask your top people to define risk smart behavior and build this into staff competencies.'
- 'Recruit people who are already risk smart.'

"Many thanks. I cannot really add much to your comments. You have covered a lot of ground and you have all given us something to think about. Well, that's all from me folks. Hope you enjoyed the session. And the answer to the big question is no, I'm not wearing a wig and sorry, I'm tied up tonight, baby."

"Excellent, Donald. And just for the record, it was not me making those naughty remarks. An organization may stop asking, Shall we start employing risk smart people? And start saying, we cannot afford to use people who are not risk smart. Thank you, Donald.

"Now we come to a slight change in the program. We were expecting Dexter Bandstanding to talk to us about ERM and internal control. Unfortunately, Dexter has gone down with flu and cannot make this presentation. He leads a small team who are developing a risk software package, and a member of his team, Maria Abimbola, has agreed to stand in for Dexter and talk us through his presentation. Okay, so we did have a contingency plan, which essentially involved me getting down on my knees and begging Maria for help. Maria, if you please."

CHAPTER 15

CONFERENCE SESSION ELEVEN

"Hello, ladies and gentlemen. I wish Dexter a speedy recovery and hope that I am able to cover all his points.

"My job today is quite simple [*displays Slide 15.1*]. I will spend a few minutes taking you through the governance equation, that is, where ERM fits into the overall governance agenda. I hear a lot of people go on about corporate governance, risk management, and internal controls in the same breath and it almost seems that these three things are interchangeable. Not so; they are aligned but they do not mean the same thing. We have got into a rather lazy habit of using throwaway lines, almost as clichés, and I think this is a shame. People need to be clear about their terminology or the governance drive can become a bit of a joke. Okay, that's my soapbox out of the way. Let's have a look at the next slide.

"I think the three concepts are linked [*displays Slide 15.2*]. Corporate governance provides the overriding framework and this is about society wanting to promote respectable, well-run organizations that essentially do what they say they will do. The word 'respectable' means different things to different people. To me it means there is a code of conduct and a value system in place that is fundamental to the core purpose of the organization. It means keeping promises and it means

---

ERM Conference – London

The Internal Control Dimension

Where do ERM and controls fit into the overall governance equation?

---

behaving in a way that inspires confidence. It's sad that time and time again companies and agencies and not-for-profit outfits have let us down and behaved badly. It's sad because it means society has had to devise ways and means of locking out miscreants and making up rules to help the situation. Governance is led by the way the board behaves and the way they respond to the needs of their stakeholders. Good performance should be carried out in an open and acceptable manner. It is about the way external audit reviews the published accounts and the way the internal auditors review the internal organizational systems. Governance asks that each party to the accountability platform perform its duty in a way that stands up to scrutiny. Anyway, you get my point.

   "ERM, however, is about risk management across the business and it starts with the risk that the business is not properly governed. And then

SLIDE **15.2** *Corporate Governance 1*

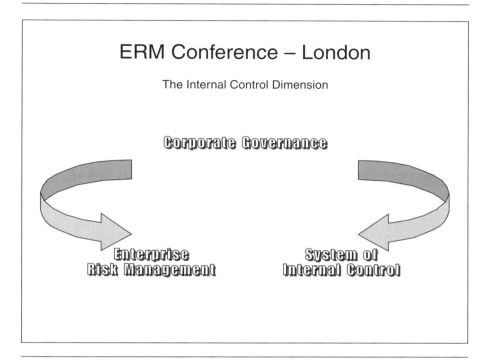

ERM will go on to addressing the risks that even where the organization is well governed, there will still be matters that affect its ability to deliver. Having worked out where these risks lie, the management can ensure that aspects that can be controlled are controlled while aspects that cannot be controlled are addressed in the best way possible. We are all open to terrorist attacks and it is hard to zero this risk, apart from shutting up shop. What is needed is for each organization to work out how much it is at risk and how best to respond in order to minimize the chances and impacts if the risk does in fact materialize. This is the type and openness of the dialogue that should be happening between the shareholders, the company board, and the management. That is the essence of corporate governance, and the show-stopping risks arise when this dialogue breaks down or is just poor.

"I want to build on this idea of controls [*displays Slide 15.3*]. In the past, companies and governments could do pretty much as they liked. So long as there was enough profit and growth, no one asked questions. And so long as the government did an okay job, all was well. We are now in a world of rapid change, and global shifts in resource allocations and cost profiles. You can get a skilled workforce that is based in some overseas countries for, say, a third of the cost of local staff, and with the right communications infrastructure, it doesn't really matter where your workforce is located. At the same time, people are demanding more from public services and we think nothing of externalizing a unit where the private sector can do the job better. Even charities and aid agencies are being asked to explain how donations or grants have helped in emerging democracies and people will stop giving if they do not get the right answers.

SLIDE 15.3   *Corporate Governance 2*

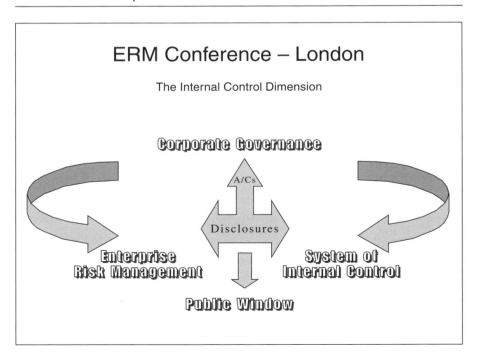

"In this scenario we can argue that all organizations now have a public window attached to what they say and what they do and what they report. If there is any mismatch between these three factors, then there will be problems. External accounts and various regulatory disclosures are all part of this framework where good governance must be seen to be happening, and the executives must explain themselves even when results are on the upside. In fact, some oil companies get criticized for making too much money by exploiting increases in oil prices while other companies get criticized for not making enough money. Sometimes you just cannot win. In the past, the public window was about companies telling people how they are doing. I think that now it's more about letting people look into the business to find out how the company is doing. What people want to see is an effective risk management process that encourages the use of good controls. It's a two-way show, and ERM is about making sure the risks that might make the corporate show look tatty are addressed.

"Let me continue [*displays Slide 15.4*]. We have been talking about risk and control in a simple way. You have a risk—you get a control. Easy as apple pie. But we need to do more than that. To get from bad risk to good control it is best to prepare a better structure. One approach is to define a basic four-way split on risks: First, strategic risk, which can be related to the way strategy is set and performance defined to implement this strategy. Second, business risk is everything that happens in the core business units or services. Third, compliance risk is falling foul of laws and regulations, or exposing the company to a legal claim of whatever nature. Last, project risk is stuff that comes from all those projects and proposals that abound in any forward moving organization. The risk here relates to not delivering the project, and as a result not being able to move forward. Having made this breakdown we can then start to talk about internal controls in a more meaningful way.

"Using the four-way split, we can align risk to control much more easily [*displays Slide 15.5*]. Strategic risk needs a strategic risk management approach in terms of an overall strategy to ensure we are doing the right things in the right way, as a long-term aim. This is looking at

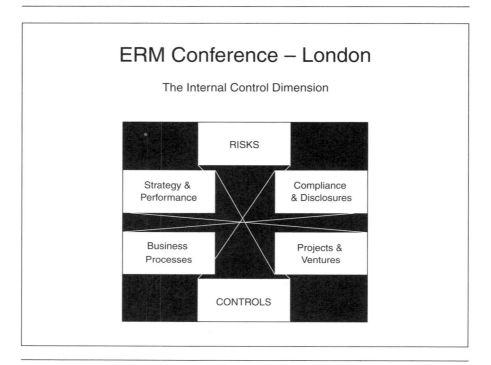

risk over the horizon and planning ahead to ensure we gain a lead or at least don't get left standing when new things break or old products come under pressure. Good companies get out of markets that are closing in and causing problems. They also get into markets that are taking off. But all this happens at a strategic level and tends to hit the top people in the organization. Good strategic risk management is about taking control of things at the highest level of the organization.

"Compliance and disclosure risk requires a different control dimension. It is more about having standard procedures that stick fast and mean no laws are flouted by staff, intentionally or unintentionally. If there is a set of accounting policies in use, then employees must stick to the rules of classifying, say, significant spending so that the accounts can properly reflect the commercial reality of the underlying transactions.

SLIDE **15.5**   *The Internal Control Dimension 2*

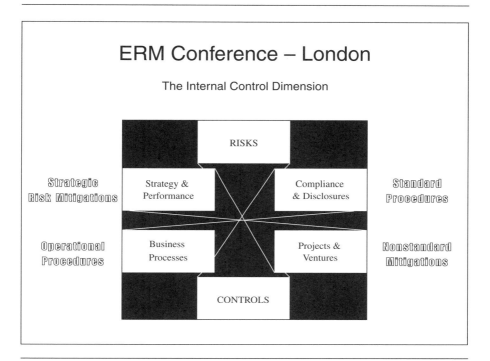

These controls are quite rigid, and areas such as health and safety, employment practices, or new product trials must be tied down by tight controls and reviews that these controls are being applied—there will be very little room for flexibility here.

"Project risk is different again. The controls that fit each project will vary depending on what the project is about. If we want to develop a new overseas office we will need controls that are built to respond to the unique risks that each different venture entails. This is where the risk appetite may be more flexible and we can take some chances to get ahead of the competition, where appropriate. We may be able to approve budgets that are spent on new ventures and write a few of them off where they do not deliver, so long as this does not exceed our tolerance levels. Having said that, we would still want each project to follow the basics of good project management and all this entails. We can accept a failed project but we would not want a project that breaches all the procedures for approval, management, monitoring, spending, and other such matters.

"The final element is what I would call the basic internal controls. Business risk requires standard operational routines that are formulated by the management and applied. Most information systems have control features built into them as do production processes. When people talk about internal controls, they mainly mean these sorts of basic operational routines that are used in all organizations: for payroll, human resources, production, sales, marketing, budgeting, financial accounting, and so on. That is, the core business and back office systems.

"I want to add one more feature to the ERM/internal control template [*displays Slide 15.6*]. That is the simple fact that ERM relates to

SLIDE **15.6**   *System of Internal Control*

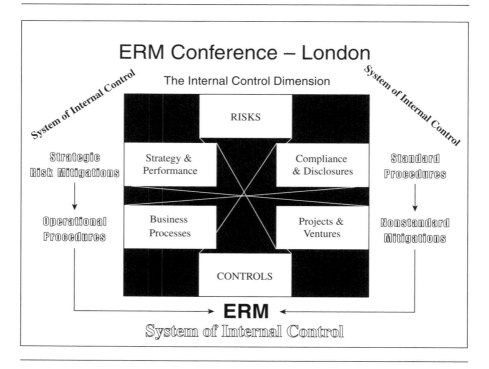

risks to each of the four elements and that each type of risk requires a different control approach. We have said this is strategic, compliance, project or change control, and operational procedures. But together they form what we call the system of internal control.

"No matter what approach we have to internal control, it is essentially about tackling risk [*displays Slide 15.7*]. If this is kept in mind, then it makes sense. But we must also ask what it is to be in control. Let me take you through each point on the slide:

- **Clear aims:** Here control starts with having a good idea of what you want to achieve. Strategic risk relates to risk that impacts your ability to get to a clear goal over a defined period. Risk can only be defined if this goal is quite clear. I have seen several organizations have trouble with confused aims and vague strategic outcomes.

SLIDE **15.7**   *Being in Control*

ERM Conference – London

The Internal Control Dimension

Being in control:

- *Clear aims*

- *Focus on risk*

- *Holistic perspective – ERM*

- *Good governance*

They want to be best, better, world-class—but at what? The really good outfits have a strong and simple message that sums up what they are. It may be that the company wants to offer a diverse range of products and is constantly taking over smaller fish to get there. This is okay so long as the corporate aim incorporates this diversity of product lines and ties them together in some sensible way.

- **Focus on risk:** We have said this a lot. Controls are only needed if they serve to mitigate a risk. The risk of stifling initiative becomes an issue where people need to check and double-check before making a decision for no good reason. Where there is a good reason, say a bad decision could cause catastrophic failure, then it's fine to have lots of checks involved. But there must be a defined risk that warrants these defined controls.

- **Holistic perspective:** This is about people seeing control as a concept that runs across the organization. If one team decides that it can no longer check query x, then it needs to make clear whether this gap will have a knock-on effect that may mean poor services elsewhere or some lost advantage to the organization. I know one company that secured night-time phone cover from a cheap agency and saved lots of money but lost important customers who could not get a sensible response when they called the company outside office hours. A brand-new risk came out of trying to manage the risk of budget overspends.

- **Good governance:** Controls should promote accountability, good performance, and a good reputation. Marketing may say that the risk of lower sales can be tackled if they suck in lots of personal data from associates' systems and send out marketing material to these potential customers. But then the risk of losing or giving away personal data to fraudsters who may be involved in identity theft must also be considered. Good governance is about good behavior and organizations are starting to think about how their operations affect others outside of their own cozy corporate world.

- **Good controls:** Good systems of internal control allow a management to say that they are in control and tell the world. This is why published internal control certificates are so important. But being in control needs to fit with all the things that we have discussed so far.

"We are at the final slide [*displays Slide 15.8*]. What I am saying is that governance, risk management, and internal control are all connected but different. Governance is about behavior; risks are what can make this behavior poor, or just wrong, and controls are there to try to make sure this does not happen. If we put our controls together, they form a system of internal control and that system of internal control helps define how we behave, which brings us right back to good governance. So to summarize the governance equation: controls kick most risks into touch and ensure that what we promise to do, mostly happens. And if this works out, then we will have good governance, at least for most of the time."

SLIDE **15.8**   *ERM and Internal Controls*

ERM Conference – London

The Internal Control Dimension

ERM and internal controls fit clearly into the overall governance equation

"Fascinating, Maria. I think we do tend to use the catch phrases 'risk management' and 'internal control' without thinking through how each bit fits together. And I have to express a special thanks for Maria stepping in at such short notice. Maria, you have gone through your presentation at great speed and we have a few minutes to spare. May I ask you to tell us a little about your risk management software project?"

"Certainly. I have been working with a team set up by the well-known risk management expert, Dexter Bandstanding. We have developed a dashboard approach to risk reporting where we have been able to reproduce an organization, in terms of its projects, operations, teams, business lines, and so on, in a form of risk map. This multilayered map records the state of risk across set categories, which I will not go into now. Anyway, we formulated our color-codes system with red, green, and three grades of yellow, that is, low, medium, and high yellow. This is because we found many people were dumping their risks into yellow as they thought this was an average position. The idea is that high-level reports show top management where there is high unmitigated risk. We then went on to design what we call a Dynamic Intervention Based Module. Here managers can take a high yellow or say red risk area and input decision points where named people are asked to deliver a solution and report back. After the change is made, which is generally speaking about better controls, the risk profile is immediately reformulated and hopefully high risks are brought down. For example, one transport company used our system and found that the risk of drivers not taking proper breaks was high and that the controls over this problem were pretty weak. The operations manager was able to use our software to send an intervention instruction regarding the way rest periods were being monitored and the risk went straight down to low amber, with regular check points to make sure the new arrangements were working.

"So far, so good. We are now working on a Predictive Futures Module whereby managers can design several different risk management strategies, to address the circumstances they have now adjusted for future impacts, and each strategy is modeled to form a series of possible risk maps, with a new set of color codes risk profiles. We are now at a stage where we are considering a Consequential Impacts Module where we can work out, if management proposes a certain change, say a new operational procedure, the knock-on effects for other control routines that can be determined, after which a new risk map can be drawn, or several alternative maps. Going back to the long haul transport company, we later placed more layers on our system that allowed the operations manager to suggest a change in rest breaks and then observe the consequential impact on say targets over drive times and excessive time-out breaks. So one change may be seen to create several other impacts and the manager can monitor this and then decide on best action.

"Essentially, we are trying to make ERM dynamic, holistic, and also multifaceted to reflect the realities of organizational life. It's hard work and we still have a way to go, but we are making good progress."

"I'm sure that this time next year you will be able to come to our annual conference and give us an update. Thank you, Maria. Well, I have a bit of a treat now. We have listened to an international group of speakers, although many have come all the way from the States to be here. Since we are in London we, that is, the planning committee, thought it would be appropriate to have a Brit as the final speaker. I had the pleasure of making contact with our distinguished guest, Dr. Belmoral, who despite being semiretired, agreed to come back and talk to us about his unique stance on ERM. Let's take a quick break and return to the conference room, where the seats are plusher than they are here. And then we can sit back and you can enjoy the thoughts and fears of Dr. Belmoral. Say fifteen minutes break, and then back to the main conference room."

CHAPTER 16

CONFERENCE SESSION TWELVE

"**W**elcome back. It is my great pleasure to welcome Dr. Belmoral, who will take us through to the close of the annual ERM conference."

"Hello, everyone [*displays Slide 16.1*]. I want to give you my thoughts on becoming sensibly risqué and why I feel this is the way forward in what might be seen as the murky waters of risk management. I'm not sure why I was invited to this conference, as most people say I'm a bit controversial. Don't ask me why. Perhaps it's because I'm getting old and I disagree with most of what people say about ERM and I have a rather odd view on some things. Anyway, I'll let you decide that one. I have got some slides for you, although I have spoken at quite a few events just off the cuff with no flashy slides. So if I digress, please let me know. It's a bit odd for most of you to just sit and listen to someone and I personally cannot concentrate on any one thing for more than ten minutes. Anyway, I've already started to digress, so let's move on.

"Many companies get themselves in real trouble and become targets to be taken over or just broken up and sold off. There is a frightening amount of risk out there. I've worked with some big outfits that get involved in major acquisitions and some take on newly formed entities that consume huge amounts of cash, with very little early payback. Some companies fall down where huge risks swing into action. Oil price

---

ERM Conference – London

Risqué Thinking and Positivity?

Becoming Sensibly
Risqué

---

increases, a new drug that fails testing procedures, a big product recall, slowing sales, and all kinds of things can trip up the best-run company. The public sector can be hit by poor confidence or the all-time favorites, late completion and huge price overruns on new projects.

"The amount of pressure that falls at the feet of CEOs, chairs, and board members is getting crazy. I have just finished working with a company that has decided to embark on a global search for a new CEO. They don't care what country the chief comes from so long as he or she has the talent and can deliver. The idea of employing traditional good souls has all but gone. In the old days, entrepreneurs used to just get together a group of friends, form a board, and run a company that more or less ran itself, with a loyal customer base and pretty stable conditions. I now talk to executive teams and they tell me that a failure to change, a lack of talent, and a failure to look outside the company to seek inspiration and challenge are the biggest risks they face. Sometimes, boards cannot quite define these ideas and this is where it gets scary. Those risks that cannot be properly expressed can cause great problems. This is where a lack of imagination can stall the ERM process. What cannot be seen in the mind's eye can escape the risk identification stage and get lost. Some call this intuition, where we instinctively know that something is missing or something is wrong, or something should be there but is not. If we can express these fears as risks, then ERM can come into play. But if we cannot, then ERM becomes a bit of a joke.

"I worked with one board and facilitated a risk workshop by asking them for their top ten risks. After we got through the formalities I suggested to them that to me, the biggest risk that large multinationals face is a lack of talent at the top. So a big risk for them is that they don't know what they are doing. Try telling that to the main board members without shaking them up a bit. Boards that cannot accept this fact are not real. I stand up and tell them that—and get paid for doing so. So board members need to be astute, experienced, motivated, and honest. Any breakdown in any of these factors will leave a gap. I simply asked the board members: How can you be sure that you meet all these elements of effective boards? And when you have set the agenda for management, how can you be sure that your top managers are delivering? Risk starts from the top. It starts with the risk of poor governance, poor board functioning, and poor strategy.

"Anyway, when I had had my go at them there was a long silence. They asked for a recess and I went outside expecting to be asked to leave. Luckily they asked me back in and asked whether I could work out a format through which they could assess their own performance, which I did. We suggested that good boards set a challenging strategy and make sure it is delivered, and flexed to take on board external changes. We also suggested that nonexecutives get involved in the company and ask lots of questions to test the board strategy. The nonexecutives are an essential part of ERM where they challenge strategy and help isolate all those risks that relate to each option so that the best one is selected. Risk assessment starts as strategy is being set and not, as some think, after we have got to strategic objectives. It worries me where risk management models start with corporate objectives. ERM should swing into action before strategy is defined, and not just after this has happened. Board reports that talk about important corporate issues and then see risk management as a separate and remote item are not really employing ERM. Boards that ask for all reports to include a robust risk assessment are closer to real ERM. This theme on integrated ERM should run across the entire organization.

"I have made a bit of a study of big corporate collapses and when these scandals break the shares plunge and the key players desert. Most often the board gets voted out and the rebuild starts. This can take forever and many of them get taken over before they can recover. I had a go at calculating some of the fines that get stuck on to delinquent companies, but now we are moving into the arena where the top people have to take personal responsibility for damage done to a company's value through negligence, fraud, or just sheer carelessness. So the top dogs build an infrastructure to protect them. But from what? Sometimes they build a legal maze that means the arrow points away from them and highjack ERM as a defense. Frightening, eh? There can be tons of risk management stuff going on but poor governance arrangements and very little real business value in all of it. I once worked on a program of facilitated risk workshops and we clocked dozens of workshops with tons of paperwork produced each month. It took me awhile to realize that the board was not actually interested in the results of these workshops; they just wanted to report that they had been resourced and done. What a waste. It gets worse. The business teams also knew that their action points would be more or less ignored and their energy levels dropped over the life of the program so that, in the end, it became hard to get these teams to sign up for their half-day workshop. Risk activity that falls outside of real business work is actually a waste of time. Not only is this a waste, but it makes ERM seem irrelevant and an opportunity is missed.

"Great ERM sees risk as opportunity. Staying away from the action is okay for staying out of trouble, but it also means missing out on chances for real progress. Rising commodity prices, cheap labor in third-world countries, demands for safer cars, or cleaner cars, or natural foods can all be seen as risks that can hurt an established business. Or, they can be seen as great opportunities to move ahead while competitors take a defensive attitude. I have the impression that people across the world feel that global risks are becoming more volatile and harder to control. Some say that humans are becoming more and more susceptible to animal diseases that can cross over to humans. And that global travel means a problem in some remote part of the word can quickly cross over many continents in a matter of weeks. Over the next decade, rather than become a global community, some countries may start to close their borders and stop certain travelers or produce from coming in. This has already started to happen with some antiterrorist measures. Maybe this will happen to the Internet, where overseas connections will be blocked unless they meet a government-set criterion. In this scenario, the world may close down and become a set of different tribal blocks, each having its own defense against physical, information, and chemical intrusion, including the ability to block intrusion from people on, say, a hit list, using biometrical identifying devices.

"Let me see. As usual, I've been going on a bit. Perhaps it's time for a few slides.

"Right there [*displays Slide 16.2*]. This slide is about positivity. Which is about being real, being astute, and being a little risqué, when necessary. I was in a bar last year and got talking to a guy. He told me he rarely went home since he read that 75% of all accidents occurred in the house and therefore he was much safer here. Eventually he stopped going to work because he heard that 20% of accidents happen there. I went back to the bar to find him to ask what the other 5% was and found out that he had died a few months ago—you guessed it, from alcohol poisoning.

"Anyway, let's get back to this idea of risk. I helped out a medium-sized retail group where one customer had fabricated a complaint that was picked up by the local, and eventually national, media. We spent loads on clearing their name but there is still a group of people who just don't trust the brand name. When the complaint first came through, the

SLIDE **16.2**   *Good Appreciation of Risk*

ERM Conference – London

Risqué Thinking and Positivity?

Good appreciation of risk and the ability to develop a realistic picture of what can be controlled and how, in conjunction with the expectations of key stakeholders

---

company denied the legitimacy of the complaint and asked for proof. They focused more on the fact that there was no truth to the claim, then on the damage the rumor could do if it got out in the mainstream. But they had not factored in the risk that an honest company can get a really bad reputation if they are not careful.

"Some companies get themselves in a bind by miss-selling investment schemes and stuff like expensive loan protection coverage or cold-calling people. Where this is the norm in some companies, there can be a real ignorance of the long-term damage that could happen through this type of exposure. Other boards try to buy time and play around with the accounts, not because they want to engage in criminal activity, but just because they panic and tell a small lie that grows and grows. This slippery slope can make honest businesspeople behave in a way that means they become criminals in suits. Active fraud is different. Cybercrime is a risk that is now putting people off on-line banking. Phishing happens where a fraudster calls bank customers at random and pretends to be from the bank, and requests, say, account numbers and personal password details to verify the customer. This is at a time when local branches are being closed and phone lines covered by low-paid call center staff. But risk has a strange nature. What is a risk to one company can be an opportunity for another. I came across one bank that is opening up branches because they sensed that people are rejecting hands-off contact. So risk to some banks was an opportunity to others who gained a lead.

"Risk concepts can be misused—like selling antiterrorist gadgets to householders or small businesses as the fear of terror attacks is now commonplace. I have seen the risk management agenda completely misused. There is the risk that TVs will break down, or your house will collapse, or you will fall over dead or injure yourself and stop working, but this is not put into perspective and some companies use inappropriate levels of fear to get a product or an insurance cover sold. It goes on and on. Moreover, I've seen a chief risk officer sell up the idea of risk to get a pay raise. People get so scared at work that they don't want to make any decision without checking with the risk people, or writing dozens of reports about the risks. Risk can be real, perceived, or contrived and it is important that we understand the difference between these three different concepts. And it is important that companies and governments are honest in the way they present these ideas. If contrived risk is presented as real risk, then ERM becomes superficial. I have seen one management team describe their new ventures as "Red Risk" projects so that they get paid bonuses to get the red risks down to yellow or green. In this company, red risks also get special budgets and the managers were given extra resources. In other companies, red risks meant that the manager was in danger of being sacked.

"But let's get back to the big canvas of ERM—you can't take your kids to the park now without taking out an insurance policy in case they have an accident. Schools, youth groups, social event organizers, and loads of others are up against a brick wall. They are canceling events because they are running scared. And kids are growing up thinking that anything outside their comfort zone is dangerous. Their parents place them in a bubble, buy them whatever they want, and real life passes them by. They grow up not being able to deal with any variation from the norm. These kids are graduating and joining your companies. They are becoming the people of tomorrow. Frightening, eh?

"Okay, let me ask you a rhetorical question. What do you think is the biggest risk to a nuclear power plant? For a new nuclear power station their biggest risk will probably be economic risk in securing huge loans to fund the millions that it takes to build the thing before it is able to generate a single penny in income. But a government that wants to sell the idea of nuclear power has a task on its hand. How to tell the public that the risks can be managed and the risk of not having an alternative source of energy is much bigger than anything else, as fossil fuel prices continue to soar? The main factor in this scenario is the degree to which the public trusts the government and the message makers. And this depends on past experience, the way the message is presented, and whether what is being said fits with what is actually happening. It's hard to tell people that crime is falling in areas where local people are being attacked by thugs on a regular basis. A government that makes too many mistakes in unreliable message giving will suffer. A board that makes too many mistakes in failing to disclose the full effects of their strategy, both good and bad, will suffer. A charity that cannot say what happened to the donations sent abroad for local services will eventually collapse.

"You need to have the right attitude toward risk. Different people hide, run, fight, think up excuses, seek help, or just react with the first thing that comes to mind. I don't mind so long as this is positive. But good companies need to have the right culture in place so that the right decisions are made. Culture is a hard concept to measure. It is about when people consult, how performance is measured, who gets promoted, how real ownership happens, reward systems, and how people work, whether in boxes or right across the organizations. A blame culture does not accept mistakes, and there is a view that ERM cannot flourish where people are not allowed to have new ideas. Culture is about like-minded communities coming together for a common cause. This is the start of ERM. That is, positive movement for the better. There is so much that can be learned from near misses. I remember noticing that the stairs in my office were a bit slippery and you know it just did not dawn on me that something could be done. Or, that I should have told someone. Anyway, after nearly spilling my coffee on a regular basis, a new person started and made a fuss. In the end, the buildings manager put in new nonslip carpets and the problem was solved. I felt really bad that I did not realize that there was a solution. Near misses are often not reported, and when something bad happens people say they thought something was wrong but did not think to do anything. This is about culture—having people stand up and feel that they have a voice even if it's not within the narrow confines of their job.

"Here is a new slide [*displays Slide 16.3*]. Let's take each point in turn:

- **Clear aims.** This is important. We need to make sure we work out where risk is relevant. Risk is what affects what you are trying to achieve. But you need to be clear about what this is in the first place. One company I worked with was obsessed with the risk of their head office being blown up by terrorists. They set up a large department of contingency planning teams and held monthly board meetings to discuss these plans. I told them that being pre-pared was fine but they had taken their eye off the ball, and if this continued they would have no business to protect because it was being run to the ground. It's a matter of balance and good sense. I worked with a charity that focused on securing donations. When I met them their main goal was to generate lots of income, which was sent back to the head office for project work. But the rules changed overnight with a change in the charity regulator's policy and questions were being asked about the value from the local ser-vices, even if the charity was securing lots of gifted money. In this charity most of the managers got caught out and were locked into

---

ERM Conference – London

Risqué Thinking and Positivity?

- Clear aims
- Clear responsibilities
- Knowing top risks
- Understanding risk appetite
- Knowing top controls
- Appreciate complex relationships
- Learn lessons
- Better framework for success

---

the old agenda and did not question what they were achieving but only what income they were generating. ERM did not work here as there were inconsistent goals and we had to spend a lot of time cleaning things up before we could move on.

- **Clear responsibilities.** Tell people that they have clear goals and a clear function at work, but that they are all part of the ERM machine. If they observe a risk that can hurt the company or for that matter that could be used to gain an advantage, then they should respond. People should get out of boxes and think about the corporate line, not just their part of things.
- **Knowing top risks.** Spend time on what needs attention. But beware the squeaky-wheel bit. You know the old saying, that the squeaky wheel gets the grease. That's fine, but remember the rest

of the wagon. Getting down and changing the wheel is fine, but we need to check the whole wagon and make sure all the wheels are oiled before they go bad. Many companies work on the squeaky-wheel basis—management waits for a problem to break and then sends in the troops. Top management only approves troops where we can show that there is a war going on. But people are less able to anticipate problems and drive their wagons around the rocks, rather than crash into them and then fix the damage. ERM is about responsibility and accountability: the ability to tell people what you've done and what you have not been able to sort out through a careful analysis of the risks and how these risks might be mitigated. Business executives are now facing up to their responsibilities. They are starting to tell their stakeholders about their strategy and how ERM works in their organization.

- **Risk appetites.** Okay, what is this? It's what makes you tick. How long do you wait before you scratch an itch? Depends on your tolerance and what else is going on. When you're busy, then the itch gets left; but if you are sitting around bored, you might scratch and scratch. Okay? That's what happens to some government people. They are so bored at work that they start to invent minor things to occupy their time and fill in form after form to justify their job. If a staff member cannot explain why he or she fills in a form, then we need to ask whether it's worth it. I remember one job I had years ago where I used to make up stuff for my support staff to do, because they would have gotten bored with the few tasks that were really important. I used to give them the easy stuff that I could have done but which would keep them busy. They ticked their schedules, saying they had done this and that, and we were all happy. There was no consideration of risk or risk appetites and areas where we could leave things alone as there was no risk involved.

- **Top controls.** ERM has taken us into a whole new world of theory: future risks, future plans, and future risk management strategies. People get into the future but there is a danger that we forget the basics. Top risks means top controls need to be in place. And if we stop thinking about these controls and focus only on areas where there is high risk with no controls, then we could mess up. We need to make sure key controls work. Design, then redesign, then review and make sure staff are employing them properly. We cannot assume that a basic control works. Take contract management. A key control is tendering that may be applied to the bigger contracts. Sound simple? This ensures the best bid wins. But if our tendering process is not kept sharp, then huge contracts may go astray and huge sums could be lost or wasted. Fraud is another matter. So the ERM process should be also about reviewing important controls that guard against risk that really needs to be bolted down.

- **Complex relationships.** Risk means controls are needed, but these controls can in turn lead to other risks. I know one company that said all new spending needed a business case and this was a key control over budgeting. But the need for these business cases was slowing things down so much that many spends missed important deadlines and people got bogged down into writing reports and not chasing business leads. Managing the risk of overspending was causing many deals to be lost and business suffered. But it was more complicated than that. People started to draw down standard business cases from templates and just changed the amounts. This meant a lot of new spending was being misclassified and people in that division were starting to get around many other procedures as a natural way of working.

- **Learning lessons.** Good companies make more mistakes than most but learn fast from them. The key is to set this learning into revising the framework for success and so make for a more successful business. I worked with one clothing retail company and their policy was, stack them high and sell them cheap. Anyway, the brand got a name as being cheap, basic, and low-income style. The board was upset when the term "low-income style" was repeated in the fashion press but I suggested that they use this as a thrust into a marketing strategy. They sent their buyers to fashion shows and got them involved in youth projects, you know, street culture.

They used these ideas to produce a brand that was about street credibility mixed with fashion ideas. People now see the brand as a badge of honor and as a result, sales have increased significantly. They now use the gimmick 'cheap and cheerful' in their campaigns. I'll talk about learning lessons some more later on.

"Right, a new slide [*displays Slide 16.4*]. What do we have here? Oh yes. I'm talking about being positive. So this is about being proactive. The scale is from inactive to reactive to proactive. So far, so good. Inactive people see risk as being about fate. The luck of the draw: What happens just happens. They feel that the hand of fate is inescapable. They get in trouble, sigh, and try to keep going. People like these have an up-to-date resume and know that if something big breaks they will have to jump and hope for the best. This type of risk management is about being happy in ignorance.

SLIDE 16.4   *Fate Contingency*

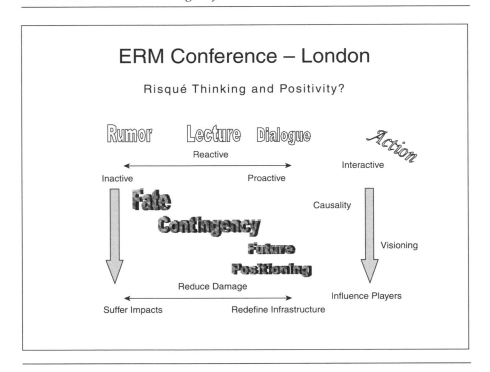

"Reactive people know that there are risks out there and when it hits they have some kind of response. These people tend to build backup plans and like to see lots of lifeboats on ships when they go cruising. Reactive people spend time reviewing problems, getting rid of bad staff, rebuilding poor systems, and just keeping afloat. This type of risk management is basically crisis management.

"Proactive people, on the other hand, try to anticipate things. They see risk as clues to the future and this helps them develop a future position that is best placed to handle what's going on.

"Inactive organizations are full of people who base what they do on rumor and things that people say in unguarded moments. Staffs learn about strategy through tips and hints as the boardroom sits in secret and throws a series of new changes out to their staff in regular surprise announcements. Everyone sits in their little silo and works in their own isolated world. Reactive organizations tell their people about strategy in a series of ongoing lectures that form downward-only communications. Proactive organizations engage in a dialogue with their people to take them on this journey to a better future positioning. This type of risk management is what I see as positive risk management. You know ERM can be seen as a bag of techniques and software that looks and sounds great. But, what I call ERM is a way of encouraging dialogue and challenge in an organization that needs to be held together by something other than formal structures.

"Okay, we've made it through the top part of the slide. Let's hit the next parts. From left to right: Inactive cultures suffer impacts and just try to keep going. Many fall over or just keep away from any of the real competitive action and hope for the best. Reactive cultures take the hits and try to reduce collateral damage. Proactive cultures see themselves as a living ERM process that continually redefines itself to meet new challenges. This positive approach to risk management is action based and understands causality in that risks could lead to reactions that have to be addressed. It is based on visioning in terms of having a clear image of the future as one where they are ahead of obstacles and the opposition. Proactive organizations feel that they can influence things, people, and issues. This is what being in control is all about and it is what makes a management able to see a future that moves it forward. Take China. In-active companies simply say what about China? And that's that. Reactive companies see China as a threat in terms of undercutting their products and positions and respond by putting up barriers and hiding behind them. Proactive outfits see China as presenting great threats and great opportunities. China is now producing tons of stuff but she is wanting partners and as she grows in wealth, she's also starting to consume luxury products, which opens up new markets. My slide suggests that ERM provides an opportunity to get rid of the old program and work to a better future. But risk management still holds a negative sway, which is why I need to keep saying that it's about keeping things positive.

"Charles Darwin was about survival of the fittest. Put simply, those organizations that can adapt better to what's happening around them, now and in the future, survive. Those who don't, won't. If ERM is not about this, then I'm a Martian.

"I see positive ERM as a way of life that is being absorbed by many organizations to make themselves more successful [*displays Slide 16.5*]. This is not easy and I notice that there is a chain of events that good organizations go through. We all have implicit risks and implicit ways of handling these risks. The next stage is to build a process to represent what was already happening in an unspoken way. That is an ERM process. This makes risk explicit and something that people start to openly talk about in terms of what impacts their work and how they deal with it. After a year or so of risk gazing we start to see risk as actually implicit in doing business and not as a separate concept. ERM can then return to being an implicit ideal as it becomes part of the way people behave at work. Next slide. Oh . . . hang on. There're some more things on this slide:

- **Regulation.** That's about seeing things through the regulator's eyes and making sure what's a risk to the regulators is also seen as a risk inside the business. Not just keeping them happy and sending in a few returns each quarter. But more than that, having an idea of what parties the regulators represent and how their needs can be met.

SLIDE **16.5**   *Risk Absorption Principle*

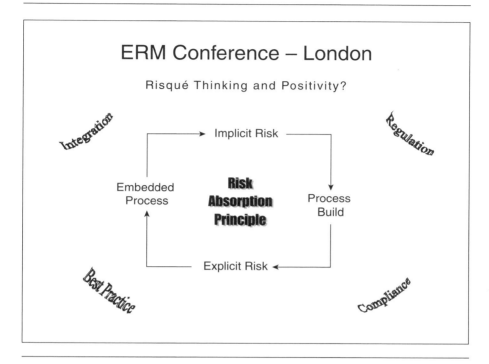

- **Compliance.** I guess this is about ensuring compliance issues become risks in that these are matters that need to be observed by all.
- **Best practice.** ERM is about best practice, not just compliance. Right?
- **Integration.** This is what we have said about embedding ERM inside the business.

"Risks come in many forms. One incident in one part of the world could affect the supply of computer chips and throw whole industries into slowdown. It could be new technology, global business, terrorism, changing customer demands, ethics, slimmer companies, government red tape, efficiency drives, fraud, and even legal claims. These and other risks need to be absorbed by the business and handled by the usual strategic decisions and operational processes.

"How you do this is up to you, as the ERM methodology is whatever works for you. This is important. Trying to force a solution onto an organization can be difficult. This is because the absorption aspect becomes hard when a foreign ERM process is developed that falls out of step with the normal business systems. That is not to say that ERM should not kick-start new approaches and better mindsets as people start to take responsibility for their actions. But it just means that ERM should come from within the corporate body and not from a big-shot consultant who has not taken the time to understand the way the organization can best benefit from a risk-based approach to its work.

"Right [*displays Slide 16.6*]. I've done the corporate spin, the ERM process and corporate systems, and the rest. Basic stuff, really; what I really want to get to is you and your feelings. I'm interested in people and how they are getting into an ERM mindset and being both positive and at times risqué. The best companies, and for that matter government agencies and nongovernmental organizations, have people who believe in themselves and what they are doing at work. I think positive ERM is about having a good balance between work, social, and family life. There are so many powerful messages on the way people handle uncertainty inside and outside work. Some new companies have been formed by people who have faced risk and have got an angle on things. I know of a close friend who worked for a big company. He got into a huge new venture, worked hard, got very stressed, and turned to drink for relief. He became an alcoholic and I saw what was the most positive person I know turn into mush in less than a year. I spoke to him when he was at his lowest and we discussed this idea of positivity. Anyway, he met and married a nice young lady, stopped boozing, and wrote a book about heavy drinking. He gave presentations to large companies about stress and the high-achiever culture and spoke about his darkest hour. And how he used his experience to dig his way out and return back to the light. He now runs a company that helps top companies get their people to balance work/life worlds and stay on top. And he's pretty rich now, although he says it's not about the money.

"I think that people and companies need to think about how to be healthy, wealthy, and wise, and how to deal with risks that impact these

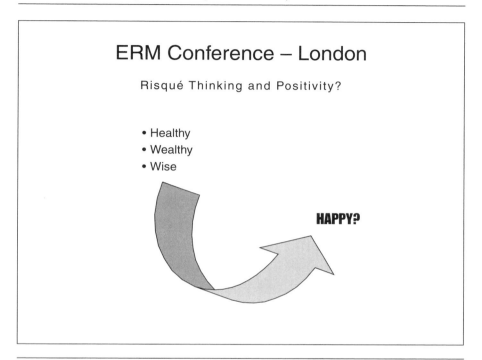

aspirations. From this, we can start to think about the idea of being happy. Happy people who work for a pleasant employer can reach for the stars. What I'm saying is that each and every one of you can do your own risk assessment and think through what you really want from life and how you can manage risks to achieving your own personal goals. And then find an employer who fits in with this analysis and make them part of your overall plans. Think about a corporate world where people felt that work was a real part of their health, wealth, and wisdom agenda, and that employers and employees were in a partnership that was right for both sides. Organizations can think about the welfare and health of their people and provide facilities to encourage them where possible. And they can work with their people to ensure that their compensation is fair and there is good investment and pensions planning advice available. Organizations can try to develop wisdom in their staff and find ways to release the talents that are buried deep inside most people but that are mostly hidden at work. I know one company that runs a library at work with Internet cafés, book clubs, and short research projects. People go there at lunchtime or after work and share their hobbies with others. My aim is for a happy, well-balanced workforce. But this is harder than you think, because everyone has their own idea of what makes them happy. I do know that fun organizations can get better results from their people.

"Right, where am I [*displays Slide 16.7*]? Positivity. I have another slide here on risk and being positive. Risk that is seen as things that cause loss is narrowminded and negative. Recovery is next. This is about taking hits and coming back again and again. It is about contingency and planning for worse-case scenarios. But it is still limited and

SLIDE 16.7   *Positivity Plane*

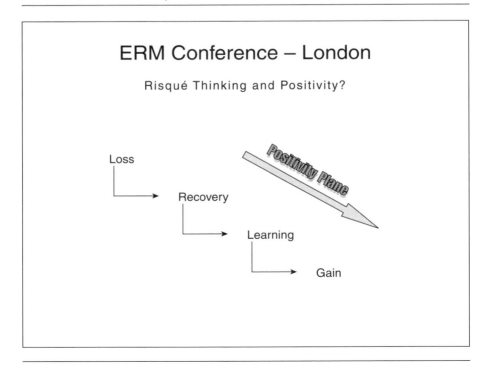

lacks real positivity. Learning about risk is a better approach and the more we learn about what affects us, the better. This is the risk assessment process that most organizations are now into. My final stage is about gaining from risk where top players get ahead by dealing with uncertainty better than others. If your board is a center of excellence in managing risk in the industry in question, this is good. ERM can drive this change and big downers like corporate governance regulations, stiff competition, best practice guides, and the strain on using capital can all be used to advantage. Every organization has a choice between differing strategies. Risk takers may focus on short-term tasks, do a little quick research, and then buy into a few new concerns or new products. Slower moving companies may build over time with lots of solid research that takes longer to get to the market but is more reliable. Other companies try to stay the same but focus on, say, supply chain management as the biggest risk to getting their product to the customer. The key is to set a strategy to fit your version of the future. And your version of the future needs to take account of uncertainty so that it means traps can be avoided and advantages are grasped. Corporate strategy is the essence of ERM as it seeks to build a resource that can get ahead of rivals. Or meet more than basic expectations, but in fact excel. Future strategy means assessing future risks and staying ahead. In this way, risk management is about positive change dealing with routine business and building a capacity to handle the unexpected as well.

"Next slide [*displays Slide 16.8*]. I've put down lots of items to discuss but we are running out of time. We will need to go through them very quickly:

- **Attitude.** I think good ERM is about having good attitudes to work. Period. Try this: Instead of complaining about everything and bad mouthing everyone you meet, why not get positive? Stop moaning, and every time you feel like complaining about life, stop and think about what's good. A few years ago I was turning into a sad old man, and I complained about everything that went on in the companies who employed me. But when I realized this was happening, I changed and started to get positive and looked for

ERM Conference – London

Risqué Thinking and Positivity?

- Attitude
- Energies
- Flexible structures
- Risk scores
- Governance
- Procedures
- Blame role
- Rewards
- Challenge

what was good in my clients and used this to help build solutions for the future.

- **Energies.** We should encourage innovation. I think that stamping down risk is fine, but there is no future in just keeping things in check. Executives should set out values regarding innovation and have a positive view on failure. Look for great performance in aspects of work where we need to reach out to higher ground. Getting people to work in loose groups is one way of using a network of shared ideas, both good and bad. But make sure you trial and review these ideas carefully before any implementation plans.

- **Flexible structures.** Flex the company to fit the culture and flex the culture to fit the risks that are significant to being successful. Talk to people about the risk of lost opportunities when they are being too scared to try new things.

- **Risk scores.** New risks have to be ascertained. Ignoring them could be disastrous, and the big issue for most management is about asking where they are going. ERM tries to deal with total risks to the organization, not just bits of risk and one-off showstoppers. Good ERM takes a positive view of threats where risk-based silos are avoided to get a common basis for risk management.

- **Governance.** The CEO and CFO have to sign off their Section 404 responsibilities on whether internal control over financial reporting is effective. There are costs, but make sure the benefits clearly exceed these costs. In the UK here, listed companies have to issue a statement that internal controls have been reviewed, while external audit review these messages. People who govern the organization need to identify and respond to risk for the owners so as to create value as an ongoing responsibility. Much of this is based on sound financial accounts and a reliable external audit process. Some areas are real hard to regulate, and say teams that deal with derivatives are by their nature dealing in risky products as they are betting on changes in the price of commodities. Corporate disclosures should also cover the ERM process and all significant risks, as well as the effectiveness of controls as part of corporate strategy. But the question is, does this conflict with the need for commercial sensitivity?

- **Procedures.** These are important. For example, if the company uses data mining to ensure its information systems are sound, then this must be applied properly as loads of information does not always mean loads of control. Procedures only work if they make sense in dealing with defined risks.

- **Blame role.** Companies can assume lots of new risks, but this is part of doing business. I can't remember much about this point, so let's move on to the last point.

- **Reward systems.** Rewards should embrace ERM and ensure that the challenge concept is built into the way risk is seen as a positive concept.

"Okay [*displays Slide 16.9*]. We're out of time. I have to say that big business is getting rather tired of governance and some of the excessive levels of regulations that are emerging from all parts of the world. Many

SLIDE 16.9   *Remaining Sensibly Risqué*

ERM Conference – London

Risqué Thinking and Positivity?

Remaining Sensibly Risqué

---

enterprises are struggling to break free from government red tape, and the great rafts of rules after rules. There will always be a few rogues and where we find them we should show no mercy. But having boards spend their time signing off on tons of paperwork just to satisfy some obscure regulation that snapped into place right after a one-off scandal has broken out is very worrying. We need to have a sense of balance and make sure the thousands of good corporations are free to prosper while the few bad apples that appear are quickly sat on.

"Okay, now for the controversial bit. I think ERM should stand for *Expeditious Risk Management.* And ongoing risk assessments should be a basic part of the way we work. It's simple. Whenever you need to make a decision, commit resources, choose between options, say yes or no, or move resources, then just take a time-out to ask yourself: Have I checked that all risks are covered? Then move on. This is an express way to get risk management into your business. Nothing more. Okay, now I've let off steam, let's get back to the presentation. What is being sensibly risqué about?

"Well, it's all that I have described. Live life to the full and get a risk language in place and messages from the top that recognize and encourage a culture of excellence, even where this follows some failure. Work out what drives innovation and use this as a springboard for success. Bring in new staff that fit this high performance profile. Not based on what you currently are, but what you want to be in the future, bearing in mind the risks that you need to handle to stay ahead. And more than anything, keep things positive. That is, your people, your systems, and your products. Get your people to do their own personal risk assessment and work out how they can fit their goals in with their work, starting with the board. Be healthy, wealthy, and wise but remember, try to have a little fun at the same time. I've tried it and it works.

"Most organizations are still getting to grips with ERM, and we need to get ERM into real life, not just as a paper exercise but in a risqué but sensible way. But it's about more than that. We need to be more creative in the way we see things in society. We need to get our children looking at their environment and what they want to see for a better future. Growing up in concrete housing schemes and seeing daily acts of violence and assuming that business is about having a greedy grab-all mindset learned from their elders does not mean they have to grow up in a world where everything is so unequal. Some countries have it all, while many others in the third world have nothing. We need to teach our children to care for their environment and be concerned about global warming and major climate shifts. If we get our youngsters to think through the risks if nothing changes and how they can take a risk in making for a better world, then although our generation has failed miserably to make the world a better, fairer, and safer place, perhaps the new generation that is growing up may be able to do better. Risk management is a huge concept that can be used to encourage positive forward movement by making clear the risks to all of us, of failing to make these changes. There is a lot at stake. Right . . . I've overrun quite a lot and we have more or less come to the end, anyway. I'll hand you back to your chairman. Wishing you all the best, ladies and gentlemen."

"Wonderful. Thank you, Dr. Belmoral; you have given us lots to think about. I agree that ERM may outgrow its business base and become a global change concept. Time is against us and we have come to the end of the conference. It's actually very late now, and I feel that we have in fact run out of time. But I wonder if there is a really quick question out there that we can deal with? Young lady over there. The one who looks like a Marilyn Monroe. Your question please."

"Does Donald wear a wig and is he married?"

"You know, Donald, rather than answer the lady, we could leave this question up in the air as a tantalizing mystery. We have had a long day today and I can see the hotel staff standing by to clear the room. You have all, I hope, filled in your feedback forms and we will use these to plan future events. So I will not delay any further. Please look at our web site for messages about the conference and information on future events. For those booked into the morning workshop, see you tomorrow. I now call this year's annual ERM conference to a close and ask you all to stand and give your speakers and give yourselves some hearty applause to end the day. Thank you."

Bill, Helen, and Jack gathered at the conference door and the three friends looked at each other, and the tired feeling was reflected in each of their faces. Bill broke the ice, "We have a busy day tomorrow and I've got to go through my notes to make sure I'm ready for the Strongbow workshop. I don't know about you two, but I'm going to hit the showers, book room service, and take a break tonight."

Jack looked at Helen, who was smiling kindly at a worried-looking Bill, and said, "Good idea. Being surrounded by hundreds of people can get to you after a while. Helen. Your call?"

"Yes, quite. I'm shattered. Tell you what; let's take a break tonight and have a bit of a do tomorrow evening."

And with that they broke up and departed to their respective rooms for some much deserved peace and quiet.

CHAPTER 17

THE WORKSHOP

People were starting to enter the large room and make their claim to a seat from the rows of chairs that were made available as they eagerly anticipated their post-conference workshop. Bill, Jack, and Helen got there early and sat together sipping their warm coffee. Jack turned toward Helen and said, "Are you going to use much of this ERM stuff from the conference back at work?"

"Oh yes, certainly. I'll be writing a short paper on ways forward and latest developments." Helen beamed a smile, "It's what I'm good at."

Bill joined in, "Don't you do any hands-on? You know, helping embed risk management into the business?"

"You mean run risk workshops and such? Oh no. That's not me at all. I'm actually quite shy and no matter what I do, I just can't stand the idea of presenting or facilitating or anything like that."

Jack gently prodded Helen in the arm, "You know so much about ERM. You can't sit in the background all the time . . ."

Helen stopped smiling and her tone became much more serious. "One time I wrote a paper on getting risk management out to the local offices, with action points, strategies, and key change issues that had to be addressed. I even linked risk management with local service plans to make sure it made sense to the people on the front line. Anyway, I couldn't bring myself to present my paper to the corporate management team and my boss had to do it. So it goes really well and my boss gets a huge bonus and I get nothing. But, that's life I guess . . ."

Bill sighed, "That's not life. That's unfair."

The room was now full and a hush developed over the group of 40 or so people as Lance Strongbow marched into the room. His huge bald dome seemed to shine with an unnatural glow as if he were some superior, ET-like alien. He grabbed his mike and snorted loudly while glancing round the room as if the presence of so many casually dressed people offended his sense of good taste. Using the mike as an assault weapon he started off, pointing to a nervous-looking young man with long ginger hair who was sitting quite close to him, "You, there. What's risk in Latin?"

"I dunno, sir . . ." came a stuttered reply.

After a pause for effect, the great Strongbow declared, "Risk for you is not knowing enough about the subject even after your conference and then turning up to this workshop and being embarrassed by your lack of knowledge. Get it?"

The young man nodded, looked down at his feet, and seemed to literally shrink into his chair.

The mighty Strongbow raised his eyes and scanned the room very slowly. He spotted Bill and with a jerk shot out his finger toward him and said, "You, sir. What is risk to you? In one sentence please. Let's make it easy and ask for it in English," adding a small chuckle at this final piece of wit.

Bill was seated toward the back of the group and carefully glanced down at the words that he had scribbled down on a sheet of paper, making sure no one could see this paper before placing it back in his pocket. Helen whispered to him, "Bill, the Latin for risk is . . ."

But Bill wasn't paying any attention and he stood up and said in a voice that resembled a senior newsreader talking to an uneducated audience about a difficult topic, "Risk management is applied by formulating a clear but iterative framework such as that used in the COSO model, but it may also underpin a type of process-driven dynamic that appears in the Australian/New Zealand standards, even if this is slightly inconsistent with the UK's IRM guidance and less integrated perhaps than the Institute of Internal Auditors' own format. Don't you agree?"

Lance Strongbow glared and looked as if he could commit murder then and there. He opened and then closed his mouth and sweat started to gather on his shaven head, but he could not get anything out before Bill stood up again and said, "Oh, and your ex, Georgina, says to say hi to old big-head. So, hi there, Lancey." At this a few giggles broke out from the audience and Lance went completely red and his neck throbbed and a few people laughed out loud. Lance Strongbow slapped down the mike with a loud bang and shouted out, "That's it. I've had enough of you. You're illiterate. It's like throwing pearls to swine . . ." before marching out of the room without so much as a glance at anyone. At this a ripple of applause broke out quite spontaneously.

When the laughter had died down the assembled group turned their gaze toward Bill as the newly found group leader. Bill froze and after a couple of seconds Jack stood up and said, "We've got an hour until lunchtime. We can either pack up and go or we can do something constructive with our time." A murmur of agreement and nodding heads appeared to support the latter. Jack then announced, "I vote that Helen Choi take over this session. She's unprepared and unrehearsed, but I believe she can do a good job."

At which Helen turned toward Jack and her mouth dropped open. Bill whispered in her ear, "Do it. It's your time to shine, okay?" and administered a discrete shove behind Helen's back that forced her up from her seat. Jack stood up to let her pass and whispered his message to her, "As we say in Jamaica, Big up your status!" At this Helen straightened her back and made her way to the front.

As she walked toward the stage, a vision of her time at home in Hong Kong flashed though her mind. Her father sitting in the corner reading his paper. Her mother sewing close by. Her brother spread out on his stomach on the floor watching TV and herself sitting quietly reading a book and from time to time glancing out of the window at the crowded street below. Her favorite uncle would often pop in to visit them. He would stand around, his large frame wobbling as he laughed, making jokes and telling wild stories of his long and eventful journeys around the remoter parts of China, and while this happened, all newspapers, books, and sewing would be put down for a while as her family listened to these stories. The last time Helen saw her uncle he had taken her to one side and said in a surprisingly soft voice, "Little one, we only have one life to live and everyone should make a little noise. Not all the time, but sometimes. That way people will know that you're still alive . . ."

Helen arrived at the front and faced her audience. She glanced at the microphone and placed it to one side. She came down from the stage and walked close to the delegates and her voice was remarkably clear as she launched into her speech, "Okay. What to do? Let's set an objective for this session. How about this: *To Consider Ways of Making Risk Workshops More Effective.*" A murmur of agreement spread across the room since this was the title of the planned session anyway.

"Let's do it. But first, a little warming-up exercise. And I mean exercise. We have four rows of chairs facing the front as if we are expecting a film star whom we can look at and admire. This is your workshop. So grab those round tables from the corner and arrange them in groups around the front, four to a table, with all chairs facing front."

This took a while to organize, but when done Helen continued, "I propose that we develop a list of attributes of good risk workshops and then select the top ten. We can each come up with an attribute. That will give us say forty items. We could then vote on them and arrive at our top ten. Then I propose we get into small groups, ten groups of four each, and spend a little time assessing how we can ensure the selected attribute can be achieved. So if say one attribute is that risk workshops should be motivating for the participants, one group can think about ways of ensuring that this happens. At the end we will have developed a benchmark that we can take away and use to fine-tune the way such workshops may be used back at work. Sounds okay?"

Having received a positive response, she continued, "I need a scribe. Someone who can plug in the laptop and display the results of the large screen."

The ginger-haired young man who had been insulted by the once-great Strongbow got up and started fiddling with the laptop. His name was Brian, and he had the system up and running in a few minutes.

Helen continued to facilitate the session and took the group through the stages she had described earlier. It took around 20 minutes to get to the top 10 attributes of good risk workshops, at which point Helen asked them to break into groups of four and select one attribute each to analyze. The smaller groups took some 10 minutes each to work through their agreed comments, and each was asked in turn to present their conclusions to the large group as the various responses were typed into the spreadsheet by Brian, until there was a complete record of the morning's session.

Helen read some of the feedback that had been received. "We seem to have a bit of a list of the top issues concerning risk workshops, and if you like I can read some of them out:

- Integrate risk management, governance, and internal control. So that the results of the workshop may be used to support statements on internal control.
- Keep the workshops positive and do not see risk as just threats but retain the positive aspects of managing and growing the business, even if there are risks attached to making change.
- Energize the group and make sure the experience is fun, motivating, and not boring or ritualistic.
- Stop when you have done enough work and do not waste time stretching things out when this is not necessary.
- Give power over to the group and do not lead them too much so that they feel like bystanders.
- Develop a better awareness of ERM among the delegates as part of the workshop process by making sure the facilitators are experienced and knowledgeable.
- Involve everyone who is part of the process. Get quiet people to open up and stop noisy people from taking over too much.
- Make sure you do lots of preparation as it is expensive to have people in workshop mode.
- Link the workshop into the jobs and actual work experiences that people have as a part of their role, rather than a separate exercise.

- Promote corporate strategy through ERM and ensure that there is good alignment between the two that is reflected in the way risk is dealt with in the workshop.
- Only hold a formal workshop where you really need to. It is much better to build risk assessments and control reviews into the way people work and not have risk assessments as a separate exercise.

"Okay, we have criteria for developing a program of good risk workshops. But, how you meet these aspirations is up to you and the way you set up your risk management process."

When the work was complete, Helen formally closed the session and announced, "That's great. You have all worked really hard and the results speak for themselves. I'll ask the conference organizer to e-mail the table of agreed action points to everyone here. Okay, it's about time for lunch. Thanks for working with me."

"Thank you," shouted Brian, which was followed by loud applause. Brian stood up, smiled broadly and continued, "We're supposed to go on after lunch. Will you facilitate some more for us?"

Helen tapped her chin with her forefinger, "You know what, we've achieved our workshop objective and that's that. The most important point about running workshops is to stop as soon as you've got a result, even where there is time left over. Companies who gauge their ERM process by the number of workshops they do have missed the point. When you get to a good end—just stop."

As she returned to her seat a new round of applause broke out and, wide-eyed, she beamed toward Bill and Jack and for once she felt really alive. Bill gave her a huge hug and said, "You are it—the real deal!"

Jack leaned forward, grabbed her arm, and shouted, "Now you can take center stage back at work. How about that?"

Helen smiled and said softly, "Not really. I told you I prefer the back office stuff. That's really me and I'll continue like that. But it's good to know that, whenever I feel like it, I can remind people I'm around. Let them know I'm still alive. It'll be part of my personal contingency plans. Guys, thanks for letting me know what I can do."

Jack was just about to launch into his standard argument about living life to the full when Bill stepped in, "I understand. It's enough just to know what you can do. I understand completely."

With that the three of them joined the line for lunch amid the buzz of excitement from the crowd that had been generated by a highly successful workshop.

CHAPTER 18

THE ISLAND

Jack, Bill, and Helen sat at their usual table and enjoyed a slow lunch knowing that there would be no further sessions to attend. Bill said, "I've got to pop over to see my aunt. I could go now and be back by tonight."

Helen asked, "Where does she live? Your aunt?"

"It's called the Isle of Wight."

"Hey, Silverton," Jack called out as the tall figure of Silverton was spotted sliding through the dining room. He came over and asked, "Yes, gentlemen? What can I do for you?" and extended a wide smile to Bill, who was looking a little embarrassed. Jack answered, "Can you tell us how to find this Isle of Wight?"

"It's not so far. You will need to motor down to Portsmouth or Southampton. No, Portsmouth would be best from London. You then take the car ferry across to the island and there you are. Two-and-a-half-hour trip. Give or take a bit."

"Thanks, Silverton," added Bill. "Could you dig up a map and a route, oh, and order a rental car for first thing tomorrow, say around ten a.m.? Something roomy."

"Certainly, sir. I'll talk to the front desk."

And with that he was gone.

Bill said to Jack, "You can drive. I haven't got my license and I'm not one for driving on the left. Especially on these tiny roads. They're worse than New York."

"Hang on a minute," Jack demanded waving his hands around, "I have an injury. That big guy who fell on me in the bar twisted my ankle. Have you not noticed my limp? I can't take on a two-hour drive."

Bill said, "You don't limp. You have that kinda hopping walk that you picked up in Jamaica."

"Rubbish. I am limping and I do not hop anywhere . . ."

Bill interrupted, "Anyway. We still need to sort things out. How do we get there?"

The two men looked at Helen who stopped eating and said, "What?"

Jack said, "Helen. Why don't you come with us? Can you drive on the left?"

"Uh, yes I can."

Bill said, "Will you join us? Your flight back is on Sunday, so how about we get back Saturday, which will give us a few days there."

Helen was taken aback. "I promised Maria that we'd hit the shops straight after the conference. But, if she wants to come and gives me some girl support, then I'll go with you."

Jack stepped in with a grin, "You mean Maria, the same person Bill visited at midnight with flowers and nothing else?"

"Yes. But don't worry, I explained all that to her and she was quite amused. Let me go find her and see if she's okay with this."

At that Helen left the table and Bill turned to Jack, "You may need to get your ankle checked out."

"Why?"

"You said it's strained."

Jack squirmed a little, "Not really. I was just trying to get Helen along with us. She's your ERM expert and imagine what we could do with her on board. She can help us with your presentation. Right?"

"You know, Jack, I sometimes worry about your ethical standards."

Jack shrugged his shoulders, "Too much ethics can get really expensive."

Helen returned along with Maria, and the two ladies sat with Bill and Jack. Helen said, "Maria agrees to come but Bill has got to behave himself."

Maria laughed and asked, "Where's this place?"

"The isle of whites," answered Jack.

"And are black people allowed to visit this island?" Maria asked.

Helen jumped in, "Don't be a clown, Jack. It's the Isle of Wight, not whites."

Maria laughed again and said, "I know—just teasing. I did my first degree in London and we used to visit the Isle of Wight every summer. It's a beautiful place and I'd love to see it again. Helen, let's hit the shops straightaway if we're leaving tomorrow. Although there are some really good shops on the island, anyway. Tell you what, I'll show you around when we get there."

With that it was only a matter of agreeing a meeting time for tomorrow morning and the ladies left. Jack got up.

"Okay, Bill. How about we hit the gym and go through the sequence and a few more techniques. You gotta get yourself a daily routine. Half-hour workout and a jog."

"You still jogging, Jack?"

"Well, not really. It's my little secret. I say I'm off for a jog but I really take an hour-long walk most days. I find jogging causes me injuries while I can walk anytime with no problems at all."

"So to manage the risk of heart attack, obesity, and so on, an hour's walk and half-hour workout a day will do it?"

"Spot on. As they said in the conference, keeps you happy, healthy, and wise. Anyway, don't tell anyone my secret or they'll think I'm past it. The gym beckons."

The next day was fine and sunny and the four friends met at the hotel lobby at 10 a.m., each with a small piece of luggage. Bill's phone rang and he said, "Sweets. Hi. How are you? . . . Your mom's fine. That's great. Sweetheart, I'm just off to the Isle of Wight with Jack, Maria, and Helen. We'll be there a few days and . . . Who? Helen and Maria . . . no, we just met them at the conference. . . . Hello . . . hello . . . hello . . ."

Bill looked at his cell phone. "The line's gone dead. Anyway, let me sort out the paperwork and we can find the car and set off."

As Bill marched off to the front desk Maria asked Jack, "Was that Bill's wife on the phone?"

"Yes"

"Wow," Maria said, impressed, "I thought the guys back home were bad but Bill really takes the biscuit . . ."

The drive down to Portsmouth was really pleasant. Maria knew her way around London pretty well and directed Helen through several crowded streets until they found the A3. This freeway took them straight into Portsmouth, which was on the south coast. They drove past much open land where rolling hills, huge trees, and large stretches of green fields gave them a sense of freedom from busy city life. Maria explained how most of the fields they saw were farmlands and they spotted the occasional cattle and sheep wandering around in sections of some of the fields. Bill admired the views, and some of the tension he had experienced over the last few days was slowly drifting off. Helen was particularly interested in the farm animals and turned her head every time they passed some horses or pigs.

Helen murmured, "I should have been a farmer. I just love the big outdoors. Hong Kong is great for city life but it's hard to kick back and get away from it all."

Bill nodded and said, "That's a bit like New York. Everything's so rushed. I've even got myself a pair of jogging shoes to get across Manhattan in a hurry."

Jack joined in, "I think we should make this trip a bit of a break. Have some time off. I know we've got to prepare something on risk management but we can surely find time to relax as well."

Bill looked at Jack and laughed, saying, "I thought you were an expert in relaxing."

Jack defended his honor. "You know I write books. Well one book, anyway. And it's not easy. When you see me sitting around thinking, that means I'm getting my ideas together. These things can't be rushed . . ."

Maria shouted out, "See that giant tree over there? The one with the knobby bits and huge limbs? It's an old English oak tree. They can live for a thousand years and it only takes one acorn to grow every thousand years for it to replenish itself. Imagine, it's actually lived through the Ice Age. Jack what are you writing about?"

"Well, I am working on a piece about risk management. The conference has kicked things off and me and Bill will get our ideas together and knock something out."

Maria looked confused. "Don't you do any research at all? I mean I've been reviewing the way big organizations are using ERM and what they've got from it. There's so much to learn."

"Oh, yes," Jack replied, "I'll be reading up on things. But I like to see risk management in action as part of everyday life. I think its about people being risk aware."

Helen stopped thinking about farms and animals and rolling hills long enough to get involved in the conversation. "Absolutely," she said, "I think risk management is about people knowing their goals, understanding their responsibilities, and then being equipped to deal with uncertainty in a way that is acceptable to their key stakeholders."

"Say that again," Bill mumbled, as he frantically scribbled something down in his notebook.

Helen repeated her views. There was a brief silence before Maria asked, "Bill, you've been making notes since we left London. What's that all about?

Bill looked up, surprised.

"Oh, I'm sorry. I thought you knew. Jack and I do this when we meet. We get into a topic and talk it through. You know. Talk about all the issues, then get it down on paper. I've recorded most of the conference sessions and now I'm just jotting down bits of information and ideas so that I can prepare a paper on ERM. This trip is about my aunt but I also need to come back with my presentation on ERM and how it can help my company. If we all got involved that would be great. Is that okay with you?"

"Sure thing," agreed Jack.

Bill said sharply, "Not you, Jack! You have to do this anyway. I mean you two, Helen and Maria."

"Sure," Maria replied.

Helen said, "I wonder how much it would cost to buy a farm out here . . ."

"Right," said Jack. "So it's agreed. We talk about this risk stuff. Give Bill some ideas and then knock out a paper that makes sense. Good."

Maria asked a question, "Just where is this place on the Isle of Wight?"

Bill pushed his hand into his pocket. "It's in the letter. Hang on. It's in my travel file. Maria, open that file next to you and look for a hand-written letter."

Maria found the letter and tried to hand it back to Bill, who was sitting beside Helen in the back of the car.

"That's okay, Maria. You keep it. The address is somewhere on the letter. Have a look."

Maria bit her bottom lip and studied the letter. "You sure you want me to read this?"

"You might as well. I've not had time to look at it properly," Bill replied, closing his eyes as the sun hit his forehead and he suddenly felt drowsy and very relaxed.

"Well. I have only been to the west of the island a few times, which is where your aunt lives—Coral Gardens, in Freshwater. It's a very nice, quiet area. It's the posh end of the island and we should be able to find it okay. Isn't it odd that you have not met your aunt before and she's your mom's twin."

At this Bill jerked awake, "What did you say?"

"It says here," Maria studied the letter, "that your aunt thinks it is such a shame that identical twins should lose touch. And that she would love to know if they still looked the same after all these years . . ."

Bill reached his hand forewards through the gap in the car seats, "Let me have a look, Maria," he said in a slightly shaky voice.

There was several minutes' silence as Bill read the letter for the first time and the car continued to glide through the countryside.

"What's the problem?" Jack asked, as the atmosphere became a little tense.

Bill did not answer and continued to read. As the other three settled down to a now-silent trip, Bill folded the letter and placed it in his pocket. He eventually said, "This is going to be weird. My mom died years ago and now I'm going to meet a woman who probably looks exactly like her. I'm not sure what to think . . ."

Helen looked at Bill in the rear-view mirror, looking as if he were a small child that had become lost in the woods, and said, "That's life. Me, I wouldn't mind seeing my uncle or at least someone who reminds me of him. He died years ago. There really isn't anything to worry about."

After a short pause, Bill replied, "You're right, I guess. It's just going to be weird. I wonder why my dad didn't tell me about this . . ."

Not one for sentimentality, Jack broke the spell, "When we going to eat? And where?"

Maria said, "We could stop on the way. Isn't that a pub over on the left?"

Helen screwed up her eyes, "The Devil's Punch Bowl," she said, as a large and attractive tavern came into view and the road slowed down as they approached a built-up part of the motorway. She looked at her watch and realized that they had some way to go before getting to Portsmouth and suggested, "Looks nice but how about let's keep going and eat on the ferry. Is the food all right, Maria?"

"It's okay. Snacks and bits to eat. But the ferry only takes half an hour or so, so they don't go in for full meals."

A little further down the road they arrived in Portsmouth, a navel port that has a long historical connection with the British royal navy. The signposts showed the route for the Isle of Wight car ferry, and they drove around several stretches of roads and roundabouts before they arrived at a port along the seafront where cars were parked in dozens of lanes facing toward the sea.

A short wiry man in a yellow fluorescent jacket thrust his head through the car window and asked, "Have you got a ticket, love?"

"No, actually," Helen replied looking slightly worried.

The short man computed this information and said, "Go over to the far lane and buy one. Please. You should be okay as we don't seem too busy today."

Bill did the honors and returned after a while grasping a yellow outbound and return ticket.

"Sorry," Maria said, "I forgot about the advance tickets. It's normally best to buy them to make sure you get a place on the ferry."

"I got 'em," said Bill, "But it's just that we have to wait an hour before we can board. That's the second ferry, as they come every half hour."

"Well. I'm getting some shuteye," said Jack, as he reclined his seat, leaned back, and slipped his cap down over his eyes.

Bill poked Jack in his arm and assumed a royal navy military attitude, saying, "Hang on, Jack, me old shipmate. We have only a few days to get this risk management stuff in the bag. We need to start the ball rolling. I mean now, right now."

Jack looked injured and asked, "Your suggestion being . . . ?"

"That we start talking risk and such. You know, like we did in Jamaica when we covered so much ground on internal control."

Jack remembered that he was under contract to help Bill deliver the goods and replaced his cap on the back of his head.

"Aye, aye, Captain. You're right as usual. Okay, Helen, go for it. Give us some stuff on risk. You too, Maria."

Helen thought about saying something smart along the lines of "Why don't you get off your big fat butt and start first?" She stopped herself and resumed her much-renowned dignity and said as if talking to an idiot, "Okay. Let's analyze the ferry operation. How would ERM fit in here? Anyone?"

Jack took up the challenge, "They will need to have sound arrangements to ensure no one sinks on route. That would be terrible, no?"

Bill chipped in, "Yes. They would have to take things slow. But not so slow as to mean they're inefficient."

Helen started to get busy and said, "That's the mistake many people make when talking about risk management. They only focus on health and safety issues and lose the big picture. Start with what the ferry company is trying to do. What is it?"

Maria entered the fray, "They want to make money from transporting cars, trucks, and people from port to port."

Jack scratched his head and the others waited expectantly for his comments. After a minute had passed he realized this and said, "You know I'm really hungry and if I'm not mistaken there's some kind of cafe place over there." He pointed to a glass-fronted building next door to the office where Bill had got the ferry tickets.

After a while, the four of them sat round a table overlooking the ferry port and ate fish and chips with buttered bread. Helen continued her discussion, "Okay. So just what is the ferry company trying to achieve?"

Maria said, "It needs to provide a profitable ferry operation that meets the expectations of all its key stakeholders."

Bill added, "Or exceeds these expectations."

Helen went on, "And can we hazard a guess at the risks that might impact this objective?"

"Well," Bill said, "there are risks such as poor demand, or for that matter excessive demand, an unreliable service, adverse weather, breach of safety rules, things like rude staff and generally a large number of unsatisfied customers . . ."

"Okay," Maria interrupted, "I guess what we need to ask is how does the ferry company assess these risks, once it has been able to identify them?"

Helen managed to pull her eyes away from the open sea and said, "It looks so calm and peaceful out at sea. I could sit here all day and just look . . ."

Jack laughed out loud and said, "You love looking at the countryside. You just love to gaze out to sea. When did you last get a vacation, Helen?"

Helen assumed a defensive posture, her arms crossed, and pursed her lips, "Actually, I'm far too busy at work to worry about taking time out. That's not a crime is it?"

Jack felt he needed to explore this further. "But we all need to get in touch with our true selves. Get away from our desks for a while."

Bill added, "You've been getting in touch with your true self for over a year now, Jack."

"Funny guy. Helen, what I mean is, don't just dream about time out, do something about it."

Helen relaxed her posture and said in an almost apologetic way, "I know what you mean. But I want to make my first million, buy a business, and then I'll be able to take time off. I'm pretty well on the way since my company pays big bonuses, but you have to put in the hours. I'm nearly there."

Maria put her hand over Helen's hand and said, "You can still have a break now and then. Well, actually right now is a break from routine. I vote we stop talking about this risk stuff and take a few days out . . ."

Bill looked horrified, "Oh, please don't say that, girls. I need you and I need your ideas. Let's keep things light and talk about concepts in the round. You know, no heavy stuff. We've had that at the conference."

"I agree," said Jack.

Helen stood up. "We'd better get back to the car and get ready. The last ferry's just pulling out and we should be on the next one."

"Boy," Jack whispered to Bill, "that was close. We nearly lost them."

The ferry operation swung into action and they were directed onto the boat with well practiced ease, as Helen lined up the car behind a jeep and the four passengers got out and went though a side door to the main ferry decks. The stairs led to an enclosed lounge area and they took a further set of stairs that took them to the top floor and the deck area. Helen went through a set of doors and out onto an outdoor deck where chairs were lined up facing the open sea.

Bill sat down, then got up, "This is my treat and you are my guests. What can I get you?"

After some discussion, Bill went back inside and returned some minutes later with wine for Maria, orange juice for Helen, and two bottles of beer for himself and Jack. The four admired the scene as the blue water swept in front of them, and as they pulled out, small yachts and a few speed boats bobbed up and down as they negotiated the slip streams around both sides of the huge ferry. Portsmouth slowly faded into the distance as the ferry chugged forward toward the port of Fishbourne, and the soft sunshine danced across the deck and onto the faces of the passengers.

After a few minutes, Maria broke the spell and said, "You know, this is the Solent. A quiet spread of water between Portsmouth and the island. That's why there are so many boats and yachts around here. People around here know these waters are calm. Whenever I got on this ferry each summer I knew my holidays had started."

The others sipped their drinks and started to see themselves as vacationers. Bill contributed to this atmosphere by handing out several small booklets. "I picked these up inside. They list the things that happen on the Isle of Wight. So, Maria, this is some kind of tourist hotspot. Right?"

"Absolutely. Times like now and for most of the summer this place is buzzing with tourists. That is, those who have found this place and know its beauty."

They each checked their copy of the booklet and each person secretly selected the things they wanted to do if they got the chance.

Bill studied his own booklet, which, although small, contained a wealth of information. There was a writeup on all the main towns on the island and a note on each of the many sandy beaches that were found on all sides of the island. Places of interest and specific events were listed, along with shops, hotels, and historic houses and even a castle. He found out that although the island itself is only 23 miles from east to west and just over 13 miles from north to south, there are nearly 30 miles of beaches and over 500 miles of footpaths. It is shaped much like a diamond and is a walker's paradise.

"Ah," said Bill, "I've found something about Freshwater. It's in the west of the island and it's actually a village rather than a town. It looks rather good. It has a bay, Freshwater Bay, that has some huge white rocks that rise out of the sea just off the bay. There's a hotel at the bay that we could book. It sits right on the seafront."

Helen was sipping her orange juice and looking far out to sea. She said, "I wonder how much it would cost to buy one of those small motor boats?"

Bill put down his booklet and snapping his fingers in front of Helen, said, "Okay, day dreamer. Let's get back to business. ERM."

As before, Helen took command and turned in her chair to face the rest of the group. "Okay, guys," she said, "tell me which of those boats you see out there you'd like to own."

After a slight hesitation as they each wondered whether Helen had put a shot of something strong in her orange juice, they entered into the spirit of things.

Jack chose a small yacht that was leaning far over to catch the wind as it slowly turned in a wide circle. Bill chose a small yellow powerboat that was speeding past the ferry, while Maria said she preferred the large launch that could be seen in the distance with skimpily dressed people sunbathing on deck. Helen looked impressed and she wrote the answers down in a notebook labeled *ERM*.

"Great," she said. "Let's move on . . ."

"What about our answers?" asked Jack.

"Okay, Jack," Helen answered, "I think you're a risk taker in your small yacht. Bill, you're in the middle, while you, Maria, in your comfy motor launch could be a little more risk averse than the others. Anyway, let's move on. What did we say the ferry company will want to achieve?"

Maria pulled out her own notebook, and said, "The ferry company will need to provide a profitable ferry operation that meets or exceeds the expectations of all its key stakeholders."

Helen asked, "And what kind of risks affect these objectives?"

Maria read on, "Poor demand, excessive demand, an unreliable service, adverse weather, breach of safety rules, rude staff, and unsatisfied customers . . . and I would add safety issues, like a ferry sinking or getting into trouble."

Bill started laughing, "You know, when I bought the food from the restaurant in Portsmouth I got talking to the manager and I asked her about risks to her business. Do you know what she said? She thinks that mechanical failure, which is a huge risk to the ferry operators, is a good opportunity for her. People experiencing delays flood her place and she sells twice as much as normal. Her biggest risk is running out of supplies, which can happen when there are big delays. So it seems as if risk to one company is an opportunity to another associated business."

Maria jumped in, "My research suggests that each organization has to develop a risk model that makes sense to the way it does its business. I found that organizations that took their lead from general guidance and outside consultants tried to develop an ERM process that did not fit their business model. The better ones reassessed their business model to take account of the need to assess and manage risk as an integrated process. So the planning process, performance management, and the way accountabilities were set and discharged were all redesigned to build in the concept of ERM. Remember, ERM as a concept is pretty straightforward. The hard part is to make it fit into the business. And the real challenge is to get it into the way people behave at work."

"Hang on a bit," said Jack, as he scribbled down the words.

Helen frowned at Jack and tapped his pen to stop him writing. "What we're saying, Jack, is that you can't take what one company is doing and present that as the way forward. You have to work out how to fit the basics of ERM into your world. ERM takes the simple idea of understanding and managing risk to your objectives and says that this should be applied across the entire organization. Integrated ERM means systems are flexed to incorporate the concepts behind ERM into the way they are designed. Embedded ERM takes this further and argues that ERM should help drive the way people take responsibility for their work, review whether their arrangements respond well to risk, and generally behave in a risk smart manner. This is where it gets hard."

Jack appeared to have little time for reflection and simply continued to write it all down.

Bill leaned back on his chair and breathed in the fresh sea air that swept across the open deck. He looked at Helen and asked, "What model would you use for the ferry company? Bearing in mind each business is different . . ."

Helen thought for a second and then grabbed Jack's notebook and scribbled down a diagram that included:

- Aims
- Decision making
- Risks
- Strategy
- Controls
- Operations
- Safety
- Performance measurement

"You understand that this is entirely conjecture. The ferry's business is about getting people and vehicles safely from points a to b in a routine and reliable manner. I guess a comfortable manner, also. Their risks may well focus on safety procedures and efficient operations as well as good scheduled maintenance to ensure the ferries behave well. The rest of the business systems support this basic premise."

Maria said, "What about risks like a drop in business because tourists stop coming to the island? That is beyond their control and outside their framework."

"Not really," Helen answered. "If this were a significant risk then the ferry company could help sponsor the tourist trade. This booklet is jam packed with events and special activities. It looks as if there are events going on throughout the year. There's rock concerts, motorcycle rallies, carnivals, historical celebrations, and much more. The ferry company could sponsor these and other events and help promote them as part of their overall marketing strategy. ERM is about being proactive and getting hold of risks and working out what to do about them. The big issue now is risks that impact business ventures and their partners and finding ways of sharing the risk between key players."

"Okay," said Bill, as he turned the diagram toward himself. "Talk us through your ERM business model."

Helen seemed upset that she had to turn her attention to the diagram and away from the sea. "Right. At the top is overall aims, which gets translated into strategy. Two big parts of the model are operations and safety procedures. That is, operating the ferry safely. It's really simple. I've superimposed risk identification and assessment across all parts of the main model, and controls spin off from this as mitigating any unacceptable levels of risk. Performance is built into the model to ensure that people perform to make things work in spite of the risks and to reward them if they are able to employ controls in such a way as to stop any significant risks from getting in the way of success—that is, achieving one's aims. ERM that is not aligned with business success and performance will be pretty pointless. That's why it is no good doing it just for the regulators. It's done to ensure that stakeholder value remains intact even where there are significant risks knocking around."

Bill smiled and said, "I like it."

Jack sighed, and using his upturned palms as a welcoming gesture said, "Yep. We're nearly there. I can see the presentation taking shape in front of my eyes."

Maria wagged her index finger at Jack, "Remember. You're not running a ferry operation. Your model has to be your own interpretation of reality."

Jack was about to reply when a loudspeaker announcement asked all drivers and their passengers to return to their cars.

Bill sat still as the others gathered up their things and Jack said, "Shake it up, Bill. What's wrong?"

Bill slowly got up and looked as if he were about to go to jail, and said, "I'm going to meet someone who looks like my mom. It's downright scary . . ."

Helen took his arm and said, "Come on, big man. Life's full of surprises. Most times when you see a new thing as an opportunity it turns out for the best. ERM works best where people embrace their future rather than worry about it."

Sharon was worried as she waited for Ruth to open her front door. There was something wrong with Ruth. At first she thought it was because her mom was unwell. But as the old lady was on the mend, Ruth was still looking pretty stressed.

"Hi, Ruth," beamed Sharon, "I was passing your road and I thought I'd drop in." Sharon had a habit of "dropping in" on people as was the norm all over the island.

Ruth stepped back and then forward as she gave her a hug.

The two ladies went straight through to the back and sat out on the veranda, which had distant views of the blue sea at Montego Bay.

After some small talk about Ruth's mother, who was due home tomorrow, and arranging cold drinks, they sat back and enjoyed the cool breeze that swept through the veranda. The concrete yard contained many potted plants arranged in a semicircle, and various trees and green bushes surrounded the garden with the sea a distant haze. Sharon said, "I'm going to miss all this," waving her hand generally in the direction of the sea. "Have you been in the sea yet?" she asked.

"No. Not yet. I used to love swimming in the ocean when I lived here. But I've been too busy with my mom and all that . . ."

"What's wrong?" Sharon suddenly asked, catching Ruth off guard, who paused as if she was trying to think up an excuse.

Before she could come up with anything, Sharon pressed home her request, "You know, you can tell me. You need to tell someone why you look as if the world's against you."

"I'm just not *sure*. Bill's a great guy and we get on just fine. It's just that he doesn't think about what he does most times. He stumbles into things, and the latest is that he's jetted off with some girls he met at the London conference . . ."

Sharon frowned and held up a finger to stop Ruth's explanation, "Hang on . . ." Sharon said, "You mean Bill's gone off with some girls and I suppose Jack's with him?"

"Uh . . . yes. Well, I mean, they are working together on their latest project. I'm not saying they're up to anything. It's just that Bill doesn't think things through. He's off running around while I'm here looking after my ma."

Sharon slipped into warrior mode as she thought about grabbing hold of her husband and what she would say to him. Her faced brightened up as she mentally told herself off for being unfair. She said, "actually, I very much doubt that Bill would admit to going off with these women if he were up to anything. There's more to it than that, surely. What is really bugging you, girlfriend?"

Ruth squirmed a little as she poured herself another cold drink to buy more time. She realized that Sharon was waiting for an answer and said, "Okay. Bill never talks about families. He works all hours and wants to get right to the top of the tree at work. . . . Looks like a family would hold him back . . ."

"Have you never talked about having a family?"

"I don't want Bill to feel trapped. You know, I'm an only child and I've always dreamed about having a big family. Well, I mean a couple of kids at least. Looks like this will remain a dream."

Sharon saw the sorrow in Ruth's eyes and realized that her gripes about Jack and the way he drifted through life were nothing compared to the issues that rebounded between Bill and his wife. Sharon had produced three pretty nice children and they were all doing well on their journey through life. They were back in the States for a few weeks with their grandparents, and all was well.

"What're you gonna do?" Sharon asked soothingly.

"Well . . . not sure. I guess it's a matter of leaving Bill and finding someone who wants a family. Or, just sticking with things as they are. Bill's a wonderful guy and maybe it's just that we can't have it all."

Sharon did not want to take responsibility for Ruth's life and refrained from offering up any advice. She simply took hold of Ruth's hand and gave it a squeeze while she said, "It'll work out. Don't worry. . . ." The dark shadows that had settled over the sea suggested that the impromptu visit was over.

The four friends drove slowly down a hill and swept into Freshwater Bay and marveled at the sight that greeted them. The bay consisted of a sweeping beach surrounded by a whitewashed seafront walkway with benches set out to ensure visitors can capture the tranquil scene. Helen stopped the car in a car park area that faced the Bay and they each got out of the car to take in the views. Over to the left two huge white rocks seemed to climb out of the sea as the waves crashed around the edge of the rocks. Helen walked across the road and sat down on a bench facing the rocks and gazed toward the sea as if she was in some kind of dream.

The others watched her for a few minutes before Jack said, "Not bad. Reminds me of Jamaica, without the really hot sun. Anyway, let's check that hotel over there and get booked in." He pointed to a white building with a long veranda set across the road and a little back from the sea.

Maria skipped toward Helen shouting, "You go and book us in. I'm joining Helen. And Bill—make sure your room is not close to mine. I don't want you popping around late at night."

Jack's laughter was so loud Bill could not think of a suitable reply and could only open and close his mouth before Jack said, "Come on, bud. Let's go check in."

Maria sat beside Helen and for a few minutes enjoyed the silence that came from taking time off from the rat race. Realizing that Helen was not going to start the conversation, Maria tapped her lightly on her shoulder and said, "What's cooking? Helen, you go crazy whenever you see a sight or get a chance to relax. You need to get off the fast lane for a bit."

Helen smiled and Maria continued, "I take a break from work every three or four months. It's important to get a balance in life."

Helen kept looking out toward the rocks and finally replied, "I know, I know. It's just that my dad always told me that I'd end up like my good-for-nothing uncle if I didn't work hard all the time. And that's what I do. My dad worked day and night and it's what's expected . . ."

"If you had to choose between your dad and your uncle, which one do you think is happiest?"

"Well, that's hard. My uncle's dead now."

"When he was alive. Which one, Helen?"

"I would say my uncle had it right. He was always so happy and care-free. When he died, my dad actually changed and now he takes time off from his business and he and my mom go away much more. But then, I guess uncle got it all wrong because in the end he fell off a boat in mainland China and drowned. Some say he was drunk. You know, hundreds of people came to his funeral. They were out in the streets and people still talk about him to this day."

Maria stood up in front of Helen, blocking her view, and using her best schoolmarm's voice, said, "Be a little more like your uncle and less like your dad used to be. How about it?"

Helen got up and said, "Come on, bossy boots, we'd better join the others and see what rooms they've booked."

They walked across the road past the car and up a small hill toward the hotel. The had to pass a pretty-looking cottage in front of the hotel that had rosebushes of red, pink, and white blossoms surrounding the front door. As usual, Helen took time to admire the flowers and slowly caught up with Maria as they approached the hotel. Inside they saw Jack and Bill sitting around a table in conversation with a good-looking businessman in a dark suit, sporting a small black moustache. Jack stood up.

"Hi, girls. This is Mr. Greenspam, the hotel owner. Meet Maria and Helen."

The manager stood up in a formal manner and shook hands. "Hello," he said, "pleased to meet you. I was just telling your friends that you really need to book in advance when you visit the island during the summer. Unfortunately, I'm actually full right now but I have asked my receptionist to contact the holiday company and see whether they can find a place for you. You want to stay here in Freshwater?"

Bill replied, "Yes, please. I, uh . . . we need to be in the area."

"How about a drink? I'll send over a bottle of wine, on the house, as way of apologizing for being full, and you can wait here for any news. And please call me Peter."

After much expression of thanks, Peter left and as promised a wine bottle and four wine glasses were brought over by a spotty teenage boy wearing the orange shirt that all staff seemed to possess.

"Nice guy. Or should I say, a jolly good chap," Jack said, as he raised his wine glass to his lips.

"Absolutely," Bill replied, and added, "looks like we have some news," as the receptionist walked toward them and said, "I have found a cottage. Well, actually, it's a smallish house just down the road from here. Freshfields. I can book it for you if you like, and the holiday people will bring round the keys in say an hour or two. Is that okay?"

Jack replied as quick as a flash, "Great. Can we get a meal now while we wait for the keys?" and turned to the others for confirmation.

Bill, Helen, and Maria shrugged their shoulders in unison and the four explorers were soon seated around the dining table tucking into a rather tasty meal of steak and various side dishes.

After the meal they retired to the coffee lounge and, spotting them seated in couches and chairs in the corner of the room, Peter came over and sat in a chair facing them. Helen was looking through the window.

As if reading Helen's mind, Peter said, "I know. We don't have a sea view here. It's such a shame. My guests would pay twice the money to have a view over the bay but it's blocked by the cottage over there," and he thrust a finger toward the cottage that they had walked past to get to the hotel.

Bill turned toward Peter and asked, "What's your biggest risk? I mean what risks impact your hotel business?"

Peter looked surprised and looked as if he was not going to answer. But he snapped out of it and said, "Okay. We run a pretty good operation here. There are no real gaps but I would say my risks revolve around the winter season. That is where people spend less time in Freshwater during the colder months."

"And how do you manage this risk?" Bill continued. "I am dealing with it. I'm working on the local guests . . . that is, people who live on the island, and I'm putting on a winter entertainment season for them. I'm also working on the business side with packages for small conferences and training events. You can block-book bedrooms and my training room for a work event. I've put a new page on my web site. I'm also into weddings, but these are normally summer bookings."

Jack rubbed his hands, "Excellent. That is good risk management. But what do you do with risk that's hard to deal with?"

Peter stood up and said, "If it bugs me, I eliminate it. Simple. Anyway, here's your keys. That tall lady over there is from the holiday company. Linda," he shouted, "Over here . . ."

An elegant older woman marched toward them and, with a charming smile, placed a brochure and set of keys on their table. Bill took her over to a separate table and they sat together to complete the necessary forms and pay the monies that were now due.

When he returned to the others Jack asked, "Well, Bill. We've driven all the way from London and we've got to this Freshwater. We've found a place to stay, so shouldn't we get over to your aunt? Isn't that what we're here for . . . as well as writing something that you can take back to work . . ."

Bill did not appear too interested in Jack's point and said, "Let's find this house we've rented. Yes?"

Helen chipped in, "At least we can find out where she lives. Excuse me," Helen called to the teenager who had brought them wine earlier, and when he had wandered over to them asked, "Can you tell us where we can find . . . what's that place called, Bill?"

"Oh, yes. Coral Gardens."

The teenager seemed to smirk a little, much to the surprise of the four people listening for his reply. He seemed to think the question was a joke and when he noted the serious looks he was receiving he switched into a similarly serious mode and pointed to the window saying, "It's right there. That's Coral Gardens. I mean the Freshwater Bay Coral Gardens. Is that what you mean?"

Helen agreed, "Yes, thanks. It looks like it's kinda shut up. Is the lady there . . ."

Bill took over, "Yes, is Mrs. Little there? Maud Little? She's my aunt."

The boy became really serious and started to answer and then stopped. He scratched his head and mumbled, "I'm not sure. Let me, uh . . . let me get Mr. Greenspam," and he left this time a little faster than his normally slow walking pace.

Bill looked toward the cottage while the other three engaged in small talk, mainly about the pretty Freshwater Bay that they had just discovered. After a while, Peter Greenspam emerged from a door marked "private" and came toward the group. He looked at Jack and said, "Are you Mrs. Little's nephew?"

Jack pointed at Bill and said, "No, Bill here is the nephew."

Peter touched Bill's arm and said, "Please come with me, neighbor," and he and Bill drifted off through the door to Peter's office.

Jack laughed and said, "Maybe Peter's the aunt's lover. And he wants to adopt Bill . . ."

Helen and Maria were unimpressed and looked at each other with unspoken words that ran something along the lines of, "What's a good excuse to get away from this oaf?"

As a way of making up lost ground, Jack started to relay his experiences in the Caribbean and told stories about snorkeling, learning to speak Jamaican patois, the local dialect, and going to open-air dances to study the latest dance moves. Just as he had got back into the ladies' good graces and had them laughing out loud, the "private" door opened and Bill returned to the seating area looking thoughtful. He stared at Coral Gardens.

"What's wrong?" Helen asked. Bill continued looking at the cottage and said, "Well, that's it. Apparently Maud's gone. She died many months ago . . ."

Helen held Bill's hand and said, "Sorry, Bill."

Bill stopped looking at the cottage and squeezed Helen's hand, "Not to worry. I mean I didn't even know her. So a wasted trip. Sorry, gang . . . I . . . "

Helen interrupted, "Let's get this straight. This trip's been great and it's the first time I've had any kind of break for at least a year. So don't worry, Bill. Not at all."

Jack, demonstrating the sum total of the diplomacy and tact he had acquired over the years, slapped his knees and stated, "Poor risk management, Bill. Your objective was to visit your aunt. One huge risk was that she would not be there and we really should have thought about ways of mitigating this risk. Like finding a phone number or e-mail address to check out things . . ."

Jack felt an odd sensation as he realized he had once again fallen outside the bounds of polite conversation and managed to change the topic. "Let's get over to our guest house. I need to go for a run and take a shower."

That said, they each walked the short distance to the car with Maria guiding Helen in the direction of the car as she started to drift off and veer toward her seafront bench. Freshfields was a short drive from the Bay, and after juggling with the keys Bill finally opened the door to a very pleasant beige colored lounge, which ended with a dining area and a small kitchen through a door on the right. They inspected the house and found it had three bedrooms and a well-kept back garden with wooden chairs set around a large garden table. The BBQ in the corner of the garden completed the cozy feel that the house had.

"This'll do," Jack declared to the agreement of the rest of the party. After a frantic hour during which bedrooms were chosen and bags were unpacked, Bill, Helen, and Maria sat around the lounge area for a well-earned break. Jack bounded down the stairs and stood hands on hips with his legs astride and announced, "I'm off for a run," and slapped his rather dumpy stomach. Bill jumped up and said, "Hang on, let me put on my trainers. I'm coming too. It shouldn't be to stressful—this running," and winked at Jack.

Helen and Maria planned their day. They would pop over to the grocery store that they had spotted close by and stay put tonight. Tomorrow they would go into the main town, Newport, and hit the shops. That gave them an entire day to stock up on clothes and such and the following day they could work with Bill and Jack on Bill's ERM presentation. Helen leaned back satisfied that this would be a good use of her time and Maria flicked through the travel guides and leaflets about the Island that were piled up on the coffeetable.

Maria scanned through a small book and said, "Did you know the Isle of Wight has a really interesting history? They say here that they think the word 'wight' means 'raised above the sea.' Wow, apparently over a million people vacation on the island every year. That's why it's so well set up for tourists, and only 120,000 people actually live here. Let me see if there's anything else interesting in this booklet. Yes, I've always wondered why there are so many places called 'Chine' all over the island. Chine means a feature with a stream has cut through solid rock. Oh, and yes, the islanders have their own motto. Let me see; it reads; 'All this natural beauty is of God.' This trip should be lots of fun."

CHAPTER 19

RISK MANAGEMENT IN ACTION

Jack performed his interpretation of "running," which consisted of simply walking at a fair pace. Bill walked alongside, and taking deep breaths said, "You know, Jack, why don't you stop this macho stuff. Just tell the truth—you are getting on in years and you find walking better than some Olympic-style running."

Jack laughed, "Whatever . . ."

Instead of walking back toward Freshwater Bay, they turned left and headed for a different beach, called Totland Bay. They passed the main street in Freshwater and looked in the various shop windows of the old fashioned stores that sold a variety of household goods and food. Bill marveled, "It's weird. There are no huge department stores here. Each shop looks like a little business run by a local family. They're all so different and unique."

Jack followed Bill's gaze at the stores they passed and said, "You're right. It's quite nice that this place isn't owned by mega-stores. I guess this is what most countries were like before big business took over the consumer market."

They continued down the street and walked across a junction and a playing field, following signs to Totland Bay. In less than 20 minutes they arrived at a small bay surrounded by tourists, gift shops, and small restaurants. Unlike Freshwater Bay, the entire beach was quite sandy, and small children and a few adults splashed around in the sea. Some were wearing wet suits as it was starting to get late and the sea was not very warm. After walking a hundred yards along the sea front they came across a cafe that stretched out onto a little pier that reached out over the sea. Jack stepped through the door and grabbed a seat at the end of the pier where the white waves splashed around them. Bill stayed standing and said, "I think we gotta go and get our drinks ourselves. What're you having?"

After deciding on soft drinks, the two men relaxed back as the sunset was starting to cast an orange glow across the water. A few small boats bobbed up and down a couple of miles out to sea. Jack looked at Bill and noticed the worried look on his face.

"Tell me, Bill, old chap. What's wrong?"

"Well, where do I start? My ma's gone and my pa's withdrawn into a shell. My aunt, whom I've only just heard about, is also gone. And my wife told me when I first met her that she had a claustrophobic relationship with her ex and . . . what did she say?" Bill searched his mind and continued in an even more rapid way, "I know —something about a caged bird never sings. I want to have a family and there's no point bringing up this subject . . . and say trap her more . . ."

"Slow down," Jack managed to say, wondering how this outburst happened.

Bill gestured with his hands and asked, "You know, I never asked you whether your parents are still here."

"No. They died years ago. But I have my wife's people so the kids have their grandparents. You know, life goes on. It's the way it's meant to be. Why don't you ask Ruth if she wants children?"

"I thought about that but I really don't want to scare her off. I know she will agree to whatever I want. But then she'll get stuck and start feeling down. I've seen it happen. You know, my first wife ran off with some fella she met at work. When you've been through that, it's hard . . ."

Jack's limited counseling skills had been exhausted and he thought about ways of changing the subject. Having received no inspiration on suitable topics he simply said, "We'd better get back. The girls will be wondering where we've gone."

The two men walked back to Freshfields and found Maria and Helen packing a few food items in the cupboard and fridge. Jack laughed, "Why buy stuff? We can eat at the hotel. Peter Green . . . whatever his name is, is a great host."

Maria turned and frowned, "Look, Jack!" she said. "You have to be independent. You can't run to the hotel whenever you want a coffee. When you live somewhere, make it home—even if it's only for a few days."

Jack put up his hands, "Okay, Maria, darling. But can I suggest we go back to the hotel for a few drinks later on?"

Helen said, "You boys go. I'm taking some time out to unwind tonight."

That said, Bill and Jack made a little small talk until it was time to hit the road. They both walked down to Freshwater Bay and the small hotel that they had discovered earlier on. Maria and Helen stayed home and relaxed around their coffee cups and made plans for their shopping trip the following day.

Bill and Jack walked into the hotel and headed straight for the bar. They found a table that overlooked the cottage that they had seen earlier. Bill thought of his unknown aunt and Jack wondered whether the hotel sold Jamaican rum. A young woman with long blond hair sat at the bar and seemed to be watching them. Jack, who could see her, said softly to Bill, "I think we have an admirer. Don't look, but that woman has been eyeing us since we came in."

Bill seemed uninterested but Jack winked at her and said, "Shoot. She's coming over . . ."

The shapely woman in her early twenties got up from her seat, her long blond hair flowed down to her shoulders and she was casually dressed in jeans, boots, and a tight sweater. She came across to them and stood beside their table. She opened the conversation, "Excuse me, but the bartender says you're Maud's nephew. Is that true?"

Bill said, "Hi. Yes, I am. Bill Reynolds is the name," and shook hands. "This is Jack," he continued, pointing at Jack, who seemed to be amused at this pleasant distraction.

"I'm Sophia. You know about your aunt?"

"Yes. Peter, the hotel manager, told me earlier today."

"Please accept my condolences. You know about the police case?"

"No," Bill shook his head.

"Look. They say Maud didn't die a natural death. That she was given an overdose. Strong painkillers. She wasn't too well and she was on medication. The police say someone gave her the overdose and they arrested someone on suspicion of murder."

Bill looked amazed and his mouth fell open but no words came out. Jack swung into action, "What's all this about?"

Sophia seemed unsure of whether to continue or not. She swayed a little and Jack noticed that she displayed the signs of being slightly drunk and wondered if he and Bill should just leave quietly.

Sophia looked at both men and, as if she had made a firm decision, sat down with a bump in the free chair.

Jack repeated his question. "What's this about?"

Looking at Bill, Sophia brushed aside the loose hair that hung down over her face and said in a hushed voice, "The police think that you're aunt didn't die naturally. And they've locked up a friend of mine. He's charged with . . ."

She stopped and held a hanky to her eyes as she let out a few quiet sobs. She managed to splutter out, "He didn't do it, I just know it . . ." before she stopped again and buried herself in her large hanky.

Jack looked at Bill and wondered what to do next when a tall slim man in a dark suit and what looked like hair that was dyed a bright orange came toward them and placed a large arm around Sophia's shoulder and mumbled, "Sorry, chaps. I work for the hotel. Name's Matches. Never without a match in me mouth—that's me. You must excuse her lads, she's drunk. I'll just get rid of her . . ."

He spat out a chewed match in an ashtray, and then ushered Sophia away and out of the front door.

After a few minutes the hotel owner, Mr. Greenspam, came through the office door and shook hands with both men before saying,

"Hello, again, gentlemen. I just heard what happened. Don't worry about Sophia. She's been drinking a lot since they carted her boyfriend off to jail."

Jack also shook hands and asked, "Did Maud . . . uh . . . was Maud murdered?"

Greenspam sat down and snapped his fingers as the spotty teenager ran forward and stood by to take his drinks order.

After ordering a round of drinks he said, "It's a sad story. Maud relied a lot on Sophia's boyfriend, James Spocket. People called him Jimmy. Sophia works at the general store down the road and Jimmy was a sort of elderly persons' helper. The local authority sent him around to help her as she was getting old. He'd organize meals, clean the place. You know, he'd do jobs for Maud and other elderly people on his rounds who lived alone. Anyway, I understand that he forged a will that meant the old lady's estate went over to him. And rather than wait for . . ." He looked at Bill and paused. "Rather than wait for her eventual. . . demise, he speeded it up. He got her to take loads of painkillers, injected the stuff, and of course, she took sick and died."

"*Jeeze,*" Jack mumbled. "How'd he get found out?"

Greenspam frowned as if trying to recall the details. "The police were tipped off that something was wrong and they did an autopsy. Then they found a stock of painkillers at Jimmy's apartment, and that was that. Open and shut case, really."

Greenspam stroked his thin moustache and said to Bill, "You're Maud's nephew on her sister's side, aren't you? I always thought she had no one left."

Bill seemed defensive and explained, "We didn't know about Maud until we got a letter she sent to my dad in the States before she died. I was supposed to make contact with her."

Greenspam tapped Bill's shoulder. "I'm sorry you had a wasted trip. I guess you're off home now. I mean back to the U.S.?"

Jack replied, "We'll stick around for a bit and then get off home."

At that Greenspam stood up and in a rather formal manner shook hands with Bill and then Jack. "I must get back to the office. Gents," he said, as he flicked his fingers in a farewell gesture and walked back through the office door.

Bill glanced across at his aunt's cottage and seemed lost in thought. Jack shrugged his shoulders as if this action dismissed the whole idea of visiting aunts and meeting long-lost relatives before saying, "We should get back to the house and see what the girls are up to."

As Bill finished up his beer, they headed for the door and bumped into Maria and Helen, who were just coming to the bar. Bill held Helen's shoulders as she fell against him.

"Hi," she said. "You two leaving? We got bored and came here to see what's cooking."

Jack asked, "Should we go back for a drink?"

Helen looked over Bill's shoulder at the people scattered around tables in the bar, talking in hushed conversations, and shook her head.

"I'd rather walk along the bay for a bit. What do you think, Maria?"

"Absolutely. It looks so nice over there," Maria said, as she pointed across the road from the hotel toward the shadowy bay in the distance.

After a brief hesitation caused by Jack standing still and trying and failing to think up a good reason why they should get back to the bar, the four of them drifted across the road and walked down to the bay that guarded the gently surging sea as it crashed in and out against the rocks. Helen went into her state of meditation as she sat on her bench and looked out across the gray sea that from time to time reflected the moon as it emerged from behind the evening clouds every so often. Jack and Maria ran down onto the beach and started lobbing small stones into the waves as the frothy sea rolled toward them. They played a game of just avoiding the surf as it surged forward and back, trying in earnest to wet their feet.

Bill sat beside Helen on a small bench and followed her gaze toward the just-visible gray horizon. They sat in silence apart from the distant shouts from Jack and Maria down at the sea edge.

Helen said, without looking at Bill, "Just before we came into the hotel drive, we saw a tall guy manhandling a young woman. He was quite rough with her and she looked really upset. I was really worried and when they saw us she ran toward the road and he turned back to the hotel."

Bill explained how the girl, Sophia, had confronted them and that her friend was inside after he was charged with his aunt's death. Bill turned toward Helen and said, "What do I do?"

"How's that?" Helen asked, and for the first time she stopped looking out at the sea and focused on Bill.

"Well. My aunt's gone and there's been some kind of criminal case. Do I leave it be, or do I talk to the cops? You talk about risk management, but sometimes things happen so out of the blue that there's no way we can plan for them. It was all so simple. Go visit my aunt. Make contact. Give her the ring. Report back to my dad. And now this."

Helen thought for a bit and then said, "Risk management is not about planning for a fixed state of play. It's about thinking through all the factors that come into play and working out where to focus one's efforts to get closer to achieving one's goals. What do you want from this visit?"

"I want to make links with this side of my family. Well, I wanted to, that is—past tense. I want to do what's right and proper and then let my dad know what happened. That's it."

"Okay. The risk here is that you'll go home and feel that something 'Right and Proper' had not been done. Right?"

"I guess." Bill was feeling tired and wanted to take over Helen's job of gazing out to sea and doing nothing more. In contrast, Helen seemed to sparkle as she geared up to the job and demanded, "You need to list all those things that you need to do before you go home—to tie up this trip to England. I mean the family stuff."

Bill conceded that there were things to do, and said, "Okay. I need to check with the cops and make sure I understand what happened. And I need to make sure there's no other family here. Oh . . . and I need to give my ma's ring to . . . to someone who should have it . . ."

Helen got up and leaned against the iron railing and said in a matter-of-fact way, "That's it. You know what you need to do. Tomorrow, I'll shop, then work on your ERM presentation with Maria, and you and Jack can work through your list of tasks. And that way we'll do all that needs doing."

Bill watched in admiration as she turned her back to him and clapped her hands to attract the attention of the playmates on the beach below them. Bill said to Helen's back, "Helen. What do you want from life?"

She cupped her hand around her mouth and shouted to the two shadowy figures down by the sea, "Come on, you guys. It's getting late!"

She then faced Bill and said, "I used to want to be right at the top at work. But you know what? What I really want is to settle down with someone nice and have a big family . . ."

Maria and Jack clambered up the few steps from the beach and joined the other two, before the four of them turned and walked slowly back toward their temporary home delete from home.

CHAPTER 20

THE JOURNEY CONTINUES

Bill smiled as he felt engulfed by a pleasant feeling of warmth and satisfaction. He was looking at a small baby that was being held by a woman whose face was in shadow. The vision of mother and child was quite blurred, and as he slept the sight drifted in and out but continued to hold a sense of warmth. As he dreamed, the picture started to fade again; this time it was starting to disappear completely. He felt a tremendous sense of loss as if his life was now empty and without any real meaning.

Sharon went across the veranda, past the mango tree, and knocked on Ruth's door. She stood looking across the garden at the side of the house where she could just make out the blue sea in the background with its thin lines of white surf bubbling at the foot of each set of waves. She knocked again and was going to leave when she noticed a window left open with a small flap of white curtains blowing through the gap. She went over to the window and called out, "Ruth . . . Ruth!"

After a few minutes the front door was opened and Ruth's mother poked her head around the door and smiled when she saw Sharon. The old lady waved her thin hand, beckoning Sharon forward, and said in a remarkably strong voice, "Come in, darling. Please come on in."

As she stepped back, Sharon came forward and skipped through the open door and into the small lounge area. She sat on a wicker chair as Ruth's mom slowly lowered herself into another similar chair that faced the first one. Sharon smiled and said, "Sorry, Mrs. Madoc. I saw the open window and thought that Ruth was home . . ."

Mrs. Madoc was small framed with a silver scarf over her long hair. She was dark, with very fine features set within a small face. She said in almost a whisper, "Ruth is home; you know, it's funny. She came home to look after me and since my operation I'm just fine. But it seems she's now unwell and she's been sick a few times. She seems so tired and irritable. She's lying down and trying to sleep. Life's so funny."

Sharon agreed and added, "I'm sure it's nothing serious. Can I go and see her?"

Mrs. Madoc pointed to a closed door at the furthest side of the main room and said, "She's through there. Help yourself. You want a cold drink, darling? Lemonade?

"Yes, please, Mrs. Madoc."

Sharon waited until her drink was poured from a large jug that had been left cooling in the fridge and then went through the door that she had been just shown.

She entered the bedroom and saw Ruth lying on top of her bed, propped up on several pillows with a book lying open beside her.

"What's up?" Sharon said, as she came in the room and sat down gently on the bed beside her.

"Not a lot," came the soft reply.

"What's wrong, Ruth? You're just not the same. Something's wrong . . ."

Ruth looked embarrassed as the drawn blinds made the room appear dark and spooky. She paused a little and then said as if talking to a doctor, "I've been feeling under the weather a bit. Just tired and . . . well, tired all the time. I'll be okay."

Sharon touched Ruth's brow and said, "You don't have a temperature. Is it a virus?"

A tear slid down Ruth's cheek and she wiped it away and suddenly said, "I think I might be pregnant."

Sharon stopped herself from jumping up and congratulating her friend. Instead she said, "And that's bad . . . ?"

"Bill has never mentioned babies to me. The only time we talked about it I said I was not ready and he quickly agreed and went on and on about not being ready and he was absolutely with me on that . . . so I stopped thinking about it, too, and now . . ."

Ruth held a hanky to her face as tears appeared anew.

Sharon held her hand, "It may not be so bad. Call him and talk . . ."

"I did call him. He said he was with his conference buddies. Jack and two girls and then we got cut off. Since then I can't get through. It's horrible . . ."

At this more tears appeared and Sharon got up, walked toward the door, and announced, "I'm inviting you and your mom to dinner. I'll go home, prepare some things, and pick you up at seven. No arguments, okay?"

At this, she disappeared through the door and made sure Ruth's ma was okay with the dinner arrangements before making for home. Her mission was to cheer up her good friend.

The next day, Jack was the first to rise and he went out for his usual "run/walk." By the time he got back the others were dressed and talking about what to cook for breakfast. Bill said, "Jack, get your shower and we can all hit the road. There's something in the guest book about a cafe at a bay close to here. There's driving directions we can follow. Me and Jack went that way yesterday when we went to Totland Bay, which I think must be quite close."

They were soon on the road, with Helen at the wheel following the directions from Bill as he clutched the guest book and read out the way to Colwell Bay.

As the car reached a stoplight he said, "It says here that Colwell Bay is a large, sandy bay ideal for swimming when the weather's right. The sidewalk is built right up against the sea front and there are small cafes dotted around the bay. There's a place called Crusoe's Cafe and Restaurant, which is a few yards along the bay with benches placed outside so that diners can enjoy the waves that crash against the sea wall a few feet away. From there one could see Hurst castle across the water on the other side of the island. Sounds interesting. It goes on to say that if one continued walking left after a few hundred yards, Totland Bay will come into sight. Another cozy bay with its own shops, cafes, and bars . . ."

The car lurched forward as the thought of breakfast drove them on toward their destination, which they reached in less than 10 minutes. Colwell Bay was as described in the book, and they soon found Crusoe's Restaurant and took their seats on the outside benches as they waited for what was described as a "Full English Breakfast." This consisted of bacon, eggs, mushrooms, toast, and beans. While waiting, they occupied their time drinking mugs of strong coffee. The meal arrived and they each dived into their dish.

Bill raced through his meal and as he finished said to the others, "Right. We need to organize. Me and Jack have got to sort out my aunt's affairs. And . . ."

Maria put down her coffee cup and interrupted Bill, "And Helen and I will shop . . ."

Helen quickly added, "Then we'll knock out an outline for your presentation. Your ERM presentation, Bill. Remember that?"

Bill was staring ahead and suddenly became really serious.

"There's something wrong with my aunt."

The three of them stared at him and three brains churned away as they thought that being dead could probably be described as having something wrong. Bill looked at their frowns and quickly added, "I mean there's something wrong with this whole business. The death. The guy that's been arrested and the matter being open and closed just like that. Me and Jack will do a little checking around. Just to make sure it all stacks up."

Helen looked worried and said to Bill, "Take care, please."

Jack slapped Bill on his shoulder and said, "I'll take care of him for you. Don't worry."

With that the four of them got up and left a tip for their friendly waitress and headed off. The girls planned to get off to the shops while Bill and Jack were dropped off back at the house to make their own plans.

Maria directed Helen as the car chugged the few miles back down toward Freshwater Bay. Helen stopped the car at the bay and sat staring once more at the scene in front of her. She said to Maria, "You know this Freshwater Bay is actually quite a small bay."

They looked at the sandy beach, which also had some stony areas, and Helen pointed toward the right where a white cliff hung over the sea with a house perched on top. Below, a large hotel stood next to the sea with balconies sweeping across most of the first-floor rooms. To the left were more cliffs, this time slightly more brown in color. The two giant rocks looked even larger in the daylight as they rose out of the sea like huge incisor teeth surrounded by the constantly swirling water.

Maria looked at Helen as she admired the views and said, "What're you thinking?"

Helen seemed to snap out of her spell. "Oh, nothing much. Do you know that Hong Kong used to be run by Britain, and my dad got us all British passports when I was young. If I wanted to, I could stay in the UK for as long as I like. Funny world, isn't it. Which way now?"

Maria gave the orders as Helen swung the car right and drove along the winding road to Alum Bay. They arrived after a short drive and drove up a hill to a large car park on the cliffs overlooking the bay. Alum Bay is further west of the island and has a much bigger cliff formation. The shops and cafes are so far from the actual beach that there is a cable car constructed over the cliffs that operates continuously, carrying people from the busy cliff top to the beach. Down on the beach is a rock formation rising from the sea called the Needles, where jagged rocks seem to emerge from the cliff as if to punctuate the white cliffs themselves. At the end of the rocks is a lighthouse. Boats from the beachside jetty ferry holidaymakers around the Needles and the old lighthouse, making a round trip through the fairly rough seas over this side of the island. The two women sat in a pinewood cafe and ordered the local favorite, cream teas, which is a scone with clotted cream and strawberry preserve.

After making light work of the dish, Helen took out a small handheld computer and frowned, "Right, what do we do now?"

Maria laughed and said, "It's obvious the boys aren't going to do a thing. They're off playing Sherlock Holmes and they'll probably get themselves in all sorts of trouble. Helen, it's up to us to put this paper together and make sure Bill doesn't get fired when he gets back to work."

"Your right, of course. But first . . ." Helen said, shutting the little PC and putting it back in her purse, "first I want to go on that cable car over there and go down to the beach."

They paid for the cream teas and wandered over to join a line for the cable car. The cars moved slowly in perpetual motion and attendants swept the customers into the double chairs as they gently came behind each person when it was their turn to get on board. The cable took the cars slowly over the cliff as they slowly descended down to the beach below. It looked dangerous from a distance but in reality it is a safe and pleasant way of avoiding the hundreds of steps that lead from the cliff top to the beach. After a few heart-stopping minutes they reached the ground and were helped off the seats by another set of attendants at the beach.

Helen looked above her at the cable cars that continued to flow downward and then upward and said in an excited voice, "I can't believe I just did that . . ."

Maria grabbed her arm and shouted above the roar of the waves, "That's nothing. It's safe. Let's sit over there . . .," and pointing to a flat rock she tugged Helen's arm and they both found a comfortable seat away from the small groups that were strolling up and down the rocky beach. When they had settled, Maria said, "Okay. Take out your hand-held computer and let's get started."

"You're nothing but a bully. I really feel like taking a break from everything right now. You know. Some time out . . ." Maria looked at Helen as she stretched out her long legs, tilted her face up to the sun and closed her eyes.

Maria counted to 10 and said dramatically, "You're supposed to be a big shot out in Hong Kong. I read somewhere that you're the corporate takeover queen for the international Asian banking sector. But just look at you now. You're so lazy."

Helen smiled and kept her eyes shut. She eventually said, "Maria, I told you I want to get to my first million but I've already earned a million-dollar bonus this year. I've not had a day off for years—the original 24/7 queen. So give me a break. The last time I sat by the sea was when my uncle took me out ages ago. He came to my office, took me to the seaside on the pretext that he wanted me to help him with something, and forced me to relax for a whole afternoon. I was so upset for the first hour that I refused to talk to him, and after that I spent what was the best day out for years. He died soon after. I think he knew he was on the way out and this was his present to me."

Maria felt a tear spring to her eyes and was not sure what to say. But Helen suddenly straightened up, snapped out her PDA, and continued to talk, "Right, ERM. What are we gonna put in Bill's presentation?"

Maria laughed with relief, mainly because she was not sure how she was going to snap Helen out of her comatose state, which was no longer a problem. She said, "I have the conference file in my shoulder bag and I'm sure that with our combined knowledge and this file here, we can get to the main issues, costs, and benefits of ERM and work up a presentation. Piece of cake."

The two women spent just under two hours in energetic conversation, punctuated by Helen jabbing at her small keyboard. They agreed and disagreed with each other in turns, while flicking through the file with its copies of slides from the conference and rough notes that they had made. After this, they finally came to a reasonably agreed set of notes along with a few diagrams that were meant to explain what ERM was about and how it could be applied in Bill's company. Helen closed her handheld computer and laid her back flat down on the smooth rock, looking pleased at what they had achieved.

Maria suddenly stood up, "Right, then, work's done. It's Fun Time. Let's get to the jetty and see if we can get on that tour boat. It'll circle the lighthouse and those huge rocks; you know, they're called the Needles. At this and in spite of her large frame, she bounded off toward the small boat that was being boarded by a group of children. They managed to get the last two seats on the boat and had to hold on tight as the engines fired up and it bobbed out toward open sea. Helen threw back her long dark hair and smiled at the children sitting opposite her as they let out shrieks of laughter and trailed their hands through the water while clapping and singing songs. Maria looked from the children to Helen and felt like an earth-mother with this brood of smaller and larger people playing around her, Helen being included as a large child. Having successfully negotiated the rocks and lighthouse, the boat returned to the jetty and each person was helped off in turn by the boat's elderly captain. As they sat in the cable car, this time going up toward the cliff top, Helen laughed out loud and shouted over the noise, "I don't want to leave this island, I want to . . ."

A strong gust of wind drowned out these last words and the cable car swept toward the ground and the two women stepped off and found their feet back on firm ground. Back in the shopping area on the cliff top, they found a shop selling the famous colored sands that are found at Alum Bay. Helen filled a small glass souvenir with various colors of sands and paid for it at reception. The two women walked slowly back to their car, which was parked on a slope at the top of the car park. As they got closer, Helen noticed two mean-looking men dressed in black motorcycle gear standing by their rental car. Helen glanced back at Maria, who was walking behind her. Maria sped up, went past Helen, and said softly, "Just do as I do."

Maria went round to the passenger side of the rental car and brushed past one of the men who shouted through his closed helmet, "Good afternoon, babes. You look fit. Want to go for a ride?"

Helen jumped into the driver's side and fumbled for her keys before she quickly gunned the engine and drove off as the men waved a sarcastic farewell. Helen shivered as she watched the two tall figures in her rearview mirror fade into the distance. Maria laughed and said something along the lines of wild dogs and some men being so alike.

Bill sat at the wooden table in the small back garden with a steaming hot cup of coffee and looked through a local newspaper he had picked up earlier. He shouted out to Jack, who was sitting at the dining table indoors.

"This place is unreal. It's so old-fashioned. There's a village hall and what they call a bazaar. And tea dances. What's a tea dance?"

"Dunno," replied Jack as he tied his bootlaces. "Anyway," he continued, "let's move. We need a plan. We need to find out what happened to your aunt and make sure we get all the facts."

Bill walked back into the house, put down the newspaper and said, "What next? Remember the girls have the car."

"Let's go and talk to that girl. The one at the hotel yesterday. And find out what her problem is. Didn't Greenspam say she works at the general store down by the high street?"

"Okay, it's not far. Let's go."

They locked up and strolled down the road and up to the high street just around the corner. It was a narrow street lined with an assortment of local stores on either side. Just up on the left they found the general store and walked past the shelves crammed with all sort of household goods to the counter at the back of the shop. There was no one there.

"Anybody home?" shouted Jack, as a noise from a back room suggested someone was about to greet them. An elderly man with a slight limp came slowly toward them and as he came closer he squinted as if he had poor vision.

"Yes. Can I help you gentlemen?"

"Can we talk to the blonde girl who works here? Uh . . . her name is . . ."
The storekeeper interrupted, "Sophia. Sophia Lovelock, you mean?"

"Absolutely," answered Jack, "Sophia Lovelock."

"She's gone."

Bill displayed the most appealing smile he could muster up, "Do you know where she's gone?" he asked in a gentle voice.

"She just left. You know she's been with me over a year and she's the most reliable young lady ever. But last night she said she had to go. She said something about being too hot. God knows what that meant. A lovely girl. I paid her what she was due and she said she was too hot and had to go away someplace. Where, I don't know."

Jack started to leave and Bill scratched his chin and said, "What did she say about being hot?"

"She said, what was it now . . . she said she was hot. No, actually she said things were too hot and she had to leave. Very sad. Her boyfriend's in jail and since that happened she has been really depressed. Very sad . . ."

Jack came back to the counter and asked, "What did he do? The boyfriend."

"Oh. I wouldn't like to say. It's a bit of a scandal. Seems he just went bad. He used to come into the shop and before he went bad he was such a nice lad. They were planning to marry, you know. Very sad."

"Do you know how to contact the girl? I mean Sophia?" Bill asked.

"No. I said I'd post her a check and she said she had to leave and would rather have cash. She looked worried. Perhaps a relative is sick. Anyway, I think she's off the island as she asked me what time the bus came for Fishbourne."

Bill said in a conspiratorial voice, "I hear her boyfriend poisoned an old lady."

The storekeeper appeared not to hear this remark and Bill continued, "Where did he get the poison from. Strong painkillers and a syringe? You don't sell syringes do you?"

The old man looked up at this and spouted out, "No, not at all. But they say he stole the painkillers from the chemist on the high street. My mate Cyril gave the police a statement. He used to run the chemist's shop. He saw the lad in his shop the day it went missing. And they found the pills at the lad's house. Some of it was hidden in his room where he lodges. Sad, sad case that."

Jack asked, "Which chemist was this?"

"Oh it's gone now. Cyril sold it and it closed down a few months ago."

"Where's Cyril now?" asked Jack.

The storekeeper seemed to realize he was gossiping to strangers and switched off. He walked around to the far side of the counter and said, "Let me know if you need to find something."

Bill felt obliged to buy a flashlight as the storekeeper had been so helpful, and they both left the store after the transaction had been completed and the store owner thanked for his help. As they walked slowly, further up the high street Jack said, "Where next?"

"I think we need to stop playing around. There's nothing more we can do so let's just leave things as they are. I was supposed to visit my aunt. She's gone and that's that."

"You're right, of course. We only have a couple of days left so I guess we need to focus on your ERM stuff."

"Agreed."

"But first let's check out that bar over there." Jack pointed to an attractive-looking pub just visible in a leafy side road set off from the high street.

The pub was a large white building with black beams down its side and potted plants scattered around the windows and entrance. Jack marched ahead as if his life depended on getting inside the building, and Bill followed on behind, wondering if it were too early to start drinking. Inside the pub the red carpets and walls looked attractive against the mahogany tables and chairs, although the furniture made it seem dark compared to the bright sun outside. Several small groups were spread around tables in the large room and a few single figures sat at the bar hunched over their drinks. Jack went straight up to the bar and asked for two local beers.

The small, tubby barman sported a long drooping moustache; he smiled and said, "That'll be Ventnor Gold. Local brew. There's a beer garden out back if you want to sit outside, chaps . . ."

Jack asked, "What happened to Cyril the chemist. I see he's sold his shop?"

"Oh yes. Old Cyril's gone off. He's gone off to the mainland to stay with his son. Did you know him well?"

"Not really," Jack said, as he paid up and pointed to Bill to head for the outside section that could be seen through an open set of double doors and the two men found themselves in a pleasant garden with a flower bed and large water can that spurted a continual stream of water into a stone fountain.

Bill looked around and said, "This is real nice. You know, you get a real feeling of peace and tranquility on this island. I could get used to it."

Jack appeared not to notice his surroundings and frowned as he sampled the beer. Finally he said, "Not bad. It tastes of hops. Now Bill, we need to think about your ERM presentation. How do you see it working out?"

"Oh. Whatever. Helen said she would work with Maria on it and we can have a look tonight. I'm sure the girls can come up with something. Let's wait for them and then you can have a go at it and I'll finish it off tonight, or tomorrow."

"Okay. You know, Bill, I'm not really going to charge you for the ERM job. I've not really done anything. To me this is just a short vacation."

Bill nodded his head with relief as this tricky point had been cleared up. He said, "Right. I mean, I'll pay your expenses and I could offer Helen and Maria a fee. Although I have a feeling they will not want to be paid. We'll talk about it later."

Jack leaned forward as if he were about to divulge a national secret and said, "You know, Helen fancies you. I can tell."

"No way." Bill leaned back in his chair with a surprised look on his face.

"Yep," continued Jack, "I can tell. Would you take her on?"

"No, no. No way. I've only been married a year. I'd be crazy to mess things up."

Jack in turn looked relieved, "I'm glad you said that. I've been married near twenty years. And I flirt most every day of the week. For fun. But I wouldn't get involved with anyone. No matter how pretty. Talking about that, we should really try to phone Jamaica. I can't get a signal for international calls. How's your cell phone?"

Bill took his small phone out of his shirt pocket and looked at it.

"Nothing doing," he replied. "Since Ruth got through to me at the conference I haven't had anything come through on it. The battery's dead and my charger is no use as it seems that they use a different power system here in the UK. You're right, though, we need to put a call through. Maybe we could find a call box. Tell me something, how do you stay married? What I mean is, don't you find it hard work?"

Jack thought about cracking a joke, then changed his mind and said, "You know, everyone has their own way. Let me put it in terms of the ERM stuff. People get together but they actually have different objectives. So their risk management strategy that they use is inconsistent as they are each going in different directions. That's why people who want to settle down together really need to communicate and find out what they each really want from life. Then they can devise a way of managing risk to their goals. For me, being married and taking care of my wife and family is my first priority. And this is where my wife stands. Family first."

"You mean your biggest risk is what interferes with this?"

"Exactly."

"And therefore your risk management strategy is . . . ?"

"Well it's being there, caring about her and doing all I can. Even where it's hard work. I'll let you into one secret."

Jack leaned in a little closer as if to emphasize the fact that this was confidential. He paused for a second then continued, "I took Sharon out to a party when we were first dating. When we had first met. And she got tired and had a headache. Anyway, I took her home, back to her parents, and she fell asleep in the car. I remember this like it happened today. I got there and she was wearing a real nice yellow dress. Sort of flowery and flowing. Anyway, I helped her out of the car as she woke up and I looked at her as she awoke and fell into my arms and I thought she was the most beautiful woman in the world. Soon after that I proposed and presto—we got hitched. Anyway, whenever times are hard and we argue but I need to keep my cool, I remember her that day, in that yellow dress and I do everything to work things out. I just put her on top of everything. And then the kids come next . . ."

Jack got up feeling a little embarrassed and headed for the bar for a refill. Bill stretched out his legs and thought about his wife. Then he thought about Helen and found these two images sat side by side in his mind. One, his new wife; beautiful, loving but sometimes reserved and distant. The other, Helen; bright, intense but kind of sad most of the time. He thought about children and the strong urge to have a large family around him to make up for the absence of his own relatives apart from his elderly dad.

Jack slammed down two pints on the table, which jerked Bill out of these hazy thoughts. Bill studied his pint and held it up to the sky as its golden color reflected the sparkling sunshine. He said to Jack, "Do you miss your parents?"

"Oh no. They went years ago. Gone but not forgotten."

"Doesn't it bother you?"

"Well . . ." Jack sat back and searched for the right words. "Well, life goes on. I remember my folks so well. They're with me and a part of me all the time. Every day and every night. But it was their time to go and I feel that they would be proud to see me push on and live my life."

"Don't you wish they were here with you?"

Jack laughed, "Bill. That is life. You're here and you live. Then you rest. I spend my time with my family and my wife's people. I say, make the most of those you have so when they go you have your memories. That's about it."

Bill relaxed back in his chair as Jack's words drifted over his mind. Jack asked, "How are you and Ruth getting on—is everything okay?"

"You know, I'm like you. I want a family. Kids, a big house, and the full works. But I don't want to pressure her. I don't want to lose her."

Jack said, "Why should you lose her?"

"It's complicated. Like I said, I want kids but she hasn't said anything about that. I told you already she said a trapped bird doesn't sing."

"Does she sing?"

"Look, Jack. You don't get it. She's happy and she sings. But if I hit her with stuff, then what next? I just can't risk it."

"Isn't risk dependent on your objectives?"

Bill got up and said, "If you start this risk psychobabble, I'll. . . . We've had days of risk this and risk that and I think I'm going mad. This is real life, my friend. Not a conference."

"Hold it down, boss. As they say in Jamaica. I'm on your side, remember."

The two men left the pub, shouting a friendly "goodbye" to the barman. As they stood outside the pub, a motorbike bounced toward them at speed and a tall man in full leathers—boots, thick gloves, and crash helmet— jumped off the pillion seat as the driver gunned the engine. The man flashed out a long metal baton from his belt and stood in front of Bill. He shouted, "Give me your money, Yank! Now!"

Bill stared at the black crash helmet and darkened visor in disbelief and stood rigid. The man stepped forward, the baton held tight in his upraised hand, and walked closer to Bill.

As he swung toward Bill, Jack launched into a flying scissor kick and smashed his left foot underneath the man's wrist as a sharp *snap* rang out. The baton flew into the air and the three men stood facing each other for a heartbeat before the motorbike plunged toward them and the attacker jumped on the back and the bike sped away. Jack and Bill lunged out of the way and looked as the bike roared away into the distance. The attacker's right hand was hanging down to one side until the bike became a black dot, then disappeared as the engine's roar drifted away.

Jack jumped up and shouted out at the invisible bike, "*Jeeze*. What the hell happened? So much for your damn peaceful island. It's just like everywhere. Full of damn druggies and crazies . . ." He literally shook his fist after the now long-gone bikers.

Bill stayed down on the grass, his legs spread out in front of him, silent. Jack looked down and said, this time quietly, "You okay?"

He quickly realized that Bill was in shock and took in the slight trembling and the dazed look on Bill's face. Jack sat down on the grass next to Bill and said, "Not a bad idea to rest a bit."

After a few minutes that seemed to last for ages, Jack got up again and asked, "Okay. Want a drink? We could do with a short one. Say Scotch?"

Bill's expression softened as he started to relax and slowly got up.

"You know, what," he said, "I think we'd better call it a day and make tracks. As you say, this place is far too deadly."

CHAPTER 21

THE END OF THE ROAD

Helen sat out in the back garden and listened to the birds, which kept up their summer songs, when she heard Bill's and Jack's voices as they came back into the house. Bill sat on the couch and Jack went through to the backyard and said "Hi" to Helen. Helen walked back into the house to ask Bill how it went and stopped as she saw Bill's posture, his wild hair, and a small cut across his right cheek, where he had fallen into the roadside.

She rushed over and sat beside him, and was just about to hold him in her arms when she thought better and simply said to Bill, "What on earth have you been up to?" She then glared at Jack and said, "What have you done, Jack?"

Jack shrugged his shoulders and said, "A little trouble. No big thing. Just the usual thing; thugs running around the place, misbehaving. Seems that it's something that happens all over the world. Where's Maria?"

Helen forced her eyes away from Bill and wondered why he had not spoken, before she said in reply to Jack's question, "She went for a walk. She won't be long. I've put a pizza in the oven and if you boys are hungry just help yourself. Me and Maria have already eaten."

This seemed to break the spell and the three friends spent the next few minutes rustling up a meal and making drinks as they tried to forget the ugly incident that had put a downer on their trip so far.

Maria returned soon after and found a Scrabble game, which proved highly successful in terms of providing much fun and laughter for nearly an hour. Bill was more or less back to normal and it was only after the game finished that Maria walked toward the kitchen and asked Bill what happened to his cheek. He was sporting a bright bandage administered earlier by Helen.

Helen laughed, "He and Jack got themselves mugged, poor things."

Maria stopped midway and sat down beside Bill. "What happened?" she enquired in a stern voice, which for once contained no threat of laughter.

Bill and Jack relayed their adventure and Jack politely described his heroics as a struggle between all of them that ended with the bikers driving off. Helen laughed out loud but Maria looked really shocked, and there was a complete silence for several minutes after the story had been told.

Helen said, "I bet they were two twelve-year-olds," and turned to Maria for support. There was none forthcoming. Maria punched the TV remote and the picture and sound from the film that was showing in the background died instantly. Maria stood up and faced the other three, "This is not supposed to happen!"

Jack laughed. "Maria, darling. We're not blaming you. It wasn't your idea to come here. Bill asked us. Things have changed everywhere since you were last here. It's no problem."

Maria remained standing and she looked like she was about to give another lecture as she had done at the conference. She eventually sat down and said, this time much more softly, "This type of thing doesn't happen here. I've just finished talking to the girl at the supermarket and she says she leaves her front door open as the island, and in particular this part of the island, is so peaceful. Something's not right. Helen, tell them what happened to us today."

Helen told them about the two bikers who had made them feel so uncomfortable earlier that day.

Jack looked at Bill and touched his watch and stood up for his turn to address the small group. He waved his arms around and said, "You know, we're supposed to be on vacation. We've had a bit of a shake up by two local thugs. But no one's hurt. This is our last night here so I suggest we cut out this morbid stuff and go out to the hotel bar to celebrate. Let's leave the car here, walk down and make a night of it. How about it?"

Bill looked unimpressed and Jack grabbed his arm and helped him up so as to give the impression of unity between them, and after throwing Maria her jacket, it seemed that they would all be heading for the bar anyway.

Tucked away at a corner table in the hotel bar the four friends shared a bottle of wine and made small talk about the state of the world and the things they liked to do for fun. Peter Greenspam rushed through the door, and on seeing the four-strong group stopped dead and went across to their table.

"Hello, there. How are you enjoying your visit? I hope you're getting around."

They responded to Peter's opening remarks and he hovered over their table a bit as if he needed to get away to do more important things. Before he could make his excuses, Helen said, "We've had a bit of a shake up. Bill here was attacked by bikers."

Bill held up his hand, "I wasn't hurt. It was just some stupid youths."

Helen looked concerned, "I think we should call the police," and looked at Peter, who stood with his hands on his hips.

Peter leaned forward and said, "I'll talk to our local police sergeant tomorrow about these yahoos. This is a small place. There's really nowhere to hide. Anyway, I'm sorry to hear about your misfortune. I hope it's not colored your views of our little island. Goodbye."

And with that he went off through the office door. Jack said, "Nice guy, that. Real friendly. Anyway girls, did you manage to get the presentation down? I mean the outline stuff for Bill?"

Helen showed them her notes on ERM, and Maria talked them through an outline of ERM in terms of how it can be formulated into a board-sponsored project of awareness, tools, procedures, reporting, and ways of embedding the concept within the existing business systems. Bill looked impressed and said that he could turn their baseline material into a presentation that would suit his business. Jack got more drinks in and a three-piece jazz group had set themselves up on the outside veranda. After a while, a female jazz singer started to sing Ella Fitzgerald songs and the atmosphere became totally relaxed and comfortable. Jack suggested they sit outside to hear the music better and Bill and Helen got up. Maria stayed sitting and stared through the window at the boarded up cottage just visible in the dark. She barked out an order, "Sit down all of you. Now!"

Three people froze and then in unison sat down.

Maria continued to look out of the window. She waited a bit and then said, "Something's wrong. Very wrong."

Jack strained his neck to study the singer, who was wearing a slinky red dress, and Maria barked out, "Jack. Don't you feel that things don't stack up?"

Bill looked concerned and, feeling she was losing them, Maria changed direction. "Let's analyze things from a risk management perspective."

Bill smiled, Helen settled down, and even Jack seemed more relaxed as the topic had become something that they knew and trusted.

"What's your point?" Jack asked.

Maria settled down and bit her lip before she said slowly, "Let's take it from the top. Bill. You come here to see your aunt and she's gone, okay. A young man has been arrested but from his point of view we get the first problem. He, this young man, had a stock of drugs in his room. Why didn't he get rid of them? His girlfriend says he's innocent."

Jack said, "That's only natural."

"But," Maria continued, "She then disappears. She had to go because, what did you say, Bill?"

Bill's head jerked upward, "She said something about it getting too hot for her. Right Jack?"

"Yep."

Maria continued, "The chemist who said the youth stole the drugs has shut up shop and gone. Right?"

"Yep." Jack replied.

"Now this is the bit that worries me. Helen and me get stalked by these bikers. And you guys get attacked. Sounds fishy?"

Jack responded, "It could happen anywhere."

Maria looked around the bar and lowered her voice, "Many years ago, I used to work in law enforcement. Jack, you used to do fraud investigations, right?"

Jack nodded. Maria carried on, "Well, then, when I did an investigation I always worried when something looked odd. Or, when lots of things looked odd. I used to check things out. That's the way we worked."

The others were enthralled and gazed at Maria as she continued her presentation. "There's too many things wrong. Bill, you told me that they don't like Yanks over here, right?"

"That right. The attacker said something about go home, Yank."

Maria frowned and said, "But how did he know you were American? Was he in the bar listening to you?"

Jack said, "Definitely not. I saw everyone in the bar. There was no way two bikers in full leathers were there."

"I can tell you that this sort of thing does not happen on this island. Tourists threatened? No way!"

Jack came in again, "I don't think those guys wanted any money. They were wearing their helmets and we could hardy hear them asking for money. And the tall guy wanted to hit Bill or at least threaten him before I stepped in. He didn't wait for Bill or for me to get out our wallets. It doesn't make sense."

Helen sipped her drink and put down the empty glass, "Well, Maria. What do you suggest we do? We're out of time."

"Let's go back to risk management. Why are we being discouraged? I mean, why are we being encouraged to stop asking questions and leave? Who wants us out of the way?"

Bill snapped his fingers a few times and said, "I agree something's wrong. But there's no one to talk to and Helen's right. We're pretty much out of time. But we do have one ally. Peter Greenspam. Next time we see him, let's ask for his help."

Jack stared outside as the fading light threw the cottage into a raft of gray shadows. The other three were engaged in their game of playing with ideas about the mystery, and he just looked out the window. Jack sipped his pint of beer and suddenly slapped down his empty glass, which created a sudden silence among the group as they looked at him Jack's eyes widened and he said with some force, "It's been staring us in the face. All this time."

Helen threw her head back and asked, "What? What has been staring at us?"

Jack smiled, "Helen and Maria. You're our ERM experts. We've been on this journey through ERM; now let's make it work for us. Why was Maud killed? I mean she was given a large dose of painkillers by someone and the cops feel that something was wrong. She was murdered, right? So why was she murdered? The guy they've put in jail made a crude will that could not possibly work and he actually hid the painkillers in his apartment. His risk management strategy was crap. Therefore we should ask whether he was set up, right?"

Maria took over from here, "Okay, I'm with you. Who gains from Maud's death?"

Jack sat forward on the edge of his chair and pointed a finger toward the window. "It's staring at us. Coral Gardens cottage. You know that it overlooks the sea and it has a great position over the bay. Second to none. So someone wants the cottage. That's all the old lady had. Let's say someone administered the drugs and then set up the young guy. Now if this happened, then what was their risk management strategy?"

Helen got a word in, "They set the guy up. And remember the girlfriend has gone and the chemist has gone. That's two risks that have disappeared."

Bill said, "Yes. The chemist said he had seen the girl's boyfriend. What was his name?"

"Can't remember. Oh yes, hang on, I think it was Cyril," answered Jack.

"You're right. Anyway, he said he saw him take the painkillers and then this chemist goes off."

Helen snapped her fingers, "Hey. You know that me and Maria were harassed by the two bikers. And you, Bill, you were threatened by them. That's about getting us to leave. Which means we are a risk. Us being here and asking questions. We pose a threat to the real culprit and he or she or they want to eliminate us . . ."

Jack interrupted, "This is dangerous. We are all at risk. Seriously, we are not wanted here and someone wants us out of the way. But who?"

Helen shrugged her shoulders. "It's getting dark and this place is really a bit isolated. It seems to me that we are just making guesses. You should know better, Jack, and you, Maria. You need hard evidence if you want to back up your wild ideas."

Jack frowned and said, "I have an idea."

He walked over to the bar and found the teenage barman slumped in a seat. "Can you make a call to your local hospital?"

The spotty youth stuttered, "They might be closed . . . .it's . . . and it's getting late."

Jack looked him in the eye and said, "I want to talk to the emergency people. What do you call them over here?"

"Accident and Emergency. Okay wait a bit . . ."

And he pulled a phone from behind the bar, looked through a booklet hanging on the wall, and dialed a number before handing the phone to Jack. Jack said in a firm voice, "You admitted a motorcyclist today.

He is a relative of mine and I want to make sure he is okay. He had an accident and broke his wrist."

After a few minutes, Jack listened to a voice on the other end and simply repeated "yes," several times before replacing the receiver. He returned to his group and sat down and waited.

"Well?" Bill asked.

Jack finally said in a quiet voice, "The hospital said that a biker did come in with a fractured wrist. They would not give me his name but said that he was patched up and discharged an hour or so ago. Funny, that. When I asked for a description she laughed and said that he refused to take off his helmet. They thought he was a bit unbalanced and wanted to get rid of him as soon as possible."

Bill slumped down in his chair and said, "Back to square one."

Jack continued, "I suggest we take care. Someone wants us out of here and it may be best to comply. We're going tomorrow, anyway. But I wonder if this person knows that. We need to stick together tonight and then get back to London. I feel we're in deep and we don't even know why."

Bill looked around the bar, and on seeing the harmless assortment of couples and groups of old men, relaxed a little before saying, "We need to find out what's cooking. Whoever wants us out is the same person who has murdered an elderly person. This is my aunt we're talking about and I owe it to her to find out what happened."

Helen sat back and shivered, "This place gives me the creeps. I mean I love this island but in the dark and with something wrong, it suddenly feels unsafe. We're strangers here and we just don't know enough about the situation. I'm with Jack. Let's get home, pack, and leave early tomorrow."

Jack said, "We could leave tonight. I saw the ferry timetable and they run all night. Could you drive, Helen?"

Maria stood up and said, "I told you that we need to find out what's going on. And you, Bill. You said you wanted to clear things up . . ."

Bill stood up and guided Maria back into her chair and said, "Not by endangering any of you. Let's get back to the house."

The four friends walked together in silence up toward Freshfields, their home away from home. It was dark and the moonlit night seemed to cast shadows over every tree, bush, and wall that they passed as they made their way back. As if on guard duty, Jack walked up front and Bill covered the rear as the two women walked together in the middle. The moon disappeared behind a cloud and the darkness seemed to press in on them as a car's engine sounded from the distance and grew louder as it came closer toward them as they walked in single file along the narrow path beside the road. The car came closer and a bright headlight beam shone up at them. Helen grabbed Bill's arm as the car swerved alongside them and Bill's blood froze. Jack tensed his muscles, but the car swept past them as the driver realized there were pedestrians nearby and moved over into the middle of the road. The engine quickly faded as the car went further on into the black night.

Helen fell back into Bill's arms and he held her tight as she shivered from the sudden cold snap that she felt from the tension that was now starting to break. Bill asked Helen if she was all right and he found himself holding her hand as they walked the few hundred yards to their cozy holiday home.

Four figures sat in chairs in silence as they drank hot drinks, and each thought about the fact that they were far from home and tied up in something strange. Jack snapped on the TV and a movie sprang to life as the tension started to slowly lift and disperse. Maria spread out the Scrabble board on the coffeetable in the middle of the lounge and said, "How about a game?"

Jack got up, put on his jacket, and said to Bill, "Where's that flashlight you bought at that old man's shop?"

Bill replied instantly, "It's there. In my jacket pocket, hanging by the front door. Where are you going?"

Jack ignored the question and grabbed the flashlight and went through the door. Helen got up and went to the front door, opened it, and saw Jack disappear quickly into the dark night.

The three remaining friends sat for a while and played Scrabble while they took turns glancing up at the wall clock as the minutes ticked away with no sight of Jack. Maria walked over to the clock and studied it intensely before saying, "I'm going to the hotel to get Jack. He must have gone for a drink. You know, I'm going to talk to that man—he drinks far too much."

Bill said, "No way are we gonna split up. I'll drive you there. Helen, you come with us."

Helen chewed her nails and said, "You go. I'll wait here for Jack. He doesn't have a key, you know. I'll keep the door closed. Promise."

Bill went outside with Maria and looked at the car parked in the drive.

"Shoot. I can't drive this car. Helen's got the key and I've been drinking."

Maria zipped up her jacket and said, "Let's walk back to the hotel. It's not far."

The two of them retraced their tracks down to Freshwater Bay and back to the hotel where they had spent the early part of the evening. They kept well to the edge of the sidewalk and felt almost safe in the dark as they appeared as shadows for most of the time. They did not speak but just concentrated on getting back to the hotel. After 10 minutes they arrived and pushed open the bar door and found the bar almost empty, as it was now getting late. The teenage barman looked up with a sigh as he saw more customers arrive to spoil his rest.

Bill marched up to the bar and said, "Have you seen my buddy Jack?"

The teenager looked puzzled as he thought this may be a trick question as he had seen all of them an hour ago. Bill repeated the question, "Did Jack come back here?"

The youngster finally said, "No."

Maria said, "You haven't seen Jack since we left?"

"No, madam."

Bill moved his face closer to the youth, "Where's your boss? Peter Greenspam?"

"He's gone out."

"Where's the other guy, Matches?"

The youth relaxed a little as he could be more helpful here, "He's been gone a while. He just disappeared since early this morning. Strange for him to be away so long."

"You sure?" asked Bill.

"Yep. He jumped on his friend's bike and that was that. Off they went."

Bill asked slowly, "You're talking about a motorbike, right?"

"Yep."

Bill looked at Maria and said, "Let's go."

"Hang on, Bill." Maria turned to the barman, "Who is this Matches?"

A loud laugh greeted her, "Hey, you want to know about Matches? Well, he's been on the Island five years but he doesn't know the Island, if you get my drift."

Bill pursed his lips and started walking out but Maria asked, "What do you mean?"

"Parkhurst, lady . . . ha, ha, ha. He's a bit of a thug and he's spent most of his time in Parkhurst."

The two of them turned toward the door and Maria waved at the youth and much to his surprise wished him a warm goodnight. As Bill opened the door for Maria, he asked her, "What's Parkhurst?"

"It's a high-security prison, here on the Island. Hang on, Bill."

Maria returned to the bar and asked the young man, who was getting ready to close down, "Who is this Peter Greenspam? Has he been here a long time?"

"Oh, he's okay—not a bit like his mad nephew, Matches. He was a big shot in the British army in Hong Kong years ago. He was an army boxing champion. They called him 'Banger Greenspam.' Anyway, the story goes that he came to the Isle of Wight to visit his nephew and saw this hotel. He got duped. The seller told him that the old girl who owned Coral Gardens would sell it to him and he could expand the hotel. But old Maud had no intention of doing that at all. She refused to sell up. Matches is out of jail on early release on the basis that he lives with his uncle. He's a real psycho. You know, this place gives me the creeps and I'll be glad to get back to University in October . . ."

Bill grabbed Maria's arm, "We have to get back," he whispered.

Maria thanked the barman, who was now smiling broadly at them, and they left the hotel bar. Maria walked side by side with Bill and in the dark she turned her head to look at his shaded profile.

"Bill. I saw you holding Helen. Is anything going on between you two?"

"Heck, no. I like Helen but I'm married and I have the best wife in the world. Every time I get close to Helen I think about Ruth and the day I first met her. That image stays with me, and you know, I can't really look at another woman in the same way as I see Ruth."

Maria nodded her head in agreement and in the dark Bill could not see the look of relief that fell across her once-worried face.

Jack switched off the flashlight, trying to conserve its battery life. It went dark and he could see the pub's lights from where he stood near some bushes. In the shadows he heard faint footsteps coming from around the corner and he pushed himself into the bush so that he was nearly invisible to any passerby. The footsteps came closer and Jack raised the flashlight over his head and tensed his body as the footsteps' owners came around the corner into sight. Jack saw two shadowy figures come in his direction, one tall and slim and the other shorter and larger, swinging what looked like a bag. He tensed his fingers around the flashlight and heard a voice: "Bill, whatever you do, never visit me at night naked."

Jack called out, "Bill. Maria. What the hell you doing here?"

Bill shouted back, "Looking for you, man."

Jack switched on his flashlight and played it slowly along the grass, and said, "Quickly. Please look at the beam and tell me what you see."

They played this game for a further five minutes before Maria whispered, "Look there!"

And they saw a pile of small white sticks spread out on the grass at the spot where Jack had seen the motorbike emerge before Bill was threatened earlier that evening. Jack studied the find and picked up a stick. "This is a chewed matchstick, and there's more of them all over here."

Maria declared, "The barman said Matches went off with some other guy on a motorbike earlier."

Jack said, "He's our attacker, and he is the one who wants to get rid of us. He works for Greenspam, right? So Greenspam holds the key. He wants the cottage. Remember, he said that he needed a sea view to make a success of the hotel. The cottage blocks this view, right?"

Bill looked up at the stars sparkling in the dark sky and heard the roar of the sea in the background. He said, "Right. You know, that Greenspam was a boxing champion. What was he called, Maria?"

"Oh yes. Banger Greenspam, I think."

Jack looked from Bill to Maria and back to Bill and said, "I've read about him. He was a contender for the European light-heavyweight boxing title years ago. He's retired now. Apparently he used to be a real dangerous character in the ring. Hang on, where's Helen? You've left her alone? Greenspam's arranged one murder. Which Matches must have done. This is a dangerous situation and we need to get back to Helen. Now!"

Helen sat in the lounge area of the holiday home and leaned back on the couch. She flicked through her guide to the Island, and studied the castle, stately homes, country parks, and beaches that were scattered throughout the guide. A jazz piano sprinkled the room with music from the small CD player and the standup lamps cast a glow over the beige colors that were a feature of the lounge. She sipped a cup of creamy coffee and thought about her life. *Fast track; fast lane; high flyer; corporate raider*—all terms that had been thrown out to define her and her lifestyle. She had bought a run-down building in the commercial sector of Hong Kong and fixed it up into an executive-style apartment block. It was now worth a small fortune and she estimated that she could maintain a good lifestyle on the rental income alone, which she had been receiving for the last few months. The final two apartments were due to be let next month and this would increase her already significant rental income. But what was it all about? Where was she going?

She slipped off her shoes and tucked her legs under her as she spread out on the couch, feeling strangely at peace as the near silence outside came as a pleasant surprise. The CD finished playing and she closed her eyes for a moment, waiting for the others to return. A noise outside made her smile as she anticipated the arrival of her three noisy buddies and the results of their mystery game that had really consumed them over the last few days. Like kids playing at spies, she thought. A soft knock on the door jerked her out of her thoughts and she slid her feet back into her shoes and got up, saying, "Hang on, Jack."

She opened the door and in front of her stood Peter Greenspam, his tie swept aside at a weird angle and his hair disheveled as if he had been rubbing his hands through it. Which is what he started to do now. Holding one hand to his forehead he said in a soft voice, "Can I come in?"

"Sure," Helen replied, as she folded her arms across her chest and stepped backward into the dimly lit room.

Sharon sat at the table as Ruth and her mother finished their meal and discussed the rising price of goods that were imported to the Caribbean. Ruth's mom had a surprisingly strong voice for someone who had just undergone surgery.

"People should buy local. Everybody wants foreign. Fast food this, takeaway that. They have no pride in their own produce. My friend works in the garment factory and they have to sew tags into the clothes saying 'made in the U.S.,' or no one will buy them. What a disgrace."

Sharon listened to her and laughed. She was going to miss Jamaica and its people when her term at the University expired.

"Anyway," the old lady continued, "people are getting too fierce nowadays. Everyone gets in a fuss for no reason at all. I just don't know what's happening. The youngsters don't have any manners at all. Apart from this one here."

And she held her daughter's hand, and managed to get her to smile for the first time that evening. Ruth got up and went to the bathroom.

Sharon leaned toward Ruth's mom and asked, "What is wrong with her? There's something wrong, right?"

The old lady nodded and sighed. She pursed her lips and said, "She's pregnant. And she doesn't want to hold Bill back. She says Bill is not ready for children and she says she needs to think of him first. I think she's as mad as a hatter. I told her to tell Bill and stop this foolishness. But she just won't listen."

Sharon listened in horror, her eyes growing wider with every word she heard. She finally said, "We've got to get hold of Bill and Jack."

The old lady pointed her finger toward the window and said, "See her there. She's going home."

Ruth's figure could be seen walking slowly out through the front gate and along the road in the direction of her mother's house. Sharon drove Ruth's mom home and grabbed Ruth by the hand, bundled her in her car, and said, "You're coming with me right now, and we are going to sort this whole thing out."

Ruth and Sharon sat around the coffeetable in Sharon's lounge in total silence. Ruth eventually said, "I need to call the hospital and give them your number."

"Why?"

"They said they would contact me if an opening for surgery became free tonight or sometime tomorrow."

"Oh, Ruth, what are you planning to do?"

"I need to save my marriage. I need to be not pregnant. You understand, surely?"

Ruth contacted the hospital and gave them her new temporary number as Sharon sat listening to the call and wondering what the hell she was supposed to do. But, this was not her decision and it was not something she could intervene in. This was about real life, real people, and real-life decisions.

At around three o clock in the morning, Sharon's phone started ringing.

Jack, Bill, and Maria started their single-file march toward their holiday home in silence. Jack was up front using his much-practiced walking skills to stay ahead and encouraged the others to keep up with his fast-moving pace. Maria fell behind and Bill felt he needed to keep her in sight as they needed to stay together right now. Jack approached the holiday home and opened the front gate. Before he got to the door he saw through the window, the dark shadow of a man with his back to him who held Helen in a tight grip as if he were strangling her. Jack kicked through the front door and it flew open. He stepped into the room and raised his fists in preparation for a fierce bout with Banger Greenspam. Hearing the loud noise, Greenspam instantly spun around and his hands instinctively flew up in front of his face as he prepared his defense. Jack stepped forward and Helen screamed, "Stop it!"

Jack froze and Bill and Maria entered the room and for a second each person stared at the other as if suspended in time. Helen stepped between Jack and Peter, her arms spread wide like a boxing referee, "Stop it. Peter's as worried as we are. His nephew has gone off the rails and he thought he might have come here."

Peter's hands went down to his side, and he said in an agitated voice, "He's gone crazy. He came to see me earlier this evening in a real state, with a bad wrist, and I dropped him off at the hospital. When I returned the hospital said he was behaving like a wild person and they had to ask him to leave once he had been treated. Anyway, he called me up and said he would take care of everything. He went on about sorting out the old girl at Coral Gardens and I told him to come home. I've asked the police to meet me at my hotel but I suddenly thought about you guys here and I needed to make sure you were okay."

They all sat down and Bill made coffee for all of them, although Peter said he had to get back to the hotel as the police would be there soon.

Jack looked at Helen, who was avoiding his gaze. Maria and Bill went into the kitchen, looking for something to rustle up for a snack and Jack got up and sat next to Helen. He said, "What did I see earlier? You and Peter. What was he doing to you?"

Helen coughed and looked embarrassed. "We got talking and he told me about his concerns about his crazy nephew, Matches. Peter used to live in Hong Kong and would you believe it, he knew my uncle. I mean, he didn't know him personally but he knew something about his death. Anyway he was friends with a senior police chief in Hong Kong and he told me that this rumor that my uncle had drowned while drunk was wrong. He drowned saving a young woman who had tried to commit suicide. Anyway it was a cover-up, as this woman was the wife of some senior politician and the authorities didn't want this information to get out. So they reported a drowning but said no more. The bit about him being drunk was just some gossip that someone started. I stood up and was so upset that I cried like a baby and Peter was trying to console me. He's . . . I think he's a great guy."

Maria burst back into the lounge area and placed a huge plate of toasted cheese sandwiches down onto the coffeetable, and this feast took some time to consume as the clock ticked away the hours deep into the night.

Jack rose first and decided to forgo his morning walk. He saw a note that had been pushed through the mailbox and read its contents:

I invite you all to breakfast at my hotel this morning.

Anytime you like

Regards,
Peter

It took less than an hour for the four friends to shower, dress, and present themselves at the hotel at Freshwater Bay for their breakfast invite. Peter was out but had left instructions for his guests to be given a full English breakfast. They had had time to pack their bags, which were left in the hired car, which was now standing in the hotel parking lot. Jack munched away at his breakfast and said, "Helen. What time do we need to hit the road?"

"Any time. Just as long as you guys get back to London today sometime."

Bill sat back and surveyed the scene outside. Coral Gardens could not be seen from his chair but he could see the smooth green hillside that led inland rather than facing toward the sea. He turned his gaze to the three people sitting opposite and announced, "I have pretty well done my presentation. I did it late last night. Well, this morning, really. Want to hear it?"

A low groan spread across the table as the others thought that they had probably had enough of ERM for a while. Helen mentally told herself off and said, "Good idea. Please go ahead, Bill."

Bill read out his list:

- Build a good understanding of risk and risk appetites within the entire organization.
- Engage the board and top managers and all employees about their responsibilities to manage risk properly.
- Review all corporate systems and processes and decision points so as to build risk assessment into and inside all parts of our business systems.
- Encourage risk-smart thinking across our entire workforce.
- Make sure our people are able to communicate what they have done to improve their controls and why.

- Keep up the momentum through defined ERM maturity targets and build on success and learn quickly from any failures.

"That's what doctor what-not, the last speaker at the conference, called ERM, expeditious risk management . . . simple."

Just as Bill finished, Peter Greenspam swept into the room and with a wide smile greeted them and sat down at their table.

"I trust all is well," he said, and seeing that they looked well fed said, "I've been at the police station all night and I need to give you an update. The police arrested Matches at the ferry as he was trying to get away. He was easy to spot with his bandaged hand. Anyway, they have reopened the murder investigation and apparently he has already implicated himself with knowledge of the crime that only the killer would know. And they are going to track down the chemist guy. The police are also running DNA tests on several matches that they found at the scene of the crime, that is, Coral Gardens, and they tell me that there may have been a miscarriage of justice against the young fellow, Jimmy, who is currently locked up. They have also tracked down that girl you met, Jimmy's girlfriend, and she was so relieved that she's coming straight back to the island. Apparently she says Matches threatened her and she got scared and left. The same thing may well have happened to the chemist who gave evidence at the trial. My guess is that Matches tried to frighten you off the island to get you out of the way. As he does with everyone else who is a threat to our business. Or, for that matter, anyone he thought was a risk to me and my buying Coral Gardens. You see, not many buyers would want a cottage that is so close to a busy hotel, so he thought I would get it at a good price. That's why he ended up in jail the first time, because of blackmail and threatening behavior. It's all looking much clearer now."

He looked at Bill and said, "Okay, neighbor?"

Bill smiled and was about to ask what will happen to Jimmy, who was locked up for a crime that he did not commit, when he stopped himself and asked instead, "I didn't know you English call everyone neighbor, like we do in the States."

Peter looked confused and said, "I suppose you will become my neighbor. I mean with Coral Gardens being so close."

Bill continued to look puzzled and Peter continued, "I just realized, you don't know how we work here. You're the nearest living relative of your deceased aunt. She made no will and that means her estate goes to the next living relative. So Coral Gardens, as far as I can see, will go to you as the next of kin."

Bill looked shocked. Peter stood up.

"I'll ask the lawyer who dealt with the case to come right over. He's got an office along the high street. If you could stick around for an hour he can talk to you about this. Helen, want to come with me?"

At that Helen and Peter left the others and disappeared through the exit. Bill looked down at his notes on his presentation and for the first time in a while felt relaxed. Jack slapped him on his back and said, "Well done. Congratulations. You now have a great holiday home. A bit far out of the way, but it's pretty dandy."

Maria frowned and said, "You guys kill me. You both have wives and neither of you has patched through a call to say hello."

Bill announced, "That won't work. It's got to be around three o'clock in the morning in Jamaica right now."

Maria ignored Bill and barked out, "Call them now!"

Jack assumed his hang-dog look and said, "Can I borrow your phone, Maria? I promise not to be long."

Jack punched in some numbers and heard a crackled "Hello" on the phone.

"Darling. This is your one and only here. What? Yes, he's here. Hold on."

Jack gave Bill the phone. Bill got up and walked to the other end of the restaurant and was there for over 20 minutes, while Maria shivered as she mentally calculated the cost of the overseas phone call. Bill returned, clapped his hands together like a performing seal, and burst out into a loud laugh. He finally said, "I'm going to be a dad. Isn't that great?"

Both Jack and Maria jumped up in excitement, making clear their congratulations.

Everything after that happened very quickly. The lawyer arrived at the hotel and confirmed that he would put proceedings into place to transfer the cottage, its contents, and a small amount money that was left to Bill, on receipt of Bill's documentation that confirms his identity and relationship with Maud. While walking to the car, Jack announced to Bill and Maria that he would write up the story of his trip to the conference and all that happened and submit the result as the manuscript for his new book on risk management. He then stated in a rush of excitement that his next book would be on corporate fraud. Bill, Maria, and Jack got into the car and waited for Helen and their return trip to London and their hotel. All of a sudden, the teenage barman jumped into the driver's seat and started the engine, to the surprise of all present. Helen appeared with Peter and walked toward the car.

Helen glowed with happiness and said, "I'm not budging. I'm staying right here for a bit. This is where my journey begins." And Peter held his arm around her waist with a wide smile on his face.

Jack shouted, "Okay, sounds good. Well done, you two."

Maria said, "Join my project team, Helen. Please. We can do most of the work via e-mail. Okay?"

Bill leaned out of the window, "I'll be back next year to check out my cottage. Helen, will you look after it until then? I'll tell that lawyer guy that he's to give you the keys. Where will you be staying?"

"At the hotel," Peter said.

Bill slipped the emerald ring that he was to give to his aunt into Maria's hand and said, "Thanks for telling us to phone home. This will remind you of your new-found friends and your home away from home."

Helen saw the ring change hands as she waved goodbye to them and managed to shout out, "Maria. I will join your team. But you just make sure Bill doesn't go sleepwalking at the hotel tonight."

The car pulled away and went through the gates toward the main road out of Freshwater Bay to start the long journey home. Bill closed his eyes and sat back. He did not dream this time; he visualized. His wife, clearly defined in her peach-colored dress that he admired her in so much, with a small child nestling in her arms. He pulled the paper out of his wallet where, at a time of stress, he had written down his goals. It read "risk presentation, office support system, promotion, election to the main board." But these were just minor things that supported his main aim: his family—his precious wife, his father, and now his child, and all those other people whom he held dear. He reflected on the huge risk he had taken in keeping them so far from him. He screwed the piece of paper into a ball and threw it out of the car window and it fluttered down into the road, rolled over a few times, and was swept by the breeze into the swirling blue waves of Freshwater Bay.

INDEX